First Friend

ALSO BY KATHARINE M. ROGERS

L. Frank Baum: Creator of Oz

The Cat and the Human Imagination:
Feline Images from Bast to Garfield

Frances Burney:
The World of "Female Difficulties"

Feminism in Eighteenth-Century England

William Wycherley

The Troublesome Helpmate:
A History of Misogyny in Literature

First Friend

A History of Dogs and Humans

Katharine M. Rogers

St. Martin's Press

New York

www.stmartins.com

ISBN 0-312-33188-6
EAN 978-0-312-33188-7

First Edition: August 2005

10 9 8 7 6 5 4 3 2 1

To Willoughby,
half a shepherd and half a retriever
and the best half of both

Contents

Illustrations and Captions

These captions refer to the illustrations located in the photo section following page 134.

1. Bas-relief of wild asses being hunted by hounds, seventh century BCE

Bas-reliefs from the palace of Nineveh glorify the king's power by portraying him killing lions and other big game. Here ferocious hunting mastiffs run down wild asses so that men on horseback can more easily shoot them. Two are bringing down one ass, while a mare looks back helplessly as another dog is about to seize her foal. For these artists, both men and dogs are merely incarnations of aggressive power.

2. Roman marble statue of a pair of dogs, possibly second century BCE

It was only in Hellenistic and Roman times that artists begin to show interest in dogs' feelings and personalities (an interest that did not reappear until the fifteenth century). These two affectionate young greyhounds elicit as much sympathetic feeling as any modern representation.

3. Pisanello, *The Vision of St. Eustace,* 1440

One day when he was out hunting, Placidus, a soldier of the Emperor Trajan known for his good works, had a vision of a stag with a crucifix between its antlers and heard the voice of Christ telling him, "I am the Christ whom you worship without knowing it. Your alms have risen before me, and for this purpose I have come, that through this deer which you hunted, I myself might hunt you." Placidus was converted to Christianity and changed his name to Eustace. St. Eustace, represented in the height of fifteenth-century court fashion, embodied the ideals of a Christian knight, including his aristocratic taste for hunting. The careful portrayals of hounds and wild animals recall illustrations to hunting treatises such as *The Master of Game*. The major types of medieval hunting dogs appear: running (scent) hounds, greyhounds, spaniels, and perhaps an alaunt (the heavier hound under the horse's hindquarters). The dogs are oblivious to the miracle.

4. Vittore Carpaccio, *The Vision of St. Augustine,* 1502

St. Augustine is writing a letter to St. Jerome and has just heard Jerome's voice telling of his imminent death and ascent to heaven. Carpaccio places Augustine in the idealized study of a Renaissance humanist, filled with books and classical statues as well as an altar. The rational organization of the space and the brilliant light that brings out every detail emphasize the intellectual atmosphere. However, Augustine's little dog, sitting prominently in the foreground, is quite oblivious to the intellectual and spiritual values; it just watches the saint expectantly, politely waiting for him to come out of his rapture and pay attention to his dog. Its animal limitations do not detract in the least from its adorable attractiveness. The Venetians loved these fluffy little white bichons and placed them in the most unlikely settings.

5. Paolo Veronese, *Feast in the House of Simon,* 1560

Sixteenth- and seventeenth-century painters, particularly the Venetians, regularly placed dogs in any pictures of biblical scenes that involved eating. Veronese represents the scene from Luke 7 when Jesus was eating in the house of Simon the Pharisee and a prostitute (identified as Mary Magdalene) came in and washed, dried, and anointed his feet. While the humans are focused on Jesus and the woman, two salukis are preoccupied with food that has been dropped under the table. The art historian Giorgio Vasari particularly praised the dogs, which he said were "so beautiful that they appeared real and alive." Dogs (and sometimes cats) also appear in the foreground of Titian's and Tintoretto's portrayals of the Last Supper, Titian's and Veronese's of the *Supper at Emmaus*, Veronese's *Marriage at Cana,* and Tintoretto's *Miracle of the Loaves and Fishes.* Preoccupied with their own concerns and oblivious to the momentous spiritual events that are going on, these animals form a link to the everyday world we know and thus make it easier for ordinary viewers to relate to the holy characters in the picture.

6. Le Nain Brothers, *The Supper at Emmaus,* 1645

On the third day after the crucifixion, Jesus appeared to two of his disciples and ate with them in the village of Emmaus. In contrast to the Venetians' typically elegant, luxurious renditions of biblical scenes, the Le Nains, who specialized in realistic scenes of rustic life, portrayed peasants in an inn. Instead of aristocratic hunting dogs, they included a short-legged mongrel, possibly a turnspit. Like other dogs in similar situations, it shows no interest in the holy conversation taking place over its head.

7. Jacob Jordaens, *The Bean King,* 1640–45 or c. 1655

Dogs were usually on hand in Flemish and Dutch scenes of revelry in order to point up the animality of the human participants. The occasion here is a Twelfth Night celebration, when a bean was placed in a cake and whoever got it in his piece became king of the feast. A crowd of revelers are having riotous fun and drinking too much; the sign on the wall reads *Nec similius insano quam ebrius,* "Nothing resembles a madman more than a drunkard." The coarse and fleshy king, some blowsy women, a vomiting man, and a small child who has been given wine are complemented by a large dog that stands in the foreground, gazing hopefully with open mouth at the child. In striking contrast to the dog, who is trying to participate, a baleful cat curled underneath the king's chair pointedly dissociates itself from the proceedings. Nevertheless, the scene appears more exuberantly fun-filled than wicked.

8. Jan Steen, *The World Upside Down,* 1663

A tipsy, disheveled couple, probably a prostitute and the father of the family, are feeling each other up in the center of the picture, a young man fiddles, a little boy smokes, a girl steals from the cupboard, the unheeded baby has knocked its dish to the floor, the housewife sleeps, and a dog does its part by getting up on the table to steal some pie. No one pays any attention to the ostentatiously pious old couple who preach reformation to them. Steen's humorous treatment livens and softens his moralizing message. He included this slim white spaniel with its characteristic brown markings in many of his paintings, from heroic and biblical scenes (such as *The Sacrifice of Iphigenia* and *The Dismissal of Hagar*) to middle- and lower-class scenes where it draws attention to sexual content (e.g., *A Woman at Her Toilet, Bathsheba After the Bath, The Sick Girl*) or exemplifies domestic disorder. He represented the dog in various sizes, from very small to medium, depending on the requirements of his composition.

9. Pierre-Auguste Renoir, *Madame Georges Charpentier and Her Children,* 1878.

In this contrasting, typically nineteenth-century view, the dog contributes to family harmony rather than accentuating animality in a disorderly household. Unlike the court mastiffs of Van Dyck (in *Children of Charles I*) and Velázquez (in *Las Meninas*), this Newfoundland is an important member of a loving family. Porthos, named after Dumas' strongest and most generous musketeer, contributes significantly to the atmosphere of well-being in this picture of a prosperous nineteenth-century home. His size conveys stability; his placidity, harmony and contentment. Georges Charpentier was an eminent publisher and art collector, who with his wife, Marguerite, regularly entertained Renoir and other distinguished guests. The Japanese decor of the drawing room, Madame Charpentier's Worth dress, and the Newfoundland are all evidence of fashion and wealth. Nevertheless, Madame Charpentier is represented less as a grande dame than as a loving and attentive mother. She presides in the rear, with three-year-old Paul beside her and six-year-old Georgette sitting on the Newfoundland, who is placed in front, as if protecting the children. His soft, luxuriant coat echoes her black-and-white dress, thus suggesting the protective, stabilizing role they both fill. Far from incidental, "Porthos is the rock and anchor of this domestic group" (James Rubin).

10. Tiziano Vecelli, *Danae,* 1553–54

A pretty toy spaniel contributes to the voluptuous sensuality of Titian's

Danae, about to be impregnated by Zeus in the form of a shower of gold. (Danae's father had shut her up away from males when he learned that her son would cause his death.) The beautiful naked young woman lies spread out invitingly, bathed in warm light. A similar dog lies curled up by Titian's provocative nude Venus of Urbino.

11. Jean-Honoré Fragonard, *The Love Letter,* 1770s

This picture is altogether more delicate in subject and technique, but here, too, a toy dog, evidently a poodle, calls attention to the sexual content of the scene. The lady's bouquet holds a love letter, and she looks back provocatively at the viewer; the dog, sitting rump to rump with her, equally engages our eyes. Although the woman may be a wife reading a letter from her husband (Boucher's son-in-law, whose name may be read on the note), her expression, together with the dog's, conveys a titillating effect.

12. Jan van Eyck, *The Arnolfini Portrait,* 1434

Here the toy terrier is definitely emblematic of erotic desire in the form of marital fidelity. The painting probably commemorates the betrothal of van Eyck's friend Giovanni Arnolfini, a rich Italian cloth merchant who had settled in Bruges, to Giovanna Cenami. He raises his right hand to confirm his oath to marry the woman, and they join hands to signify their mutual consent. In the mirror on the back wall can be seen two men, one of them van Eyck himself, who are coming to witness the betrothal oath. Other symbolic items in the painting, besides the dog, are the marriage bed behind the couple and the single candle in the chandelier, burning even though it is daylight to signify the everlasting nuptial flame or the eye of God.

13. Tiziano Vecelli, *Captain with a Cupid and a Dog,* c. 1552

Dogs in portraits often contribute to the self-image that the subject wishes to project to the public. Men are typically represented with large hunting dogs that reinforce an image of wealth, manly prowess, and lordly dominion. Titian's portrait enhances the officer's virile, assertive appearance with the powerful hunting mastiff that stands foursquare and determined behind him. But this portrait conveys an ambivalent message, for the plain, straightforward dog contrasts with fantastic elements reflecting artificial human civilization—the man's elaborate costume, the cupid holding an extravagant helmet, and the dreamy landscape behind them. The subject has been variously identified, most often as Giovanni dell'Acquaviva, a man who lived most of his life in exile but claimed the title of Duke of Atri.

14. Anthony Van Dyck, *James Stuart, Duke of Richmond and Lennox,* 1634

This aristocrat wanted to project a very different image. The subject is a tall, slim, elegant man standing with a narrow-headed greyhound gazing adoringly up at him, so as to encourage the man's blatant self-conceit. At the same time that the greyhound enhances the elegance and the social superiority of the man, it confirms the impression that both are stupid aristocrats. Could there be a satiric undertone? James Stuart, twenty-one years old at the time, was a distant cousin and close confidant of King Charles I. The portrait was probably painted to commemorate his investiture into the Order of the Garter, for it shows him wearing the insignia, a gold and silver star on his cape, and the garter itself below his left knee.

15. William Hogarth, *A Painter and His Pug,* 1745

This self-portrait lies at the opposite extreme. Both Hogarth and his dog, Trump, are plain citizens—solid, square, free of affectation, and direct of gaze. Both give the impression of firm, honest judgment, unpretentious self-respect and self-confidence. Hogarth joked about the close resemblance between his face and the dog's, and, by placing them on about the same level, he suggests that they are equal companions. He reworked an old portrait of himself as artist to include Trump, and this picture became very widely known when he engraved it and made it the frontispiece for the bound volumes of his prints. Fourteen years later Hogarth drew the identification even closer. In the course of a feud with the poet Charles Churchill, he remodeled this engraving into *The Bruiser.* Keeping the composition and the portrait of the dog the same, he replaced his own portrait with Churchill's (represented as a bear) and expressed his own feelings by making the dog urinate on Churchill's *Epistle to William Hogarth.* The eighteenth-century pug was less exaggerated than the modern breed: its legs were longer, its face less flat, and its eyes less protruding.

16. Anthony Van Dyck, *Children of Charles I,* 1637

The seven-year-old Prince of Wales, the future Charles II, stands in the center, facing directly forward. He is flanked by Mary, James (the future James II), Elizabeth, and baby Anne. The enormous mastiff that sits beside the prince suggests protection for the precious royal child; at the same time, the position of his little hand on its head, indicating dominion over something much larger than he, indicates the great power he will wield when he rules over his future kingdom. One of the Stuart family's favorite toy spaniels looks up from the lower right corner toward the younger children. In contrast to the poised, formally posed older children, accustomed to royal status, the dogs (and the baby) behave naturally and without self-consciousness.

17. Diego Velázquez, *Infante Felipe Próspero,* 1659

There is pathos in the contrast between the natural dog and the two-year-old prince, sole heir to the throne of Spain. The solemn, elaborately dressed child stands stiff and constrained by his social obligations, while the toy spaniel has felt free to drape itself comfortably over a chair. The dog suggests the soft natural child under the stiff figure of state and reminds us that this important person is also small and vulnerable. The little boy died two years later.

18. Édouard Manet, *Tama, the Japanese Dog,* c. 1875

Manet has marvelously caught the spirit of this tiny dog, whose name means *jewel* in Japanese. Tama is clearly a cherished animal with every reason to think well of himself; he packs self-assured, alert vitality into a small, fluffy body. When Renoir painted the same animal, he emphasized soft prettiness and affectionate compliance and conveyed less life. Tama belonged to Henri Cernuschi, an early collector of Far Eastern art. Manet emphasized the dog's exotic origin by placing a Japanese doll in front of him. Japanese Chins had been introduced in the West in 1853; at that time, they were less flat-faced and less profusely furred than today's breed.

19. Théodore Géricault, *Bulldog,* c. 1815

This equally lively canine portrait represents a formidable individual rather than an indulged member of the family. This is the old-style bulldog, an animal that would face bulls or dogs or anything else. However, Géricault emphasizes its alertness, forcefulness, and determination rather than its ferocity. Wary rather than aggressive, it boldly meets the eyes of human viewers, confronting them as equals. While Tama could count on favorable attention from people, this bulldog will insist on maintaining its space.

20. Rosa Bonheur, *"Barbaro" After the Hunt,* undated (mid-nineteenth century)

In contrast to the conventional sporting dog portrait, Bonheur's painting shows an engaging mongrel and emphasizes his personal feelings rather than his function as a hunting dog. Barbaro reacts to his bath (indicated by the bucket and brush) with the characteristic half-apprehensive, half-mutinous look of a dog resisting authority.

21. Alexandre-François Desportes, *Dog Guarding Game,* 1724

Bird dogs have been bred and trained to control their impulses in deference to human wishes, and this pointer, virtuously resisting its desire to eat the meat in front of it, illustrates the dog totally subject to human discipline. Its tongue is hanging out for a taste of the pile of game that it has presumably helped to catch, yet it forces itself not to touch it. Its strained pose—feet planted and head twisted around to gaze at the meat—indicates its mental tension. Framed by a column base and a luxuriant rosebush, this scene clearly demonstrates the dominion of man over animals and all of nature. The painting celebrates the beautiful, skilled dog and its subjection at the same time. King Louis XIV, who had a hunting staff of 115 men, 250 horses, and 200 couple of hounds, maintained Desportes as official painter of the royal hunt.

22. Constant Troyon, *Hound Pointing,* 1860

Influenced by Romantic exaltation of wildness and freedom, Troyon painted this pointer (not a hound) as a natural dog. He stands alone in a vast, undefined landscape and dominates the scene, like an impressive independent wild animal. The lean, fit dog is climbing up a bank, alertly scenting for game and oblivious to anything human. He exerts his muscles to hunt on his own, rather than to restrain his natural desires. The brilliant light on his body helps to make him a heroic figure, the monarch of all he surveys.

23. Frans Snyders, *Wild Boar Hunt,* mid-seventeenth century

In contrast to the usual idealized, stylized pictures focusing on the shapeliness and grace of hounds and quarry, Snyders realistically shows us hounds at their work. The dogs are aggressive killers, sinking their teeth into the boar. But it is not only the beleaguered boar who is suffering: the dogs have to throw themselves on a ferocious and well-armed animal. One has fallen under the boar's sharp front hoof and is trying to protect itself against the tusks by biting. Two others have been thrown onto their backs and are howling in agony. Presumably the pack will win, but only after more pain and risk of death.

24. Thomas Gainsborough, *Pomeranian Bitch and Pup,* 1777

Gainsborough portrays this canine mother and her offspring alone in a woods, as if they were independent animals. They belonged to his friend the musician Carl Friedrich Abel; in his portrait of Abel, Gainsborough showed the dog lying comfortably on the floor by Abel's feet, companionable rather than adoring. The Pomeranian of Gainsborough's time, recently introduced from Prussia, had not yet been miniaturized; it weighed about thirty-five pounds.

25. Jean-Baptiste Oudry, *Bitch-Hound Nursing Her Puppies,* 1752

This canine mother, on the other hand, is shown in a human setting, emphasizing her dependence on humans. Her strained pose and alert, anxious expression suggest that she cannot be sure of the security of her family. It was startlingly unconventional for Oudry, official painter of the sporting dogs of Louis XV, to portray a nondescript mother dog in a barn, and even more unconventional to invest her maternal devotion with an emotional intensity that makes it seem as strong and important as a woman's. Oudry even directed a ray of light on her head and the paw she has raised to accommodate the pups so as to suggest a heavenly illumination of sacred maternity. He showed his picture alongside heroic human subjects at the Salon, where sympathetic spectators accepted his hound as a model of human motherhood.

26. Robert Alexander, *The Happy Mother,* 1887

This realistic picture of a canine mother and her puppies is made anthropomorphic by its title. Although the family are working-class collies living in a barn, there is no suggestion of poverty, discomfort, or insecurity here, as in Oudry's picture. This mother is serene, comfortable, and relaxed, as well as loving. Motherhood is presented the way sentimental Victorians liked to see it—as undiluted carefree happiness.

27. Sir Edwin Landseer, *A Jack in Office,* before 1833

The pose and especially the title make this picture anthropomorphic, but the dogs are realistically portrayed. At the same time, their expressions and poses vividly convey the emotions dogs share with humans. A bulldog has been left to guard his master's meat truck, and hungry dogs—some starving, some greedy—gather hopefully around. The portly bulldog is assured and self-satisfied, usefully employed and confident of human support; and he is securely positioned above the others. Thus, like a human jack in office (an insolent upstart in authority), this low-class dog dominates all the others. The most conspicuous and pathetic of the suppliants is an emaciated pointer bitch, staring desperately at the remaining piece of meat in the basket but not strong or bold enough to make a dash to seize it. Her swollen teats indicate that she is pregnant or nursing. An upstart mongrel puppy has got away with stealing a skewer of meat and looks up hopefully for more. A large poodle sits up and begs, hoping perhaps to charm or distract the bulldog. Two other dogs lurk in the background. This picture, like most of Landseer's work, was enormously popular.

28. Susan Meddaugh, illustration from *Martha and Skits,* 2000

Meddaugh's books on Martha, a dog who begins to speak after eating alphabet soup, are particularly beguiling dog stories for children. Meddaugh highlights the qualities Martha shares with humans, while keeping her a plausible dog. In *Martha and Skits,* the puppy Skits (modeled on Meddaugh's own dog) is introduced into Martha's household. She thinks his antics are adorable until he overturns her food dish.

29. Rufino Tamayo, *Animals,* 1941

Dogs can, of course, be ferocious animals as well as friends of man. Tamayo's dogs—all gaping jaws, bared fangs, glaring eyes, and thrusting claws—have no softness about them at all. They are fittingly placed in a bleak landscape, where there is nothing to be seen but barren ground, rocks, and bare bones, suggesting either prey that has been picked clean or a dearth of food. (In the original, the hardness of the shapes is matched by harsh colors: black dogs and rocks against reddish ground and a fiery orange sky.) The dogs seem to be as miserable as they are hostile. Their savagery may reflect Tamayo's feelings about human savagery in World War II.

30. J. M. W. Turner, *Dawn After the Wreck,* c. 1841

This is an equally bleak landscape, but here the dog seems akin to humans rather than alien, as it howls for friends it has lost in the shipwreck. The single simplified shape in the midst of vast barren expanses is a powerful image of desolation, which extends beyond the individual's grief to the loneliness of all sentient beings in an uncaring world. Making the suffering figure a dog universalizes the emotion, and yet we feel such kinship with it that we experience its emotions as human.

First Friend

1

What Dogs Mean to Us

FROM THE BEGINNING of human memory, dogs have been living with virtually every human society on earth. Some Native American myths take the association back even earlier. The Creator God of the Chahto people of California took along his dog as he went around creating the world and humans and constantly talked to it. Apparently the Chahtos could not conceive of a (quasi) human going around without a dog. The Creator God of the Jicarilla Apaches first created a dog. It promptly asked for a companion, and the god created the first man and pronounced him "Pretty good." "He's wonderful!" said the dog. When the man started to move and laugh, the dog "jumped up on him and ran off a little, and ran back and jumped up on him . . . the way dogs do today when they are full of love and delight."[1] For more than ten thousand years, humans have depended on dogs to help them hunt, herd their flocks, and guard their homes. During this time, the social primate and the social carnivore have formed the deepest emotional bonds. The dog became a member of the human family; the human felt a more intimate companionship with the dog than with any other animal.

The dog found a pack that fulfilled its emotional and physical needs, with a wise and powerful pack leader who could offer it more effective care and protection than an alpha wolf could. The human found a child who remained dependent and admiring and never grew up to criticize or abandon its parents, a servant who cheerfully accepted a state of servitude and was grateful for a pat or a plate of scraps, a companion who could be relied on to delight in the company of its human friends. Carlotta O'Neill remarked that the family Dalmatian, on whom Eugene O'Neill wrote a tender epitaph, was "the only one of our children who has not disillusioned us."[2]

We count on a dog's love and trust; we are confident that we understand what it is feeling and thinking and that it sympathizes with our feelings. And yet at the same time, it offers a connection with the natural world outside of human conventions and human interpretations. It responds directly to sounds and scents we cannot even perceive, without attempting to fit them into human intellectual or cultural frameworks. Dogs offer Mark Derr "a certain calm, a connection to the broader world we call nature, a world beyond human control. They remind me that the human way of viewing reality is circumscribed by our senses, our bipedalism, our brains."[3]

Humans are bound by egotistical self-consciousness and by their need to apply standards of rationality or sophistication, morality or social appropriateness. We find release in the company of dogs, who are happily oblivious to such inhibitions. Sigmund Freud normally would not sing because he knew he could not carry a tune. But while stroking his beloved chow Jo-fi, he often found himself humming an aria from *Don Giovanni*.[4] When we need to talk to someone even though we have nothing significant to say, we can prattle on to our dog and know it will not think we are silly. We can caress and murmur sweet nothings to it without suspecting ourselves of mawkishness. We can reach out and touch a dog when we feel an impulse for physical contact, as we would never think of doing to a human. We can relax with dogs as we cannot with other humans, except small children. "Our need to self-censor vanishes in their company . . . in a sense, we are allowed to enter the physical world the way they do: openly, without self-consciousness."[5]

By their amiable obliviousness to human reservations and sensibilities, dogs can dissolve human tensions. Jerome K. Jerome describes an unfortunate party where the six ladies invited belonged to different sets. They sat in two antagonistic groups until the family Newfoundland barged in. He saw that one group was sitting on one side of a screen, one on the other, thought, "That's not a neatly arranged drove of people," and forthwith knocked down the screen. After the resulting confusion, laughter, and apologies, "those six ladies were hopelessly herded together, the dog sitting eying them with contentment." Then "he went in and out among them; he literally bullied them into friendship."[6]

Untroubled by the human need for critical evaluation, dogs can single-mindedly enjoy their dinner or their walk without fretting about higher or more important things or being bored by pleasures that happen the same way every day; the same chow and field are new and exciting each time. Dogs can focus totally on the smells and sounds of their surroundings, without thinking of what happened two months ago or what might happen two months hence. With your dog, "You find yourself exercising two skills that are so elusive in the human world: the ability to live in the present, and the ability to share silence. Snapshot of peace."[7] Although we cannot simply delight in the pleasure of the moment without thinking about it, as dogs do, their enthusiasm can make us forget our preoccupations for a while and share their pleasure. Harold Monro watches his dog running joyfully ahead of him on a walk and regaling itself with the exciting smells, and tells it, "You carry our bodies forward away from mind / Into the light and fun of your useless day."[8] Dogs are loving and beloved friends whose company we can enjoy free of the artificial conventions and complicated demands of human society.

The fact that we cannot communicate with dogs through words can actually improve our rapport. Dogs respond intensely to our feelings without even expecting an explanation, as a human listener inevitably would. W. H. Auden appreciated his dog's absolutely unquestioning sympathy, given with no need to know the dreary details of an unhappy situation or who is to blame for it.[9]

Jerome playfully explained the advantages of an inarticulate companion over the most congenial human: a dog will "not quarrel or argue with you. They never talk about themselves but listen to you while you talk about yourself, and keep up an appearance of being interested in the conversation. They never make stupid remarks," or tactless or unkind ones. "They never tell us our faults . . . a dog . . . never makes it his business to inquire whether you are in the right or in the wrong, never bothers as to whether you are going up or down life's ladder."[10]

Dogs are not troubled by the ambivalence that plagues almost all human relationships; as Freud said, they love their friends and bite their enemies. They offer us love that is not complicated by the calculation and critical examination engendered by human thought processes. And therefore we can feel the same simple love for them that they do for us. Cathy, the young businesswoman in Cathy Guisewite's comic strip, has only one totally unambivalent relationship in her life: with her dog, Electra. She and her sometime beau Irving cannot avoid quarrels and misunderstandings, but they have no problem feeling and expressing love to their dogs. When Irving is going away for a few days and leaves his dog, Vivian, with Cathy, he hugs the dog, assures her he will call her twice a day, and tells her how very much he loves and will miss her. To Cathy, who stands expectantly with open arms, he mumbles, "Sorry. I'm just no good at goodbyes." On his return, Vivian sits in a chair and resolutely ignores him. Cathy explains, "She's punishing you for going away. . . . She actually thinks that if she just lies there glaring and sulking, you'll come groveling!" "Of course I'll grovel! Come here, Baby! I'm groveling!" he responds, while Cathy thinks, "So much to learn from our animal friends."[11]

Because we feel dogs are so close to us, abuse of a dog can arouse at least as much indignation as abuse of a person. Indeed, our sympathy may flow more freely because our positive feelings for dogs are not tainted by the ambivalence we feel toward people. In the spring of 2000, when a woman angered another driver on the Washington Beltway, he came to her car window, seized the bichon frise who was sitting beside her, and hurled him into the stream of traffic, where of course the dog was instantly killed. This shocking episode attracted far more attention than a similar case in which an enraged woman driver shot another woman. Neither victim deserved to be murdered, but a dog—especially a small, white, cuddly one—is so manifestly innocent, as opposed to the moral complications of any human being. Members of the public, who rarely take an interest in the numerous "traditional" murders of humans that take place in our country, gladly contributed a huge reward for finding the man who killed the dog.

The effectiveness of John Berger's novel *King: A Street Story* depends on the positive feeling for dogs that his disreputable characters share with his conventionally respectable readers. Berger successfully engages our sympathy with his erratic street people by narrating their story through their dog, King. Because their relationship with him resembles ours with our dog, we have to feel a certain kinship with them. Because we accept the dog, we are more inclined to share his acceptance of the alien, distasteful lives he describes so matter-of-factly.

American politicians have long been aware that an attachment to dogs endears them to their constituents. Fondness for their pet suggests good-heartedness and wholesome traditional values, as well as kinship with the ordinary voter. Four fifths of our presidents have kept pet dogs, and Calvin Coolidge went so far as to say that "Any man who does not like dogs and want them about . . . does not deserve to be in the White House." Politicians can rely on the public's warm feelings for dogs to defuse awkward situations. When Franklin Roosevelt's opponents accused him of misusing a naval ship to transport his Scottish terrier, Fala, he skillfully used the dog to put them in the wrong. "These Republican leaders have not been content with attacks on me, or my wife, or on my sons," he said with mock solemnity; "they now include my little dog, Fala. . . . You know, Fala is Scotch, and being a Scottie, as soon as he learned that the Republican fiction writers in Congress and out had concocted a story that I had left him behind on the Aleutian Islands and had sent a destroyer back to find him—at a cost to the taxpayers of two or three, or eight or twenty million dollars—his Scotch soul was furious. He has not been the same dog since. . . . I am accustomed to hearing malicious falsehoods about myself. . . . But I think I have a right to resent, to object to libelous statements about my dog."[12]

Although Richard Nixon did not really like dogs, he saved his place on the Eisenhower/Nixon ticket in 1952 by going on television to reveal his family's warm feelings for them. He deflected the charge of accepting improper campaign contributions by admitting that the Nixons *had* accepted a gift: "A man down in Texas heard Pat on the radio mention . . . that our two youngsters would like to have a dog." So he sent them "a little cocker spaniel in a crate . . . all the way from Texas. Black and white spotted. And our little girl Tricia, the six-year-old, named it Checkers. And you know, the kids love the dog, and I just want to say this right now, that regardless of what they say about it, we're gonna keep it."[13] Barbara Bush enlivened her husband's stiff public image by presenting him from the viewpoint of the family dogs. *C. Fred's Story*, supposedly written by the Bush cocker spaniel, and *Millie's Book*, by his springer spaniel successor, reveal a warm, likable man who was devoted to his family and indulged his spunky dogs. The photographs show him solicitously opening the door for C. Fred, or stretched out on the White House lawn playing with Millie's pups, or in bed in his bathrobe with Bar, Millie, and four little grandchildren. Bill Clinton came to the White House with a cat, but soon found it desirable to add a Labrador retriever to the household.[14]

Humans who love dogs are apt to be as uncritical of them as dogs are of their human friends. Ninety-one percent of 1,063 dog owners interviewed in Melbourne in 1980–81 said their dog was good—obedient, well-behaved, gentle, affectionate, effective as a watchdog, and intelligent. "One of the outstanding results of the survey was an absolutely uncritical attitude of owners toward their dogs," the authors summarize; and, they add, surely we would not get such a glowing evaluation of spouses or friends.[15]

Not only do we love dogs uncritically, we praise them for devotion and selflessness far exceeding our own. People long for demonstrations of absolute virtue—unlimited, unshakable love or unhesitating self-sacrifice and courage—and of course rarely find them in their fellow humans. Although dogs, too, are not so totally selfless as people like to think, they can better be fitted into the ideal. Dogs have less developed egos than humans and thus are less demanding of ego gratification. They are readier to risk their lives without thinking of consequences. It is safer to rely on their love, constancy, sympathy, and goodwill than on those of most humans. We demand and get sacrifices from them—in war and medical laboratories, for example—that we would not think of expecting from ourselves or other humans. Stories in which dogs enact extreme heroism or self-sacrifice seem more plausible than analogous tales with human characters.

People are so eager to believe in dogs' superlative constancy that they seize on and magnify any evidence they can find. Dogs rarely have the opportunity to save people's lives, yet we lovingly collect such accounts as if they were typical canine behavior. In classical times, Plutarch and Aelian gathered tales of dogs who chose to die alongside their masters' bodies. The Victorians delighted in the story of Greyfriars Bobby, a terrier that supposedly devoted fourteen years of his life to mourning at the grave of his master, and erected a life-size statue of him in Edinburgh. Such stories are not confined to the Western world: Bobby has an exact counterpart in Japan. Hachiko, an Akita belonging to a professor at Tokyo University, used to meet his master every night at the Shibuya subway station. In 1925, the professor died at the university. Nevertheless, for the remaining nine years of his life, Hachiko would go to the station and wait every night. This model of fidelity so moved his admirers that they set up a statue to him at the subway exit where he used to wait.

Canine devotion and obedience furnish a useful model for pious authors exhorting humans to take a proper attitude toward God. George Washington Doane, a nineteenth-century American bishop, was confident that his dog, Cluny, "thinks that I am God," because the dog depends on him for all benefits as he does on God. But the dog is far quicker to obey his god's commands, accepts "wise corrections" better, is more grateful and more trusting.[16] The dog may also be cited as a model for subject classes of humans. A fourteenth-century bridegroom was unusually explicit. This wealthy bourgeois of sixty wrote a book to instruct his fifteen-year-old bride in her duties of submission and constant attention. She should model her behavior on the dog, who always keeps near its master and avoids all others, who "always has his heart and his eye upon his master" even when they are separated, who "even if his master whip him and throw stones at him . . . follows, wagging his tail and lying down before his master, seeks to mollify him."[17] The idea that uncritical canine affection was becoming in women persisted into Victorian times and was protested by Jane Carlyle, Charlotte Brontë, and George Eliot.

As such human parallels suggest, admiration for canine virtue has a patronizing side. If the dog is canonized, it is for its devotion to human superiors. Buffon digressed from scientific discussion in his *Natural History* to eulogize the dog, but he eulogized it for its perfect subjection to man. William Youatt opened his book on *The Dog* by praising "the disinterested and devoted affection which this noble animal is capable of displaying when he occupies his proper situation, and discharges those offices for which nature designed him"—namely, to be "our destined servant," although also "our companion and friend."[18]

Edmund Burke spelled out the disparagement latent in our loving encomiums on dogs when he used them as an example to contrast the beautiful that inspires love with the sublime that inspires awe. The impact of sublimity depends on fear, he argued; we admire power that could endanger us, but feel contempt for power "that is subservient and innocuous." Dogs may be impressively strong and swift, but because they subordinate these qualities to "our convenience and pleasure," we love but do not respect them.

> *Dogs are indeed the most social, affectionate, and amiable animals of the whole brute creation; but love approaches much nearer to contempt than is commonly imagined; and accordingly, though we caress dogs, we borrow from them an appellation of the most despicable kind, when we employ terms of reproach; and this appellation is the common mark of the last vileness and contempt in every language. Wolves have not more strength than several species of dogs; but, on account of their unmanageable fierceness, the idea of a wolf is not despicable; it is not excluded from grand descriptions and similitudes.*[19]

Dogs are so close to us that we think of them as almost human. But of course they remain animals without our speech and reason, so we do not see them as equals. Therefore we tend to regard them not as independent animals but as lesser humans—not only less reasonable and less moral, but not deserving of the well-being and amenities proper for ourselves. Common expressions reinforce the idea that dogs are and should be subject to worse conditions than humans: for example, "work like a dog," "sick as a dog," "not fit for a dog," "in the doghouse." "Go to the dogs" is to go to ruin. "It shouldn't happen to a dog" suggests that bad experiences are less unsuitable for dogs than humans. A person should never have to lead "a dog's life," and to "die like a dog" is the ultimate degradation.

Because dogs are thought of as second-class people, "dog" and "bitch" are the epithets that leap to mind when we want to denigrate a human. Calling someone a dog is almost invariably an insult, in civilizations from our own to that of the ancient Aztecs. Although the Romans were generally fond of dogs, they called parasites and spiteful people *canis*. "Puppy" is an impudent young person or upstart; "dog," "hound," and "cur" describe contemptible or surly men; "bitch" is used so automatically to abuse women that it has almost lost its canine denotation.[20]

Seeing dogs as lesser humans, we feel free to treat them as we would like, but do not dare, to treat people. We casually adopt them and discard them when we no longer enjoy their company; we breed them into distorted shapes to suit our fancy; we urge them to show courage by fighting to the death; we "break" them to conform to our arbitrary rules of conduct. In literature and legend, we constantly make them demonstrate their worth by self-sacrifice. Our gratification in appreciating such canine virtue can extend to an unpleasant fascination with canine suffering. People can find beauty in the suffering of innocents they perceive as inferior; they can appreciate it without unpleasant agitation of their feelings because they see the sufferers as separate from themselves and not equally entitled to justice. (In the same way, the victimization of less privileged human groups—poor people, people of color, women—has often been accepted as somehow fitting.) Several classic stories feature dogs misjudged by their master, even though he is supposed to be the rational party. The medieval wolfhound Gelert saved his master's baby by killing a huge wolf that menaced it, but when Gelert's master came home to find a blood-covered dog and an empty cradle, he leapt to the conclusion that the dog had killed his child and consequently executed the dog, who had in fact risked his life to save it.[21]

Three notable recent anthologies of dog stories show a strange preoccupation with canine suffering. Nine of the thirty-one stories in Roger Caras's *Treasury of Great Dog Stories* subject their canine protagonists to casual vivisection, persistent abuse by a drunk, enslavement in return for friendly overtures of help, and similar fates. The stories in Michael J. Rosen's and Jeanne Schinto's collections, *The Company of Dogs* and *The Literary Dog*, are more contemporary, sophisticated, and free of sentimental appeals; but half of them center on victimized dogs. Such anthologies must be aimed at readers who like dogs, and yet they are filled with canine unhappiness.

Whether it is distinguished or conventional, depressing or joyful, literature on dogs typically deals with realistic animals in realistic relationships with people. Because dogs are familiar to us as junior humans, we rarely imagine them as supernaturally gifted or demonic. Toy dogs entered fairy tales when pet-cherishing French aristocrats began rewriting the tales in the late seventeenth century. But they were rarely endowed with the magical qualities attributed to wild animals, cats, and even horses. In Madame d'Aulnoy's "The White Cat," the cats act like the transformed aristocrats they are, while the dogs are just pretty little pets. A tiny dog does talk in her "Story of Pretty Goldilocks," but it is only to fulfill the natural dog's role of bringing comfort and encouragement to his mistreated master.

Lina, a repellent-looking monster who behaves like a dog and soon is accepted as one, brings warmth to *The Princess and Curdie,* George MacDonald's unpleasant fairy story about human depravity. But although she is immensely endearing and contributes vitally to the hero's mission, saving his life on several occasions, she shows her worth by typical canine devotion, subservience, and self-sacrifice. Dogs speak and take human roles in Lewis Carroll's kingdom of Dogland in *Sylvie and Bruno,* but the King smiles and wags his tail when Sylvie pats him on the head. They remain dogs, despite the trappings of human society. In Walt Disney's early cartoons, all the animals are humanized except Pluto, Mickey Mouse's bloodhound-type dog. L. Frank Baum's Oz books are filled with wonderful humanized animals with much to say, but Toto, Dorothy's terrier, consistently behaves like a dog and does not speak.[22]

In C. S. Lewis's Narnia, where there are Talking Animals superior in intelligence and status to ordinary ones, the Talking Cat, Ginger, schemes with human intelligence. But the Talking Dogs are "just as doggy as they could be." There was no question of their loyalty in *The Last Battle,* but there was some apprehension that they would not have the wit to recognize the right side. Fortunately, they did; and, "they all stood up and put their front paws on the shoulders of the humans and licked their faces, all saying at once: 'Welcome! Welcome! We'll help, we'll help, help, help. Show us how to help, show us how, how. How-how-how?'" Even in Heaven, the dogs were too busy racing around and sniffing at the ground to take part in the conversation.[23] Ginger is a sophisticated, self-possessed villain with catlike qualities; the Talking Dogs are regular dogs that have the ability to talk.

When dogs appear in science fiction, they continue to play traditional canine roles. In Arthur C. Clarke's "Dog Star," the narrator's Alsatian mix saved his life by alerting him to an earthquake in Berkeley; years after her death, when he was the director of an observatory on the moon, her barking, heard in a dream, woke him just in time to minimize the effects of a lunar earthquake. Lester del Ray imagines a future in which humanity has destroyed itself and Dogs and Apes have evolved toward human levels. Although the Dogs are more intelligent, the Dog narrator predicts that the Apes will succeed to the primary position of humans because dogs have followed man for 200,000 years and cannot become leaders now. "No dog was ever complete without the companionship of Man. The Ape People will be Men."[24]

Dogs most often figure in horror fantasy by reacting with terror to evil spirits that humans do not perceive. One of the first signs that Dracula has arrived in England is the strange behavior of a normally quiet dog, who could not be restrained from barking and howling throughout the funeral of the captain of the doomed ship and finally collapsed.[25] In Algernon Blackwood's "A Psychical Invasion," the psychic expert John Silence brings his dog and cat to the exorcism of an evil spirit. Both animals perceive the spirit more intensely than the man does, and the virtuous dog dies of terror (while the cat's initial response is agreeable titillation).

Frightening supernatural black dogs do appear in folklore and literature, as is only to be expected considering that Satan was supposed to use animals as his agents and that dogs could and occasionally do hunt down and kill people. At a time when everyone was familiar with the sight and sound of packs of hounds in relentless pursuit of their prey, it was not remarkable that spectral packs tore over the countryside or through the sky, usually led by a notorious deceased sinner or by Satan himself. Satan led the Devil's Dandy dogs, a pack of black, fire-breathing, fiery-eyed dogs, over the lonely moors of Cornwall on stormy nights. They would tear to pieces any person they met unless he could fend them off with prayer. The Gabriel Hounds were a pack that ran through the sky (based perhaps on flocks of migrating geese, honking and beating their wings).[26]

The few dogs that did harm people were not endowed with preternatural ability or calculated malevolence, and were usually sinister omens rather than conscious destroyers. A huge black dog with fiery saucer eyes—called Skriker, Trash or Gytrash, Black Shuck, or Padfoot—was supposed to haunt lonely roads at night and pad along beside or behind people. It usually portended disaster but did not harm anyone who did not speak to or touch it. Similarly, the Mauthe Doog or Moddey Dhoo, a great, shaggy black dog that haunted Peel Castle in the seventeenth century, did no injury as long as he was left alone. Every night he would come into the guardroom and lie down before the fire. "No one knew whom he belonged to nor how he came, and he looked so strange that no one dared to speak to him, and the soldiers always went in pairs to carry the keys to the governor's room after the castle was locked up." But one night a soldier, reckless with drink, "snatched up the keys, dared the dog to follow him, and rushed out of the room alone. The dog got up and padded after him, and presently a terrible scream was heard and the man staggered back," cold sober. He never said a word during the three days he survived before he died in agony.[27]

However, supernatural dogs could be as benign as real ones. They might bring criminals to justice, like the huge dog with green eyes that so terrified two murderers in their hiding place in a wood that they ran back to the village and were hanged. Another great dog insistently blocked the way of a captain who was trying to join his crew for a night's fishing and thus prevented them from running into a sudden gale that would have wrecked their boat. When a cottager in Somerset, lost and groping through a sudden mist, "touched shaggy fur," he "thought that old Shep, his sheep-dog, had come out to look for him." But when the dog led him to his cottage door, he heard Shep barking inside. "He turned to look at the dog who had guided him, which grew gradually larger and then faded away." Other spectral black dogs, the Church Grims, guarded churchyards from the devil and witches. Even a headless dog, which naturally terrified those who saw him because he was so gruesome, had his head shot off while defending his master and was not aggressive to people.[28]

Arthur Conan Doyle was inspired to create the apparently supernatural "Hound of the Baskervilles" by the legend of a ghost dog who returned to haunt the squire who had murdered him and his mistress on Dartmoor. In

Doyle's story, the Baskerville family has been haunted by a huge and appalling hound that originally appeared to tear out the throat of a seventeenth-century Baskerville who had hunted a girl to her death on the moor. It has now apparently come back, terrifying the neighborhood with its baying; it has pursued the last baronet to his death and menaces the current one. Watson describes the "dreadful shape" of "an enormous coal-black hound, but not such a hound as mortal eyes have ever seen. Fire burst from its open mouth, its eyes glowed with a smouldering glare, its muzzle and hackles and dewlap were outlined in flickering flame."[29] However, Sherlock Holmes soon reveals that the evil is located not in a demonic dog, but in a human murderer. The next heir to the title bought a bloodhound-mastiff cross from a London dog dealer, starved it to make it vicious, daubed it with phosphorus to simulate a supernatural fiery glow, and set it on the baronet's trail.

Michel Parry's collection *The Hounds of Hell: Weird Tales About Dogs* reveals the difficulty of turning a dog into a really horrifying figure. Of his sixteen stories, three are not about real dogs, alive or dead. Five others feature canine ghosts that fulfill the traditional duty of avenging their murdered masters and do not horrify because they are executing justice. One tells of a harmless phantom dog that is heard but not seen, and in another the ghost is positively benevolent, barking at sentries asleep on duty to save them from punishment. Only three stories make use of realistic dogs to create horror. In Ray Bradbury's "The Emissary," a dog's characteristic loyalty and helpfulness, together with his bad habit of digging, produces disaster. The dog brightens the life of a bedridden child by bringing him scents from the world outside and then human visitors, notably his favorite teacher. After she is killed in a car accident, the dog comes bearing the smell of earth and death, and something worse will follow. "Dog was a bad dog, digging where he shouldn't. Dog was a good dog, always making friends. Dog loved people. Dog brought them home." An even more haunting story, Arthur Bradford's "Roslyn's Dog," derives its horror from the bleak lives that people too readily assume are acceptable for dogs. A young man feels sorry for his neighbor Roslyn's dog because she stays alone all day in a small chicken-wire pen. When he sympathetically communes with her, she magically contrives to shift him into her shape and place; and when we last see him, he is reduced to greeting Roslyn exuberantly when she comes every morning to leave him his bowl of dry kibble.[30]

Two anthologies of *Canine Crimes*, edited by Jeffrey Marks and Cynthia Manson, suggest that dogs (unlike cats) cannot be presented as convincing criminals. In all but one of the stories in *Canine Crimes*, dogs are just unwittingly involved in the detective plot, as when a retriever's greed for sweets leads her to find a drowned woman (Valerie Wolzien's "Nosing Around for a Clue").[31] Cynthia Manson's *Canine Crimes II* includes one effective horror story, Pauline C. Smith's "The Dog"; but as in "The Hound of the Baskervilles," the evil is really located in a human. Fred, an unpleasant, possessive man, has just died, after studying transmigration of souls and telling his wife that he will return. When she and their niece come home from his funeral, they find a large, ugly dog sitting on the front stoop, showing "a fanged grin" and a bald spot on his head, just like Fred's. They take one look and dash around through the back door. They hear the dog scratching, first at the front and then at the back. Then he leaps in through the bathroom window, where Fred knew the screen was loose. Although they manage to kill the animal, they can never quite convince each other that he was nothing more than a dog with mange on his head.

Negative images of dogs, reflecting contempt for the member of society who is less than human, complacent acceptance of canine suffering, or fear of dogs' capacity to inflict injury, are few and mild in comparison to our positive images, ranging from amiable companions to models of love and self-sacrifice. Through the thousands of years that dogs have been part of the human scene, we have seen them as our familiar friends among the animals, our happiest connection with nonhuman nature. At the same time, we often think of them almost as people, with motives and feelings like our own. Even in our fantasies, we tend to imagine dogs as the helpful, reliable creatures we know so well in actual life. The dog's merits have shone even brighter by contrast with its wild cousin, the wolf. Unlike the wild ancestors of other domesticated animals, the wolf survived and remained known, if not familiar, to those who loved and valued dogs. Although wolves were extirpated in England during the Middle Ages, they fed on corpses on European battlefields and actually killed people on the streets of Paris up until the seventeenth century. And their memory was kept fresh by folktales such as "Little Red Riding Hood." The cat arouses ambivalence in humans because it has the qualities of an alien predator *and* an amiable pet, but canine qualities can be conveniently split between the savage wolf and the loving, obedient dog.

2

How the Partnership Started

I N R U D Y A R D K I P L I N G ' S fable about the domestication of animals, "The Cat That Walked by Himself," Dog smelled meat cooking at the human hearth and went to the cave to investigate, where he found only the Woman awake. He asked her what smelled so good, and she threw him a roasted bone. When he asked for another,

> The Woman said, "Wild Thing out of the Wild Woods, help my Man to hunt through the day and guard this Cave at night, and I will give you as many roast bones as you need." . . .
>
> Wild Dog crawled into the Cave and laid his head on the Woman's lap, and said, "O my Friend and Wife of my Friend, I will help your Man to hunt through the day, and at night I will guard your Cave." . . .
>
> When the Man waked up he said, "What is Wild Dog doing here?" And the Woman said, "His name is not Wild Dog anymore, but the First Friend, because he will be our friend for always and always and always. Take him with you when you go hunting."[1]

Kipling's fable comes remarkably close to the account that scientists have pieced together of the domestication of the dog. The dog was our first domestic animal, it probably joined us voluntarily, and women may have been the first to make a pet of it.

It is now generally agreed that all dogs, from the Saint Bernard to the Pekingese, evolved from wolves. Structurally and behaviorally, they are closer to wolves than to any other canids, and there is no evidence in the fossil record of any other animal that could have developed into the dog. Dogs still retain many lupine characteristics. Breeds such as the German shepherd look much like wolves—with the wolf's long muzzle, strong jaws, large erect ears, long hanging tail, and long, strong legs for distance running. They have the wolf's excellent senses of sight, smell, and hearing.[2] Dogs are predators and vigorously defend their territory. They all have the wolf's strong loyalty to their pack and their leader, precise recognition of status and hierarchy, and complex patterns of communication, including vocalizations, facial expressions, and bodily postures; they express affection and playfulness, anger and fear, dominance and submission in the same way. They bark at intruders on their territory, howl when they want companionship, whimper when they are afraid. A subordinate wolf greets a dominant one by wagging its tail enthusiastically while maintaining a low body posture, just as a dog greets its master. Both wolves and dogs identify one another primarily by secretions of scent glands inside their anus, so they make acquaintance by sniffing one another's rear ends. Wolves and dogs can still interbreed.

Actually, the social characteristics that wolves had developed were also developed by humans of forty thousand years ago, who shared a similar lifestyle. Both were successful predatory species that adopted social structures in order to hunt cooperatively and thus be able to kill animals larger than themselves. Both humans and wolves organized themselves into large family groups, held together by affection and mutual support and acknowledgment of a leader. To maintain their complex social relationships, wolves as well as people developed acute awareness of the feelings of others, elaborate greeting displays, and other ways of communicating shades of respect or assertiveness. Wolves and humans have sufficiently similar natural behavior patterns that they can readily adapt to living in a combined group.

Raymond and Lorna Coppinger suggest that wolves started the process of domestication themselves, when they gathered around human camps to scavenge for garbage. This provided an easier and steadier livelihood than hunting, and the humans would have been glad to have someone clean up their living site. The canids could also profit from the warmth and protection of human fires. Obviously, only wolves that were naturally less wary and fearful than average would approach humans, and humans would tolerate only those that were relatively unaggressive and willing to accept subordinate status. They would kill or drive away intractable animals, while nurturing docile, friendly ones. As time passed and scavenging off humans became their regular way of life, the wolves would become less wary and ferocious—more tame, in fact; and they would no longer require the initiative, strong jaws, and formidable teeth of animals that must pull down big game. The most reliable way to date the transition from wolf to dog in the fossil record is to examine jaws and teeth. A dog's jaw is shorter than a wolf's and its teeth are smaller. People would have preferred less well-armed animals, and dogs did not need the wolf's formidable hunting weapons. Humans unwittingly created a new environmental niche, and wolves evolved to fill it, incidentally becoming more and more like dogs as they did so.[3]

Wolves living around the human community would tend to breed with each other and pass on their particular traits, whether the relative tameness that predisposed them to move into the human environment or random characteristics such as the tail curled over the back, which is widespread among dogs and never found among wolves. At some point, dogs would develop into a new species; that is, "a group of interbreeding natural populations that is genetically isolated from other such groups as a result of physiological or behavioral barriers."[4]

The remains of gnawed bones show that humans occasionally ate canids, especially pups. But it is probable that they also made pets of them. Wolf cubs are endearing, and a woman who had lost her baby might well adopt a cub and suckle it until it could eat food scraps, as women in primitive tribes still do. Being an eagerly social animal, the little wolf would make friends with members of the group, play with the children, accept leadership from those it perceived as stronger and more knowing, and try to please them. If two of these pets mated, or a female bred with a wild male and reared her puppies within the human camp, her pups would grow up as members of the human pack.[5]

Humans would naturally encourage animals that retained the immature canid characteristics of docility and friendliness. Along with puppylike personalities, dogs developed puppylike physical characteristics as well, such as shorter faces and drooping ears, as opposed to the long muzzles and erect ears of all the wild canids. Wild canids' ears become erect very soon after birth, huskies' ears a bit later, and German shepherds' ears later still; most breeds, of course, retain lop ears. A Pekingese has the short face, round head, large braincase, big eyes, floppy ears, short legs, and soft fur of a young wolf cub. Other changes, for example in coat color, might have been encouraged by casual human preference. Wild canids have adaptively cryptic coats, while conspicuous solid colors or spots would not matter in animals living under human protection.

A relatively small change in the genes can alter the rate of development so that an animal retains neotenic characteristics—that is, reaches sexual maturity before it has developed fully adult structure and behavior. For example, slight differences in the pattern of production of thyroxine could produce wide-ranging changes in functions controlled directly or indirectly by the thyroid gland: rates of growth in relation to sexual maturation, as well as fecundity and reproductive timing (through the sex hormones), the degree of docility and stress tolerance (through the adrenal hormones), and even coat color and length. Moreover, a change in any one of these characteristics would affect the others.[6] Wolves reach sexual maturity at about two years, dogs at six to fifteen months. The result is that dogs, like young wolves, look to others (humans/adults) to direct and care for them; are usually content to remain dependent followers in the pack; are playful, curious, eager to make new friends; and ready to deal with new situations. Clearly, such animals are more desirable as pets and helpers to humans than are adult wolves, who are independent, apt to be aggressive and ready to claim dominance, and wary of strangers and strange situations. Because dogs live in protected but often changing environments, they need not be so wary as wild canids but should be more adaptable, rather than balking at every stranger or new situation.[7]

This prehistoric scenario has been confirmed by the work of Dmitry Belyaev on silver foxes in Siberia, which shows how quickly genetically predisposed wild canids can be tamed and how this process produces unintended side effects similar to those that appeared in dogs. Belyaev, who was in charge of a huge fox-fur farm in Novosibirsk, wanted to develop a strain of foxes that would more readily tolerate contact with people. Of a study population of 465 foxes, he selected the 10 percent who were most calm and curious toward people and displayed the least fear or aggression. He bred among this group and continued selecting for succeeding generations. After only twenty generations he had "naturally tame animals that . . . would search for their keepers, climb on them, . . . sit on the windowsill waiting for someone to approach, roll over to get their tummies rubbed, and let people carry them around and give them their shots." They would wag their tails and answer to their names. In addition, many of them spontaneously developed drooping ears, like dogs and young foxes, and mottled coats and tails that turned up at the end, like dogs. They barked like dogs, as foxes almost never do in the wild. These surprisingly speedy and seemingly diverse changes were produced by inducing neoteny, so that the foxes reached sexual maturity while continuing to behave like immature animals. Belyaev and his associates "compressed into a few decades an ancient process that originally unfolded over thousands of years."[8]

Belyaev's tame female foxes came into heat twice a year, instead of once, just as dogs can breed twice a year and wolves only once.[9] Dogs breed promiscuously, unlike monogamous wolves; dog mothers do not give their puppies prolonged care, as wolves do, and dog fathers usually take no role at all. Dogs do not need the firm family structure of wolves, since humans have taken over parental care after weaning.

The dog's long dependence on humans has affected its cognitive abilities as well. Because they retain juvenile playfulness and malleability, dogs can learn new things better than adult wolves, with their relatively fixed mature behavioral repertoire. Wolves, who must maintain themselves in nature, excel in independent problem-solving, while dogs, after untold generations of living in human society, excel in responding to human signals and instructions. Harry Frank kept a female wolf pup, a three-quarter wolf-dog hybrid, and a male malamute in a kennel separated from their outdoor compound "by a door that required two distinct operations to unlatch. First the handle had to be pushed toward the door, and then it had to be rotated. Our malamute watched us perform this task several times a day for six years and never did learn to do it himself; our wolf-malamute hybrid was able . . . after watching us for only two weeks; and our older female wolf learned the task after watching the hybrid once." Moreover, she modified his technique to suit herself, using her paws rather than her muzzle, as he did. On the other hand, the wolf could not (or would not) learn to follow human commands.[10] Wild canids do not appear in circus performances.

Some see the dog as a degenerate wolf—dogs are "just smart enough to do a job and just dumb enough to do it"[11]—but surely it is a question of different rather than lesser abilities. It is an achievement to understand the body language and expectations of a very different species as well as dogs do those of humans. And it is also remarkable that dogs are capable of adapting to such a wide variety of human environments. A study by Brian Hare and others showed that dogs are much more skilled at reading human signals than our closest relatives, chimpanzees. If food is hidden in containers in such a way that it can be found only by responding to human signals—glancing at, pointing to, or touching the correct container—dogs have no trouble finding it, while chimpanzees pay no attention to the cues. Rather than trying to control their environment themselves—usually not possible for them—dogs develop a keen understanding of human behavior so as to communicate wishes to humans and manipulate them to achieve what they want. For most dogs, humans are the most important feature of the environment. "Evolution hasn't honed the dog's problem-solving skills, just its people-reading skills."[12]

Although dogs' senses and instincts have been somewhat dulled by domestication, Konrad Lorenz points out, they greatly excel wild animals in two qualities more relevant to intelligence: adaptability and curiosity. The same, of course, is true of people.[13] Stanley Coren describes numerous instances of dogs' creatively adapting to situations set up by humans. Peggy, a placid Newfoundland, was being tormented by a hyperactive Maltese; finally she picked up the little dog by the scruff of its neck and dropped it in the bathtub, thus resolving her problem without resorting to violence. Coren lists sixty-four words or phrases that his dogs definitely understand, as shown by their appropriate responses, and argues that there are probably more; John Paul Scott believes dogs can learn to discriminate over one hundred words or phrases.[14] And this is an animal who in nature among its own kind would communicate primarily through body language. The performing dog who appeared to be answering complicated arithmetic problems by barking the appropriate number of times was not, of course, doing calculations. He had, however, figured out on his own that his trainer's posture changed subtly when the correct number was reached; when the man relaxed, so slightly that he was unaware that he was doing so, the dog stopped barking.[15]

In order to do many varied jobs for us, dogs have been bred to be far more specialized than wolves. While the wolf excels as an all-round independent hunter, dogs excel wolves in certain aspects of the hunt. In sight hounds, the wolf's fast endurance running and good long-distance vision for moving objects have been developed into even faster speed (with less endurance) and keener sight (with some loss of scenting ability). In scent hounds, the sense of smell has been marvelously developed, with some loss of visual acuity and speed. Almost all dogs will fight if sufficiently provoked, and they fight as wolves do. But breeds like scent hounds, selected to work together in packs and live together in kennels, are more peaceable than wolves; on the other hand, terriers have been selected to resist pain, attack without warning (as they must to kill rats), be more aggressive than wolves to other canids, and fight to the death, while wolves usually desist when one party has acknowledged defeat.[16]

When wolves become mature, they have a fixed hunting sequence: locate prey / eye-stalk / chase / grab-bite / kill-bite / dissect / consume. Since dogs never fully "grow up" in lupine terms, this sequence remains more flexible and can be modified, so that some motor patterns are lost and others hyperdeveloped. A border collie, for example, controls sheep as wolves control prospective prey, by eying, stalking, and chasing them; but it must not proceed to biting them. A retriever locates game and grab-bites it, but must inhibit the three last steps. Dogs could never compete with wolves as independent predators; feral dogs can survive only where there are no wolves, as in Australia, or around towns and cities.

It is still hard to understand how wolves could be turned into Chihuahuas or dachshunds. Partly it is a matter of the clustering of neotenic genes. In addition, humans could capitalize on naturally occurring mutations that were useful to them, even though these mutations might prevent survival in a natural setting. Acromegaly, which occurs regularly at a rate of one in ten thousand among dogs (as among humans), produces giants who have generally increased bone growth with disproportionately large extremities—huge hands and feet or paws and large skulls with heavy lower jaws and brows. In

dogs, the lips, cheeks, and ears grow out of proportion to the skull, producing wrinkles, hanging jowls, and long floppy ears. Acromegalic dogs may
weigh a hundred kilograms or even more, while the normal upper size limit
for wolves is about sixty kilograms. This abnormality would be selected
against in nature, but humans looking for effective guard dogs would value
the animal's strength and fearsome appearance and not mind its unwieldi-
ness. Another regularly occurring abnormality in dogs and humans is achon-
droplasia, where cartilage hardens into bone too early, producing curved,
stunted limbs and large heads with pug noses.[17] These characteristics, which
would be disastrous in an all-round hunter, could be valued by humans who
wanted a short-legged hound that they could follow on foot or an engagingly
grotesque toy dog. Breeds from all over the world display some or all of the
acromegalic or achondroplastic characteristics.

Once dogs were established around a human settlement, their instinctive
urge to defend their territory would make them useful as watchdogs. Regard-
ing the camp or village as their den and its boundaries as their territory, they
would bark an alarm if strange animals or strange humans entered the area.
Because humans found their barking useful and encouraged it, dogs bark
more often and more readily than wild canids. Sharp-eared, keen-scented,
lightly sleeping animals would have provided an invaluable defense for a
group of sleeping humans.

It would soon have become apparent that these wolf-dogs could help in
hunting as well. Instinctively, they would use their wonderful sense of smell
to locate game and use the wolf's hunting techniques of running down animals, bringing them to bay, and joining in group attacks on large prey. They
would drive game within reach of human weapons, which in turn increased
the efficiency of canine hunting by making it possible to kill or cripple prey
without coming to close quarters. When men began to use bows and arrows
rather than stone axes in hunting, dogs greatly increased their efficiency by
tracking down wounded animals and retrieving bodies.[18]

It is probable that early hunter-gatherers and early dogs lived together as
Aborigines lived with dingoes when Europeans arrived in Australia. Although
most dingoes "lived and hunted as wild carnivores," Aboriginal families kept
some "as pets, used some as hunting partners, ate them when meat was scarce

and also showered them with affection." What dogs could contribute to the welfare of a primitive society is illustrated by the case of the Onges, a tribe in the Andaman Islands who acquired dogs only in 1857. They had had to live on fish and shellfish until dogs gave them access to meat by enabling them to catch wild pigs.[19] In a Bushman community that included seven hunters, the one man with a trained pack of hunting dogs brought in 75 percent of the meat.[20]

Finally, dogs proved invaluable allies when humans began to domesticate herd animals, perhaps about 9000 BCE in the Middle East. People needed help in protecting their sheep and goats from the predators that were still everywhere; dogs provided the necessary vigilance. They might have started to do this spontaneously, as today the dogs that hang around Masai villages follow the men driving the cattle herds and alert them by barking if a lion approaches. At some point humans learned to use dogs' instinctive skills to herd livestock as well: they could drive animals and separate selected ones from the herd in the same manner that wolves hunt reindeer and other large animals. As F. E. Zeuner points out, "The wolf knew how to round up ruminants long before man thought of doing so."[21] Dogs could also drive wild ungulates from crops. If dogs did not actually make it possible for humans to settle in towns and feed themselves through agriculture, they certainly made it easier.

At present, the earliest definite dog fossil known is a jawbone from Germany, dated at 12,000 BCE. Jaw fragments from Idaho, identifiable by their relatively small size and crowded teeth, date from 9500 to 8400 BCE. Two distinguishable varieties of dog were found in Danish peat bogs dating from about 7000 BCE, a smaller and a larger. Figurines recognizable as dogs by their upcurled tails, dating from 4970 BCE, have been found in Iraq. Canine remains dating back to 5000 BCE have also been found in the Far East, eastern North America, and Peru. By 3000 BCE, dogs were distributed all over Europe. They were so obviously useful that they quickly spread from tribe to tribe and were soon found wherever people lived. The most convincing evidence that dogs had become pets appears in certain early burials, where dog skeletons are found with humans. In a grave in northern Israel, dated at 10,000 BCE, the skeleton of an elderly woman was found with her hand resting on the chest of a four- or five-month-old puppy.[22] Surely they had been companions in life.

Dogs must have been domesticated in the Northern Hemisphere, since wolves never lived south of the equator, but not in the far north, where the native wolves are much larger than the medium small early dogs. Probably they were originally domesticated in the Near East and southern Asia, where there are two subspecies of small wolves, the Indian, *Canis lupus pallipes*, and the Arabian, *C. lupus arabs*. The Near Eastern wolves weigh fifty to sixty pounds and look very much like present-day dingoes and the local pariah dogs. Most authorities believe that dogs were domesticated at different times and places, by different peoples and from various local subspecies of wolves. Juliet Clutton-Brock has sketched probable relationships between different types of dogs and four geographical races of wolves. The Indian wolf is the probable ancestor of dingoes, pariah dogs, greyhounds, and mastiffs. Northern (spitz) dogs are descended from the North American wolf; shepherd dogs, terriers, and sporting dogs from the European wolf; and prehistoric American dogs, chows, and Oriental toy dogs from the Chinese wolf.[23]

Discounting early archaeologists' attempts to separate Stone Age dogs into breeds, Scott emphasizes their similarity. They probably resembled modern dingoes, which have retained many primitive characteristics: medium size, between wolf and jackal; grayish-yellow coat; erect ears; and, usually, hanging tails. They would have been all-purpose hunting and watchdogs.[24] The up-curved tail of many dogs was probably an early mutation, since it is so widespread—found in such widely distributed breeds as Egyptian greyhounds, chows, American Indian dogs, and basenjis. Humans might have cultivated this trait simply because they liked it or as a convenient means of distinguishing between dogs and the wolves that were still prevalent. The distinguishing coat colors of domestic dogs would have served the same purpose.

Northern or polar breeds (now often known as the spitz group) developed in isolation. Their history cannot be traced because they were kept by preliterate peoples. However, the skeletal remains of dogs found at a site in northern Kazakhstan dating from 3600 to 2500 BCE are similar in size and form to the modern Samoyed breed developed in the same region. They were presumably used, like later Samoyeds and huskies, for pulling sleds or carrying packs. Northern peoples started harnessing dogs to sleds in fan arrangement from the eighth or ninth century.[25] Dogs, the only draft animals that could endure the cold and wind, made it possible for humans to survive in the far north, where they could only live as nomads and therefore needed animals to help them carry their belongings. The northern dogs still retain wolflike characteristics, such as erect ears and thick, heavy coats; and they are less dependent on humans than many breeds, for sled dogs look to their canine leader. They all have wedge-shaped skulls framed by display ruffs, square robust builds for prolonged trotting, and a tail carried over the back.

Dogs would soon become differentiated, as they were subject to varied selection pressures in varied and changing human cultures. Even in a primitive society, breeding could be partially controlled by killing undesirable dogs, encouraging desirable ones to breed, and confining a bitch in season to keep her from mating with an undesirable dog. Genetic variations such as abnormally large size would arise by accident, and if humans considered such traits desirable, they could encourage these animals to reproduce.

Although systematic breeding in the modern sense would not have been possible before modern understanding of genetics and carefully maintained stud books, preliterate peoples were entirely capable of keeping varieties separate. The Tahltan people of coastal Northwest America had dingolike all-purpose "Village Dogs" and smaller spitz-type dogs kept for their long, thick, soft fur. These were sheared several times a year, and their hair was woven into blankets, which were a major indicator of wealth and status. The Tahltan did not need a sophisticated knowledge of genetics to observe that the hair of offspring produced by interbreeding would be shorter than that of purebred wool dogs. To preserve their valuable fur, these dogs had to be prevented from interbreeding with the village dogs, despite the difficulties of restraining dogs without chew-proof leashes and adequate fencing materials. When they could not be closely monitored, as in the summer fishing and hunting season, the wool dogs were sequestered, with buried dried fish for food, on a small offshore island. Clearly, it was possible to control dogs' reproduction when there was a sufficiently compelling economic motive. The type disappeared when European trade blankets superseded dog-hair blankets as the preferred status item.[26]

The dog is the only domestic animal found in practically every human culture, ranging from Arctic pack ice to equatorial jungles. When people came from Asia to populate the Americas, they brought dogs with them, as

did those who sailed to the Pacific Islands and Australia. In most of these societies, dogs had a special status. At a site in Kazakhstan dating back to 3600
BCE, for example, dog skeletons were found buried at the thresholds or foundation pits of houses, suggesting that they had ritual significance as
guardians of homes. The same practices were found from England to
China.[27] Often this symbolism extended to the spiritual realm, as dogs
guarded crucial gates and bridges in the land of the dead. Like earthly dogs,
they had a vivid sense of who should be admitted to a territory and who
challenged. In Zoroastrian tradition, Yima's two "four-eyed" dogs (with a
spot above each eye) guarded the Chinvat Bridge between this world and the
next, where gods and demons struggled for possession of souls. The dogs
would fight to save a good soul, but they let wicked souls, especially those
who had harmed a dog in life, fall into the abyss. In Icelandic mythology,
Garm, the dog of Hel, goddess of the dead, was chained by the entrance to
the underworld and demanded an offering. Charitable people who had given
bread to the hungry in this world would find bread in their hand to give
Garm so he would let them pass unscathed. The Iroquois also imagined a
bridge guarded by a great dog, over which the dead must cross. He denied
access to unworthy people, especially those who had abused or neglected
dogs in this world.[28]

A good indication of the symbolic importance of dogs is the strong emotions aroused by the thought of eating them. Most Westerners today would
as soon eat humans, though of course it is acceptable in many parts of the Far
East. Some North American Indians ate dogs, others regarded the practice
with such horror that they stigmatized the first group as "Dog-Eaters," and
for still others, dog was a special ceremonial food used only on sacred occasions.[29] The fact that, from very early times, in many cultures and many geographic areas, dogs were buried with humans or in separate graves of their
own suggests that they were not merely useful animals, but were cherished
companions or had ritual significance.

Tens of thousands of years ago, wolves that were genetically less wary and
fearful, less aggressive, less dominant than their fellows moved into the new
environmental niche presented by human settlements. Gradually, at first without any systematic program, humans came to influence this population by

supporting the dogs with characteristics they considered desirable and killing the others. For the first thousands of years, dogs all over Europe and Asia remained quite similar in conformation, although they varied a bit in size. By the time people were recording their experiences in Egypt and the Middle East, however, there were already several recognizable varieties of dog.

3

Dogs in the Ancient World

C AREFUL SELECTIVE BREEDING of dogs probably began in Sumeria, with a demand for specialized hunting dogs. Once people had domesticated animals as their main source of meat, hunting became a sport more than a necessity. At the same time, societies became stratified and a leisured class emerged that could indulge in hunting for pleasure. From the ubiquitous pariah-dog stock, they developed long-legged, lightly built sight hounds that could run down antelope in open country. These dogs could run faster than wolves—a modern greyhound can reach forty-three miles per hour— and they did not pause to trail their prey by scent, but pursued it by means of their excellent vision. This method worked best in desert countries, where scenting is poor because of the dryness and visibility good because of the lack of underbrush. The dogs had deep chests to increase their lung capacity and long, narrow heads to decrease wind resistance. They were bred and trained to chase any rapidly moving object, an exaggeration of the normal canid response. Because they simply cannot resist a running animal, they were kept leashed at the beginning of hunting expeditions to prevent them from charging after the wrong prey, and even today they are liable to pursue and bite joggers. The earliest skeletal remains of sight hounds were found in Mesopotamia, date from 3500 BCE, and resemble the modern saluki. This dog is still cherished by Arabs in the region, who despise and abuse other types of dog. For centuries they have bred their salukis with the greatest care, keeping an oral record of their pedigrees.[1]

At a very early date, acromegalic mutant dogs were developed into mastiff types. Once these dogs appeared, probably in northern India or Tibet, it would have been apparent that their huge size and powerful heavy jaws made them invaluable for guarding livestock and property, as well as for helping soldiers in war and hunting formidable game such as lions and wild oxen. They were eagerly sought after by other peoples and were soon distributed by trade and migration throughout the ancient world. When they arrived in Greece, they were called Molossians (from Molossis in northern Greece). A seal from Ur of 3000 BCE represents a mastiff type with a heavy body and huge feet, large semi-dropped ears, and a tail curled over its back, guarding the throne of a king or god.[2] The most notable dogs in Mesopotamian art are the huge ferocious mastiffs shown hunting lions and wild asses on bas-reliefs from the palace of Nineveh (seventh century BCE). They effectively promote the Assyrian self-image of brutal domination, helping the king assert his power to destroy whatever opposes him. Mastiffs also served as flock guards and watchdogs; the mastiff is described on Assyrian tablets as the "chained-up mouth-opening dog."[3]

The ancient Egyptians, who loved dogs as well as other animals, were the first to represent them in a rich variety of roles. The Egyptians not only hunted with sight hounds and guarded their property with mastiffs but also cherished small dogs with the exaggerated juvenile features of modern toy breeds. The first clearly distinctive variety is a greyhound-type dog that still retains large erect ears, similar to the modern pharaoh and Ibizan hounds except for its upcurled tail, who would run ahead of hunters in chariots to bring down swift game or would drive it within the reach of a hunter's arrows. By 2000 to 1800 BCE, Egyptians had greyhound types with lop and erect ears, mastiffs with erect (probably cropped) ears, and several types of smaller dogs, including basenji types.

The Egyptians gave their dogs names like Ebony, Grabber, and Cooking-pot. They mourned the family dog as they would a close human relative, by shaving off all their hair.[4] It became a convention in New Kingdom (1550–1085 BCE) wall paintings to show a dog sitting under its deceased owner's chair at a dinner party, like the bitch with enlarged teats who sits under the chair of Nebamun's wife at the feast depicted on his tomb wall. She seems to be an intermediate type between greyhound and mastiff, with a long pointed nose, drop ears, heavy shoulders, big paws, a long fringed tail, and a light coat with reddish spots.[5] The dog was one of the few animals that the Egyptians did not deify—perhaps because they felt it was so close to humans.

The surviving fragments of ancient Egyptian literature include an officer's letter home from a godforsaken garrison town, where his only consolation is his little wolfhound, who protects him from the fierce packs of street dogs. The literary folktale of "The Doomed Prince" shows the value Egyptians attached to the friendship of dogs. At the prince's birth it was foretold that he would meet his death "by the crocodile, or by the serpent, or by the dog." So the king had the boy raised in isolation in a luxurious house in the desert. One day he looked from the roof and saw a dog following a man along the road. He inquired what it was and asked for one like it. So the king sent him "a little pet dog, lest his heart be sad." When the prince grew up, he got permission to go out into the world and risk whatever fate the gods ordained; so they "gave him all sorts of arms, and also his dog to follow him," and sent him on his way. He married a princess, and when he told her of his predicted fate, she advised him to have his dog killed; but he replied, "I am not going to kill my dog, which I have brought up from when it was small." Later he encountered and was saved from the serpent (and in other versions, the crocodile), but unfortunately the papyrus breaks off before we learn whether the prince came to grief through his dog.[6] In any case, he was so attached to his pet that he would endanger his life rather than part with it.

Our first explicit record of intense feeling between man and dog appears in Homer's *Odyssey*, on Odysseus's long-delayed return to Ithaca, when he was disguised by Athene as an old beggar and unrecognizable to humans. But a listless old dog stretched outside the gate pricked up his ears and raised his head when Odysseus approached. Argus had been a marvelous hound, quick at picking up a scent and infallible in pursuit of game. Odysseus had trained him carefully, but had had to leave him behind when he sailed for Troy. At first the young hunters took Argus out after goats, deer, and hares; but now he was lying abandoned on a dung heap and infested with vermin. "But directly he became aware of Odysseus' presence he wagged his tail and dropped his ears, though he lacked the strength now to come any nearer to his master.

Yet Odysseus saw him out of the corner of his eye, and brushed a tear away without showing any sign of emotion to the swineherd," to whom he remarked how odd it was to see such a fine hound lying neglected. Having at last set eyes on his master after nineteen years, Argus collapsed in death.[7] Homer notices that a dog's nose would not be deceived by a beggarly appearance, and he touchingly recognizes the mutual love between dog and man; Odysseus, a tough warrior, wept over his dog. The dog's great worth is related to his aristocratic status: his plight, like that of the disguised Odysseus, is poignant because he is intrinsically superior to his situation.

It was hunting dogs, the companions of gods and heroes, that moved the Greeks to enthusiasm. There was already a clear class distinction between noble hounds, used for the aristocratic pastime of hunting, and street dogs, working dogs, and lapdogs. The Greeks developed scent hounds (like Argus), probably from relatively light, agile hunting mastiffs selected for keenness of nose, speed, and endurance. (Scent hounds still retain the mastiff's hanging ears and loose, heavy skin.) The Greeks, who generally hunted on foot, preferred hunting hares for sport; but they also pursued red deer and dangerous game such as wild boar. Hunting was not just an idle sport in the ancient world, where dangerous wild beasts still roamed the countryside. When a huge boar ravaged the fields of Mysia in Greece, the people appealed to King Croesus to send his son with some elite fighting men and dogs to drive it from their land.[8]

Hunting was sufficiently important to the Greeks that they left several treatises on hounds (and none on any other type of dog). Xenophon saw hunting as an essential part of education, especially as preparation for war. His *Cynegetica* (*On Hunting*) prescribes in detail how hounds should be cared for and trained and how they should behave on the hunt. He writes mainly about hunting hares with Laconians, evidently a type of scent hound. After the hounds drove her out of her shelter, the hare would run, using both speed and cunning. Hares can outrun most hounds, and they also confuse the trail by doubling back and taking great sidewise leaps that leave no trace. The hunter would follow the dogs on foot, exhorting them by name, but not too often lest he overexcite them. The hounds should be given short names, so they could be called easily—such as Psyche, Chara (Ecstasy), Oenas (Blueskin), Medas (Crafty), or Thallon (Vigorous).

When tracking, they should "hold their heads well down and aslant, smiling when they find the scent and lowering their ears; then they should all go forward together along the trail" toward the hare's hiding place, "circling frequently, with eyes continually on the move and tails wagging." They should let the huntsman know when they are close by displaying "unaffected agitation and overpowering delight at being near the hare. They should pursue with unremitting vigour, giving tongue and barking freely, dogging the hare's steps wherever she goes." In the end they would either drive her into a strategically placed net or wear her out until the huntsman could kill her. In contrast, inferior hounds may have poor scenting ability, or slink lazily off from the hunt to lie in the shade, or fail to give visual signs that they are on the trail, or run about at random, or rush boldly ahead on a false trail.[9]

Six centuries later, Arrian, who wrote his *Cynegeticus: The Book of the Chase* under the pen name of Xenophon of Athens the Second, described coursing, a form of hunting that the Greco-Roman world had adopted from the Celts after Xenophon's time. In coursing, *vertragi,* sight hounds, chased hares using speed. These hounds had the long body, narrow head, long supple neck, and tulip ears of a modern greyhound; they differed only in their rough, soft coat. A hare was started, and greyhounds were slipped from their leashes to chase it. The hunters would follow on horseback, and the sport consisted in watching the skill with which the greyhounds pursued their twisting, doubling quarry; the object was a challenging chase, and the hunters were often pleased if the hare escaped.

Unlike scent hounds, greyhounds were often treated as pets. Arrian said the best greyhounds "are fond of people" and do not regard any man as a stranger; "they submit when the huntsman calls, not from fear, but with affection for him who raised them and to honor him." They should sleep with a person, "because hounds are made fond of people this way, and they rejoice in human skin and love the person they sleep with no less than the one who feeds them." Xenophon had advised that hounds be well cared for, but he never suggested a personal relationship with them. Arrian, on the other hand, wrote a eulogy of his Hormé, or Impulse, a swift, diligent, high-spirited hound who was also gentle and very fond of people: "never before did any other hound yearn as she did for either me or my companion and fellow hunter, Megillus. . . . if I were at home, she would pass her time with me and escort me when I went out somewhere and follow closely after me when I went to school [i.e., the gymnasium] . . . and when I returned, she would go ahead, frequently turning around so as to make sure that I didn't perhaps turn off the road. But when she saw me, she would smile and at once go ahead again." At dinner "she would lay hold of him [Megillus] with her feet, first this way and then that, reminding him that some of the food must be shared with her also. And truly there would be such a great outcry as I think I have never before known in another hound, for whatever she wants she indicates with her voice. . . . And so I think I should not hesitate to record the name of the hound . . . because truly Xenophon the Athenian had a most swift, most wise, and most wonderful hound, Impulse by name."[10]

Not only did the Greeks like dogs, they respected them enough to use their characteristics to illustrate those of superior humans. In *The Republic,* Plato explained the combination of qualities he required in his ideal ruling class by comparing them to watchdogs. Like watchdogs, the Guardians could be gentle to their own people at the same time that they were spirited, courageous, and ready to fight. The fact that "Well-bred dogs . . . are by instinct perfectly gentle to people whom they know and are accustomed to, and fierce to strangers," Socrates argues, proves that "the combination of qualities we require for our Guardian is, after all, possible and not against nature." In an even more remarkable comparison, Homer compares Odysseus' righteous fury at the wanton women of his household to that of "a bitch that snarls and shows fight as she takes her stand above her helpless puppies when a stranger comes by."[11]

Some of Socrates' philosophic descendants were actually called Cynics—meaning doglike (*kynikos*). Because the epithet expressed respect as well as distaste, it was soon adopted by the Cynic teachers themselves. They preached a return to nature to counteract the artificiality and hypocrisy produced by human social institutions and conventions. They deliberately flouted normal standards of civilized behavior to jolt people out of their customary ways of thinking. In the positive sense, they were like dogs in their honesty, their independence of factitious needs, and their indifference to wealth and unnatural social distinctions. To their opponents, they were doglike in their rejection of decent manners. They professed to be as oblivious to class distinctions as dogs: according to a famous anecdote, the Cynic teacher Diogenes, who called himself the royal dog, snubbed Alexander the Great. He also is reported to have demonstrated his naturalness by unabashedly masturbating in the marketplace. Attitudes toward dogs and Cynics were similarly ambivalent: both were propertyless and disreputable and hence inferior to cultivated gentlemen; on the other hand, both were superior in their virtuous independent rejection of the false values of ordinary conventional people.[12]

War mastiffs, bred and trained to be ferocious, were used by Near Eastern peoples, Greeks, Romans, and Gauls to tear at foot soldiers and slash the legs of horses. They often wore leather armor, which might be fitted with knives to cut the legs of men and horses or with lighted torches to terrify the horses. At one point in a war between the Paeonians and the Perinthians, Herodotus relates, "the two sides challenged each other to three duels, pitching man against man, horse against horse, and dog against dog." Xerxes' expeditionary force against Greece marched with a large number of Indian dogs, a breed so fierce that they were supposed to have been sired by tigers.[13]

Many mastiff strains, however, were formidable without being belligerent and were trained to do peaceful jobs. Livestock dogs were essential to Greek and Roman farmers, primarily to protect the flocks from predators, both wolves and thieves. Eumaeus, the swineherd in the *Odyssey,* kept four fierce, powerful dogs to guard the 360 pigs in his charge; they flew at the disguised Odysseus when he appeared at the farm, but stopped when he knew enough to sit down and drop his staff.[14] Unlike modern flock guards, they worked closely with shepherds, commonly one dog to one shepherd, and were more strongly attached to the shepherd than to the sheep. A man bought some sheep in Umbria, with their dogs but without the shepherds, who delivered the sheep and returned home. The dogs left their purchaser and went back home to their shepherds—a journey of three hundred miles taking many days.[15]

Columella, an experienced farmer, eulogized these animals in his *On Agriculture.* Having discussed the flocks, he "will speak of the dumb guardians of the flocks, though it is wrong to speak of the dog as a dumb guardian; for what human being more clearly or so vociferously gives warning of the presence of a wild beast or of a thief as does the dog by its barking? What servant is more attached to his master than is a dog? What companion more faithful? What guardian more incorruptible? What more wakeful night-watchman can be found? Lastly, what more steadfast avenger or defender? To buy and keep a dog ought, therefore, to be among the first things which a farmer does, because it is the guardian of the farm, its produce, the household and the cattle." The sheepdog should be white so that it can readily be distinguished from wolves even in poor light; the farmyard dog should be black, so that it will be more alarming in daylight and better able to approach a thief unawares at night. Farmyard dogs should not be too mild, lest they fawn on everyone, including thieves, nor too fierce, lest they attack members of the household. They should be ever vigilant, yet not so excitable as to be agitated by every noise or groundless suspicion. They need not be speedy, as they should spend their lives around the farm buildings; they should be kept chained during the day and let loose at night. A flock guard needs to be fast enough to fight and chase a wolf, but not so fast as a hound. Dogs should have short convenient names such as Ferox (Savage) and Celer (Speedy).

Although Columella properly appreciated farm dogs and advised treating them well, he did propagate a superstition that has produced canine misery ever since. He recommended not only cutting off the tails of puppies forty days after their birth, but doing so by biting off the spinal cord that extends down the tail, taking it between the teeth, drawing it out a little way, and then breaking it off. This keeps the tail from growing "to an ugly length" and was also supposed to prevent rabies. The extraordinary theory behind this practice was that rabies was caused by internal worms and could be prevented by pulling out something that looked like a white worm. D. H. Lawrence's story "Rex" proves that Columella's direction was still being followed to the letter in the twentieth century: the Lawrence children lamented when their fox terrier's tail had to be docked—in fact, bitten off—but their father insisted that Rex would look like a fool otherwise, and further, that docking "had made a man of him."[16] Thus the unnecessary docking required by American Kennel Club standards to this day goes back to Roman superstition.

Mastiffs in general were sufficiently calm and gentle that the Romans called them *mansuetus,* tame—the origin of the English word *mastiff.* Guarding breeds tend to be placid, since guarding mostly requires sitting around and waiting in case something happens. They generally prefer to avoid a fight by threatening behavior. Lucretius chose Molossian hounds (the preferred Roman mastiffs) to illustrate his theory that human speech must have developed from animals' ability to express different feelings, including tender ones. "When first their gaping flabby jowls are drawn back in a grim snarl that bares their hard teeth," Molossian hounds "give vent to a stiff growl. Very different is the sound when the growl has grown to a loud-mouthed reverberating bay. Different again is the soft crooning with which they fondle their pups when they fall to licking them lovingly with their tongues or toss them with their paws, snapping with open jaws in a playful pretence of gobbling them up with teeth that never close. And different from all these are their howls when left alone in the house, or the whimpering with which they shrink and cringe to avoid the whip."[17]

The Romans wrote formal instructions on managing dogs that earned their keep—house dogs (*villatici*), shepherd dogs (*pastorales*), and sporting dogs (*venatici*—divided into war dogs, *pugnaces*; scent hounds, *sagaces*; and sight hounds, *celeres*).[18] But both Romans and Greeks left much evidence of their attachment to dogs, often toys, who were valuable only as companions. Pet dogs that look like small spitzes are depicted on Greek vases, sometimes doing tricks or playing with women. The earliest toy breed, the Maltese (called *canis melitei*), was a white fluffy dog, familiar to Aristotle's readers.[19] The Romans in particular bred miniature dogs, including the ancestors of the present-day Italian greyhound. An epigram in the *Greek Anthology* celebrates the successful whelping of Kalathine, who was small enough to travel in a lady's handbag (*kalathos*); Artemis granted her an easy delivery, for she hears the prayers of dogs as well as women; "the goddess . . . knows how to save her canine fellow-huntresses."[20]

Emotionally expressive visual representations of dogs first appeared in the realistic art of late classical times. A Hellenistic marble statue of about 200 BCE perfectly catches the self-pitying air of a sick greyhound. Another fine and lovingly realistic marble statue represents two young greyhounds sitting together, one tenderly licking the other (first or second century CE?). Companion dogs were often memorialized in epitaphs and on monuments. A bereaved master "tells how he carried his little darling 'Patrice' to the grave in floods of tears, after fondling her joyfully in his arms for fifteen years. No

longer will she give him countless kisses or snuggle happily against his neck."
He has placed her in his own marble tomb "so that he shall ever have her
company when his own time comes. Clever as a human in her ways she was."
She would share his meals, sitting on his lap and begging for tidbits. "When
he came home tired she would greet him with the joyous wagging of her tail
that told him of all her love for him." Dogs were touchingly included on
monuments, both of children and of virile men. The stele of ten-year-old
Abeita shows her reading a scroll while her dog tries to attract her attention; a
hunter's grave relief shows him hunting hares on horseback with "Julius, my
colleague"; and the stele of the gladiator Chresteinos includes a picture of his
dog, Holdfast.[21]

Such devotion naturally provoked ridicule from those who saw it as silly
dotage. Martial's epigram on Issa, Publius's darling lapdog, is so fulsome it
suggests that he was slyly poking fun at Issa's owner. She is adorably naughty,
"more winning than any girl." "If she whines, you will think she's talking";
she feels her owner's "sadness and his joy. She lies resting on his neck and
slumbers, without a breath perceptible." She would not think of wetting his
bedcover when she sleeps with him, but gently paws him to put her down and
take her up again. "Such is the inborn modesty of this chaste little dog, she
knows nothing of love; nor can we find any husband worthy of so tender a
maid." Trimalchio, the vulgar rich man in Petronius's *Satyricon*, shows off his
enormous watchdog and his adorable small pet, whose effigy will be included
on his tomb. Women were supposed to be especially liable to foolish doting
on lapdogs. Lucian describes the mortification of learned Thesmopolis when
his rich lady employer entreated him to take her pregnant Maltese bitch on
his lap when they went to the country. "It was impossible to behold anything
more ridiculous than how the dog with its little snout peeped out from beneath his mantle just below his long beard, and I suppose now and then be-
dewed his lap (though Thesmopolis did not boast of this circumstance),
yelping in a small harsh tone, as is the way with these maltese curs, and licking the bushy chin of the grave philosopher."[22]

The Romans could treat dogs with utter callousness: they pitted dogs against
wild beasts in the arena, and they held a disgusting annual sacrifice in which
they crucified a dog in vindictive commemoration of the occasion on which

the dogs failed to warn Rome that invading Gauls were climbing the Capitoline Hill (when the geese did). But in general both Romans and Greeks loved and valued dogs. Late classical writers on natural history filled their books with examples of canine intelligence and virtue. When Plutarch set out to demonstrate that "all animals partake in one way or another of reason and understanding," he took much of his evidence from dogs. Dogs do many things that go beyond smelling out and seeing and "can be carried out or perceived only through the use of intelligence and reason." Hunters are well acquainted with their "self-control and obedience and sagacity on hunting parties." And their cleverness can go beyond behavior that comes naturally and extend to elaborate acting: in one Roman play, a dog pretended to take a soporific (supposed to be a poison) and collapsed as if dead; then it woke on cue, as if recovering from a sound sleep, and ran joyfully to the right person. Even the aged Emperor Vespasian "was much moved."

As for the dog's loyalty and devotion to duty, Plutarch tells how King Pyrrhus found a dog guarding the body of a murdered man, where it had stayed for three days without eating. Pyrrhus had the corpse buried and brought the dog away with him. A few days later there was an army review, which the king inspected with the dog by his side. "But when it saw its master's murderers filing past, it rushed at them with furious barking and, as it voiced its accusation, turned to look at the king so that not only he, but everyone present became suspicious of the men. They were at once arrested and when put to the question . . . they confessed . . . and were punished." This story became a medieval classic as "The Dog of Montargis," in which the greyhound of a knight called Aubrey de Montdidier, the only witness to his murder, accused the murderer before the king by attacking him without apparent provocation and then defeated him in a trial by combat, after which the man confessed and was executed. Plutarch also tells how a watchdog at the temple of Asklepios saw a man steal some of the offerings and followed him out of the temple, keeping at a distance because the man threw stones at it. For several days it followed, barking at the thief and fawning on passersby, until those who were investigating the robbery were informed and caught the man. "On the return the dog led the procession, capering and exultant, as though it claimed for itself the credit for pursuing and capturing the temple-thief."[23]

Aelian, a century later, added further tales of canine loyalty and responsibility, as well as some facts and many superstitions (dogs will not eat dog flesh, dogs are subject to only three diseases, and so forth). His praises can become as anthropomorphic as those of any sentimental modern writer. One of his several examples of dogs who refused to survive their masters is the Maltese lapdog of the harp player Theodorus, who threw itself into its master's coffin and insisted on being buried with him. A lapdog in Sicily barked insistently to alert his master that there was an adulterer hidden in the house. The sacred hounds kept at the temple of Hephaestus at Etna in Sicily could make moral distinctions, greeting honest visitors to the temple, biting any criminal who tried to enter, and chasing away fornicators. A good hound will not touch a dead hare or boar that it happens to find, "refusing to claim credit for another's labours and declining to appropriate what does not belong to it. . . . [Thus] it appears to have a natural love of distinction: it is not meat that it wants; it is victory that it loves."

One of Aelian's tales demonstrates a dog's steadfastness through senseless suffering. Unfortunately, the history of human attitudes toward dogs reveals many examples of inflated admiration and sentimental pity coupled with callousness. Readers are ostensibly invited to marvel at the dog's superhuman heroism, while in fact they are sadistically relishing its gruesome mutilation. Some Indians set out to impress Alexander the Great by presenting him with one of their fierce hounds, who were supposed to be sired by tigers. The dog paid no attention to a stag, or a boar, or a bear, but it rushed on a lion. It clung to the lion even after men had cut off its tail, then one of its legs, then the other legs one by one, and finally its torso. "Alexander was grieved and amazed that the Hound in giving proof of its mettle had perished . . . and had met its death by reason of its courage. Accordingly the Indians, seeing Alexander's grief, presented him with four hounds of the same breed . . . and when . . . [he] received the four he forgot his grief over the first."[24]

Classical literature and mythology do occasionally touch on the sinister potentiality of dogs. The horrifying tale of Actaeon reverses the self-confident manuals of the hunt by showing a man turned from hunter to prey when the goddess Diana, furious that he has seen her bathing, transforms him into a stag. It is very frightening when the loyal, compliant dog turns on its master. As Ovid relates the story in his *Metamorphoses*, Actaeon is at first simply distressed at finding himself a stag, because he has not imagined what will happen if his hounds discover him. When they do, the animals he is used to commanding pursue him "with the lust of blood upon them." "First of all / The Killer fastens on him, then the Grabber, / Then Mountaineer gets hold of him by the shoulder." They keep him at bay "until the whole pack gathers / And all together nip and slash and fasten / Till there is no more room for wounds." Meanwhile his human companions urge on the pack, sorry that Actaeon is "missing the good show / Of quarry brought to bay." Finally the dogs "circle him, dash in, and nip, and mangle / And lacerate and tear their prey, not master . . . and so he died."[25] The tale not only turns the tables on the hunter, but raises the disturbing possibility that the dogs might not have actually mistaken Actaeon for a stag: could they have been rebelling against the dominion of their human master?

In actual life, dogs could be turned from reliable friends to dangerous enemies by a hideous disease: rabies. The Greeks dreaded the Dog Days, July 31 through August 11, marked by the rising of Sirius, which they called the Dog Star or Orion's Dog. This was the season when humans suffered fevers and sunstroke, drought endangered the crops, and dogs went mad. Rabies was traditionally supposed to be caused by sultry heat or by being bitten when the Dog Star was shining.[26]

Like many other peoples, the Greeks and Romans associated dogs with death, perhaps because they eat dead bodies. Scavenging dogs were a familiar sight throughout the ancient world, as indeed they must have remained until systematic programs to control stray dogs were organized in the nineteenth century. Thucydides' statement that they shunned the corpses of victims of the great plague shows that they must have been prowling the streets of Athens. The appalling possibility that when a man dies his body will be eaten by dogs is ever present in *The Iliad*. It intensifies the horror of Hector's parents as they watch Achilles abusing his body. Priam's vision of the ruin of his family culminates in the defilement of his body after his death, when "my dogs in front of my doorway" will rip him raw, tear at his gray head, and lay bare his secret parts:

> *those dogs I raised in my halls to be at my table, to guard my*
> *gates, who will lap my blood in the savagery of their anger*
> *and then lie down in my courts.*[27]

The ultimate horror is that it is Priam's own dogs that are turning against him, like the hounds against Actaeon.

Hecate, goddess of the underworld, was often depicted with dogs and sometimes as a bitch herself; and dogs were sacrificed to her. The ravenous three-headed dog Cerberus guarded the entrance to Hades, as dogs guard similar thresholds in other mythologies. Hesiod described him in *Theogony* as "the brazen-voiced hound of Hades, fifty-headed, relentless and strong," who fawns "with his tail and both his ears" on those who go in, but devours anyone who tries to get out. In *The Aeneid* Cerberus appears as an immense three-headed monster whose barking resounds through the underworld, but who can easily be bribed with a drugged cake. Dante transformed Vergil's description into a vivid punishment for sinners when he appropriately placed the dog over the gluttons in hell. The red-eyed, slavering, swollen-bellied beast ravens and howls over the gluttons that wallow in their putrid slush, and tears at them with his sharp claws. He threatens Dante and Vergil, but when Vergil throws lumps of the slush down his three throats, he is pacified like any hungry cur that "will set the echoes raving / and then fall still when he is thrown a bone."[28] However, the dog-loving Romans sometimes visualized even Cerberus as a loyal family pet. In a group statue of Hades, Persephone, and Cerberus in the Vatican, two of the dog's heads gaze up adoringly at Hades, while the third looks at a servant bearing a food jar.

Aspects of dogs that are occasionally mentioned in Greek and Latin literature become central in literature of the Jews, who saw dogs not as companions but as filthy street scavengers that ate any dead bodies that were not properly buried. Biblical history has a repellent background of city streets swarming with pariah dogs ever ready to eat up corpses and lick blood off the stones. The ultimate ignominy was to have one's body cast out and eaten by dogs, like Jezebel's. She was thrown out of a window by her own servants on the orders of Jehu. He meant to bury her after he had trampled on her bloody body, but by the time he got to it, the dogs had eaten everything but her skull, her feet, and the palms of her hands. It was this gruesome end that made her one of the most memorable villains in the Bible. Medieval Bibles have graphic pictures of curs sinking their teeth into Jezebel's body.

The other conspicuous role of the dog in the Bible is as a term in degrading comparisons. People abase themselves by calling themselves dead dogs and defend themselves against suspicion by protesting that they are not dogs. The Psalmist repeatedly compares his enemies to dogs. Fools and sinners who relapse are like dogs returning to their vomit. As a pastoral people, the Jews must have depended heavily on flock guards, but biblical writers are almost exclusively preoccupied with the unclean, unworthy pariah dog. Allusions to graceful greyhounds and useful watchdogs and flock guards pale by comparison. Since idealization of dogs in ancient times focused mainly on hounds, the Jews' apparent lack of interest in hunting helps to account for their lack of enthusiasm for dogs.[29]

When dogs lick the sores of the beggar Lazarus in the gospel of Luke, it is the ultimate sign of his indignity and wretchedness. In Greek society, on the other hand, dogs were sacred to Asklepios, the god of healing, and were kept at his temples, where they walked or lay among the sick people who came there, licked their ailing parts, and were credited with many cures. Possibly they relieved infection through the mild antibacterial properties of canine saliva, and probably they promoted psychosomatic improvement through calming and reassurance, as therapy dogs do today. The only hint in the Bible that a dog might be a companion is found in the apocryphal Book of Tobit, which is very late and shows definite Persian influence. (The Persians esteemed dogs, and their sacred book, the *Vendidad*, insists that even strays be properly treated.) Even in Tobit, the dog is only barely mentioned as following the boy Tobias on his journey.[30] Tobias's dog did not become important until Europeans enlarged its role in accordance with their own interest in dogs. In pictures by Pollaiuolo and Titian in the fifteenth and sixteenth centuries, the dog is represented, improbably, as a toy dog of the sort loved by Renaissance painters.

By Roman times most of the major types of dogs known today had appeared. The Romans spread their mastiffs and other dogs throughout their empire and also avidly imported dogs from other nations. They were especially impressed by British mastiffs, even more ferocious than Molossians and supposedly strong enough to break the necks of bulls. When Julius Caesar invaded Britain in 55 BCE, he was opposed by these animals, fighting side by side with their masters; later, the Romans regularly imported them to fight in the arena. Both Romans and Greeks took pains to develop superior dogs. Socrates bases an argument in *The Republic* on the evidently obvious fact that his opponent, Glaucus, takes care in selectively breeding the many hunting dogs at his house.[31] Of course, there was nothing like systematic breeding in the modern sense, which would achieve a particular conformation that could be counted on to reproduce true to type. Rather, superior dogs would be informally mated in order to do their jobs of running fast after hares, guarding property, or charming by small size and prettiness. Strictly speaking, dogs up through the early modern period should be described not as breeds, but as, in Juliet Clutton-Brock's term, varieties.

The Romans had sight hounds, mastiffs, scent hounds, and toy dogs, as well as the ubiquitous pariah dogs. All but the last were selectively bred and carefully trained. The type of sight hounds was already set, although their originally erect ears dropped in most greyhounds. Mastiffs still had widely varying dispositions, from ferocious fighting machines to watchdogs who were gently protective of the household. Those that guarded the flocks were less specialized than modern flock guards, for they also herded (or helped humans to herd) the flocks out to pasture in the morning and home at night; and they were more disposed to fight than modern flock guards. Scent hounds, too, were not so specialized as they became in medieval times. There were relatively few toy breeds. Although spitz dogs are nowhere described in ancient literature, the Pomeranian-like pets on Greek vases and the prick-eared, long-nosed, heavily furred watchdog on a famous *Cave Canem* mosaic in Pompeii suggest that spitzes had somehow made their way from northern regions to the Mediterranean world.

4

Hunting Dogs

THE ARISTOCRATIC PREOCCUPATION with hounds evident in classical times became even more conspicuous in the feudal society of the Middle Ages. Hounds were essential in medieval hunting and derived status from the class who practiced it. Hunting was a major occupation for the aristocracy, demonstrating their courage and martial skills in the absence of war; and for the most part hunting was restricted to them. Hence hounds were valued, idealized, and well treated because they belonged to aristocrats; lower-class people were not supposed—indeed, were sometimes even forbidden—to keep them. Greyhounds and large scent hounds are the only dogs to appear with any frequency on coats of arms.[1]

The principal game animals in England were the hart (stag) and various less formidable deer, the hare, the boar, and the fox. In a typical medieval hunt, dog-keepers would go out beforehand with lymers, particularly good scent hounds, to locate suitable game in the area, and one particular beast would be chosen and driven from its lair. Then the running hounds would be released couple by couple to track and bring it to bay, and the heavier hounds and human hunters with spears or long knives would come up and kill it.[2] The main sport and pleasure was watching the hounds pick up the scent and encouraging them with voice and horn to follow staunchly the tracks of the targeted beast in spite of all its wiles. Thus hunting was a partnership between men and hounds. The typical scent hound, with long muzzle and long drooping ears (which maximized smell input while minimizing hearing), was fully developed in this period. Hounds became increasingly specialized in medieval times and later became further specialized into bird dogs, the present-day sporting breeds.

The classic text is the *Livre de Chasse* of Gaston Phébus, Comte de Foix, an enthusiast writing at the end of the fourteenth century. A few years later, Edward, second Duke of York, Master of Game at the court of Henry IV, translated it as *The Master of Game*. The pack consisted essentially of running hounds or raches, ranging from St. Hubert's hounds, ancestors of the bloodhound, to medium-sized harriers for hunting hares, to small beagles for hunting rabbits on foot. Running hounds should have carefully chosen parents and be properly trained: men must take them out for walks, "be always near them," reward them properly with the neck, bowels, and liver of the deer, and scold or beat them when they go wrong. They follow the trail of a designated animal "all the day questeying and making great melody in their language and saying great villainy and chiding the beasts that they chase. And therefore I prefer them to all other kinds of hounds." (Questeying or questing—that is, baying—is the melodious howling of hounds when tracking; they bay to indicate they have the scent and draw the rest of the pack to follow them. The sound phrases get shorter with excitement as the dogs near the quarry.)

Lymers were not a distinct breed, but promising dogs chosen from among the running hounds and differentiated by more personalized training. They would live with a dog-keeper, sleeping in his room rather than with other hounds in the kennel. They would be taught to obey that particular man, who would take them out regularly on a lyam, or leash, and teach them to follow the scent of selected beasts and to ignore others. Lymers did not participate in the chase, but would be led along in case they should be needed to set the other hounds back on the right track. After the kill, the running hounds would get their proper portion of the flesh, and the lymers would be served separately, each by itself. Lymers, sometimes called sleuthhounds, were also used to track human criminals, especially cattle thieves along the English-Scots border. Anyone who denied entrance to the sleuthhound tracing stolen goods would be held for abetting the theft.[3]

Greyhounds of modern type (but preferably white) were used to run down fast game such as deer. They were brought to the field on leashes and "slipped" when the game was started. They were fast enough to overtake any beast and strong enough to seize and sometimes to pull it down and kill it. Greyhounds included not only the breed we recognize today but also stronger, rough-coated Irish wolfhounds and Scottish deerhounds. By late Roman times, the British had crossed smooth-coated greyhound types with heavier dogs to produce these large, rough-coated hounds, adapted to the British climate. They played an important role in Celtic legend as the companions of gods and heroes.[4]

Unlike other hounds, greyhounds were often pets like Arrian's dog, who constantly accompanied their masters in bedrooms, at dinner, and at church. Pictures of mounted aristocrats regularly include a greyhound running beside the horse. Accordingly, the greyhound "should be courteous and not too fierce, following well his master and doing whatever he command him. He shall be good and kindly and clean, glad and joyful and playful, and goodly to all manner of folks save to the wild beasts to whom he should be fierce, spiteful, and eager." A greyhound "is a most reasonable beast, and best knowing of any beast that ever God made," sometimes even more so than man, as we see from stories of greyhounds that brought to justice the murderers of their masters. A greyhound "hath great memory and great smelling . . . great diligence and great might . . . great worthiness and . . . great subtlety . . . good obedience, for he will learn as a man all that a man will teach him . . . Hounds are hardy, for a hound dare well to keep his master's house, and his beasts . . . and . . . goods, and he would sooner die than anything be lost in his keeping." His greatest fault is that he does not live long enough—generally only twelve years, of which he can only hunt for nine.[5]

Sir Walter Scott regularly enlivened his wonderfully vivid portrayals of the Middle Ages with a dog. Roswal, a noble Scottish deerhound modeled on Scott's own beloved Maida, is the most engaging character in *The Talisman*. He is the only valuable, aristocratic possession of the hero of the novel, who appears to be an impoverished Scottish knight attached to the army of Richard I in Palestine during the Crusades; the dog actually supports his household by bringing in venison. His manners are lovingly described: he had the tact to remain subdued while in the hut with his master's old sick squire, but pressed after the knight when he went out and "thrust his long rough countenance into the hand of his master, as if modestly soliciting some mark of his kindness. He had no sooner received the notice which he desired, in the shape of a kind word and slight caress, than, eager to acknowledge his gratitude, and joy for his master's return, he flew off at full speed, galloping in full career, and with outstretched tail, here and there, about and around, crossways and endlong," all over "those precincts which his sagacity knew were protected by his master's pennon. After a few gambols of this kind, the dog coming close up to his master, laid at once aside his frolicsome mood, relapsed into his usual gravity and slowness of gesture and deportment, and looked as if he were ashamed that anything should have moved him to depart so far out of his sober self-control."

In the end Roswal detected a villain, as the dog of Montargis did. King Richard accepted his testimony without question and, when the French king questioned valuing the word of a prince less than "the barking of a cur," Richard retorted: "recollect that the Almighty, who gave the dog to be companion of our pleasures and our toils, hath invested him with a nature noble and incapable of deceit. . . . He hath a share of man's intelligence, but no share of man's falsehood. You may bribe a soldier to slay a man with his sword, or a witness to take life by false accusation; but you cannot make a hound tear his benefactor: he is the friend of man, save when man justly incurs his enmity."[6]

Jean Froissart's tale of King Richard II's greyhound provides a counterexample to such stories of faithfulness, but it also demonstrates the importance of the animal to its noble owners. The king had a greyhound "who always waited upon" him "and would know no man else . . . he would straight run to the king and fawn upon him, and leap with his forefeet upon the king's shoulders." But one day in 1399, the hound left the king to caress Henry, Duke of Lancaster, who did not even know him. Richard rightly interpreted this as an omen that he would be deposed and Henry would become king.[7]

Although the Master of Game described greyhounds working with a pack of scent hounds, they came to be used more for coursing on their own, as they had been in classical times. The sport consisted of watching the skill with which the greyhounds pursued their twisting and turning quarry. The basic rules were set by the Duke of Norfolk on the orders of Queen Elizabeth, who enjoyed watching greyhounds coursing deer. In organized competitions, the prey animal would be released in front of the hounds, who would then be unslipped. No more than two greyhounds were to be set on a hare, and she got a head start of 240 yards. The hound who did the most toward killing the quarry was the winner; it was speed and skill in turning it from its course that counted rather than the actual kill. James Woodforde, a prosperous eighteenth-century parson, generally kept three greyhounds and two spaniels. He went out coursing hare and rabbit on his own and participated in competitive meets.[8] Coursing has become less practical in recent times, with less land and hares available; and in 1927 an ingenious American figured out how to make it a sport for the masses. Now greyhounds pursue an electronically controlled artificial hare on an elliptical track for the excitement of thousands of spectators.

The third group of hunting dogs Edward discussed in *The Master of Game* is mastiffs, called alaunts. Although many alaunts were watchdogs and butcher's dogs, alaunts gentle, who were relatively lightly built and hence faster, were used for hunting. They could handle heavier game than greyhounds or running hounds; only alaunts could drive a boar from its covert to be killed by the human hunters. Their ears were made sharply erect by cropping, since cropped ears are harder to grab and hold by prey animals, dogs, or (in the case of watchdogs) humans. Apparently their breeding as tough hunters made them liable to viciousness, for they would chase and bite livestock, other hounds, and men—sometimes even their own masters. Rarely do we see one that will "love his master and follow him, and help him in all cases, and do what his master commands him." Plate XVIII in *The Master of Game* shows alaunts gentle built much like the modern Great Dane, which used to be called a boarhound. Five of the eight are muzzled. Geoffrey Chaucer's King Lycurgus, a huge, ferocious he-man who drove a chariot drawn by bulls, was surrounded by twenty white muzzled alaunts as big as steers, used to hunt lions and deer. Plebeian mastiffs could also be used for hunting, especially by "men who hunt for profit of the household to get flesh."[9]

Finally, *The Master of Game* discusses spaniels, a new type of dog that had been developed from scent hounds for hunting birds. At first they were called hounds for the hawk because they would find and flush partridge and quail from cover so that falcons could intercept them in flight; later, when guns were developed, the birds would be shot. Bird dogs have the ancestral fleshy jowls, hanging ears, and good scenting power. They were more people-oriented than scent hounds (as are their descendants, today's sporting group): "they love well their masters and follow them without losing, although they be in a great crowd of men, and commonly they go before their master, running and wagging their tail, and raise or start fowl and wild beasts."

"On the other hand they have many bad qualities . . . [they] are fighters and great barkers," and they distract the running hounds by scampering hither and thither and running and barking at livestock, misleading the greyhounds into chasing after geese and cows. Therefore Edward would not have them around unless he wanted to hunt with hawks or nets.[10] His Plate XIX shows a varied group of dogs, although all have long drooping ears, medium-length muzzles, and feathered tails. During this period, spaniels were general-purpose sporting dogs—flushing, setting, and water retrieving.

Bird dogs came into their own in the early modern period and were differentiated and refined for their various purposes. They learned to focus on their proper game and no longer disturbed the hunt. In 1575, George Turbervile praised them enthusiastically in his verse prologue to the *Book of Falconrie*:

> *In roysting wise about they range, with cheerfull chappes to ground,*
> *To see where in the champion may some lurking fowle be found*
> *A sport to view them stirre their sternes, in hunting too and fro.*[11]

A spaniel was expected to beat "a cover over and over, and not leaving a furrow untrodden or unsearched," until he circled in on where the birds were hiding. He was to search "most coragiously and swiftly, with a wanton playing taile, and a busie labouring nose, neither desisting nor showing less delight in his labour at night than he did in the morning."[12]

By the sixteenth century, water spaniels were developed to swim after waterfowl that had dived. A small white one that lies in front of the Virgin in

Dürer's *Madonna and Child with a Multitude of Animals* shows the characteristic long shaggy hair, shaved off the back half of the dog except for a pompom left at the end of its tail. Other spaniels were developed into setters, taught to lie down quietly (set) after they found birds such as partridge and quail, so a net could be dropped over both birds and dog. When guns became good enough to be useful for hunting, in the later seventeenth century, pointers were bred and trained to point their bodies toward the birds and freeze, so as to guide the hunter's aim when the bird rose. (Wolves will also point with their nose toward the source of a scent, but they will not hold the pose as the pointer does.) Retrievers were not differentiated until the later nineteenth century.

Unlike hounds, who follow their nature when they hunt, bird dogs have to subject their instincts to human direction. Nicholas Cox describes the obedience required of "a Setting-dog." Hunting partridges, he runs "the fields over with such alacrity and nimbleness, as if there was no limit to his fury and desire, and yet by art under such excellent command, that in the very height of his career by a Hem or sound of his Master's voice he shall stand, gaze about him, look in his Master's face, and observe his directions, whether to proceed, stand still, or retire." Even when he is close enough to take his prey in his mouth, he must stop short without noise or motion and wait for his master's directions. Accordingly, the training of a bird dog, unlike a scent hound's, is designed to increase personal attachment: "The first thing you shall teach your Dog, is to make him loving and familiar with you, knowing you from any other person, and following you where-ever you go. To effect this the better, let him receive his food as near as you can from no other hand . . . and when you correct him to keep him in awe, do it rather with words than blows." Only then teach him the techniques for finding and setting birds without springing them.[13] Nowadays, the sporting dog's attachment to people and eagerness to please are more often put to use in helping disabled people.

Enlightened owners have always recognized the human's responsibility in training a bird dog to do its demanding work. P. R. A. Moxon insisted that it was up to the trainer to make his signals clear to his retriever, to "see his point of view and when something goes wrong ponder deeply if it is not your fault rather than the dog's—for in 99 cases out of 100 it will be! Win and retain your pupil's respect and love and half the battle is won—show him you are a fool and a bully and training might just as well cease for good!" In Corey Ford's more recent essay, "If You Could Only Talk," a hunter berates his pointer after a disappointing day's shooting: "You bolted. You false-pointed. You overran your nose. You froze solid on a rabbit. You ranged clear out of sight a couple of times, and the chirp of my whistle didn't mean any more to you than if I'd been a cricket. . . . You did everything a bird dog shouldn't do; you even thought up a couple of new tricks on your own. And now you could lie here beside me with your head across my leg, rolling your eyes up at me contentedly and thumping your tail a couple of times whenever I happened to stir, just as though you didn't understand that anything was wrong." He concludes reproachfully, "You don't know what it is to have to be patient . . . and make allowances for some one who doesn't understand, and hold your temper time and again when he makes a mistake—" Finally the dog replies: "Don't I? . . . Don't I know what it is to have someone shout and whistle and wave his arms at me . . . just when I'm trying to follow a tiny thread of scent down the wind?" to find and hold a bird only to "see you miss it clean, and have to stand there wagging my tail and trying to look pleased?"[14]

Terriers, "earth dogs," were developed to hunt "vermin"—especially the rats that infested farms and the foxes that killed poultry. In fact they performed a vital function as ratcatchers through the nineteenth century. Anne Brontë's Agnes Grey is distressed when the rough terrier Snap, her "little dumb, rough-visaged, but bright-eyed, warm-hearted companion," is sold by his heartless owners to "the village ratcatcher, a man notorious for his brutal treatment of his canine slaves." Besides doing useful work, terriers were used in sports available to the lower classes—hunting fox and badger on foot or competing in rat-killing contests, to see which dog could kill the most rats in a specified time or which could kill a specified number in the shortest time. At a match in 1825, Billy killed ninety rats in seven and a half minutes by a lethal nip to the neck as they tried to run past him. Because terriers started out as poor men's dogs, they do not appear in aristocratic literature such as *The Master of Game,* although Dame Juliana Berners did list them among her fourteen types of dogs in 1496.[15] Terriers acquired prestige after they began to assist at upper-class hunts by digging out foxes or badgers that had gone to ground (retreated into their burrow) after the hounds had cornered them.

Typically, terriers are compact dogs with short legs. They had to be small enough to go down a hole and brave enough to face a desperate, well-armed animal. A twelve-pound terrier must eagerly go down into the tunnel of a badger that may weigh thirty-one pounds. The nineteenth-century developer of the Sealyham terrier, Captain John Owen Tucker Edwardes, placed his puppies on the farms of his tenants, where they would learn to hunt rats. Later he would go to see them, along with two belligerent adult terriers and a shotgun. If the puppy failed to stand up unflinchingly to the older dogs, it was shot. At a year old, it had to enter a polecat's burrow without hesitation and dispatch it; the polecat would kill a slow or weak dog, and Edwardes would kill any dog that retreated as soon as it came out of the burrow.[16]

The Master of Game directs that the hounds were to be very well looked after indeed. Plate XV shows servants treating sick or injured running hounds and greyhounds—giving them medicine, treating their feet, and petting them. Bread was the hounds' staple food, but they also got meat after the hunt—a specified part of the kill, or if that was not enough, meat that was specially killed for them. They got special diets if they were sick or injured. Once when some hounds did not get well on their special diet, they were sent on a pilgrimage to St. Mesmer to hear a mass and have offerings of wax candles and silver made for them.

The hounds were housed better than the peasant population. They were to have a roomy kennel with doors at front and back and an enclosed green yard that got sun all day, with the back door always open so they could go in and out as they liked. There should be six stones within the kennel for the hounds to urinate against and a gutter to carry off urine and water. The building should have a loft for warmth in winter and coolness in summer, and a fire should be kept to warm the hounds when they were cold or wet. The kennel should be cleaned out every morning, with new straw thickly laid every day. A child should stay there night and day to keep the hounds from fighting. Plate XXII shows a kennel that looks like a country cottage, surrounded by a yard with a picket fence and filled with kennel men.[17]

Hunting as practiced by Gaston de Foix and Edward, Duke of York was obviously a rich aristocrat's sport. And so it persisted, although its practice spread to include the gentry. Cox in 1677 recommended hunting to "private Gentlemen" as well as aristocrats; it not only improves health and strength, but "inclines men to good Acquaintance, and generous Society." It was the mark of a gentleman to love hawking and hunting, and therefore dogs. Maintaining a hunting establishment continued to be enormously expensive, even though it was not so luxurious as that described in *The Master of Game*. Twenty-five to thirty-five couples of hounds and several terriers were required and had to be housed in a clean, airy kennel in a sunny yard with a clear stream. Then there had to be two huntsmen and two whippers-in, with two or three horses for each one, and a host of minor helpers such as dog feeders and earth stoppers to block the escape routes of foxes.[18] Rich aristocrats prided themselves on their packs and commissioned portraits of themselves on horseback surrounded by their hounds. Often in the compositions of Ben Marshall and George Stubbs, each hound was an individual portrait.

In 1735, when Squire William Somervile celebrated hunting in his georgic poem *The Chace*, upper-class hunters pursued hares and foxes with the aid of small running hounds—beagles or foxhounds—who were released all at one time to unravel the shifts of the quarry "wile by wile." Foxhounds have to be capable of amazing endurance. Twice a week during the hunting season, they might have to run forty to sixty miles. They are expected to sustain a chase from six to eight hours, or even twelve, running sometimes at top speed and sometimes over hedges and walls and through heavy brush. Somervile prescribed that the hounds were to be carefully matched and bred, principally on the basis of their hunting skills. Look at how ready a dog's fathers were to climb rocks, plunge into water, or thread through thorny brakes; shun "the vain babbler," who noisily charges along the wrong trail, distracting the other hounds, or "the shifting cur" that strays off from the pack. But consider the sire's shape, color, and size as well. When pups are born, select those that show their parents' good qualities and drown the rest. Farm them out until they have arrived at full strength; then train them, taking proper time, with the aid of experienced dogs. The pack should be well matched in size and voice.

Somervile describes the hunt with infectious enthusiasm:

Where all around is gay, men, horses, dogs,
And in each smiling countenance appears,
Fresh-blooming health, and universal joy.

As men and dogs follow the hunt over gates and ditches and through thorny hedges, all are caught up in the excitement and forget their cares.[19]

Not everyone, of course, shared this enthusiasm. The poet William Cowper, a gentle, sedentary soul who loved his pet spaniel but deplored the dog's eagerness to hunt birds, made quiet fun of this uplifting sport in a letter of March 3, 1788. After the hounds had killed the fox and the huntsman flung its corpse into the branches of a tree, "The gentlemen sat on their horses contemplating the fox, for which they had toiled so hard, and the hounds assembled at the foot of the tree, with faces not less expressive of the most rational delight, contemplated the same object."[20]

Colonial landowners imported foxhounds to America so that they could pursue the traditional sport of their counterparts in England. George Washington kept written records on the individual dogs of his pack at Mount Vernon from 1758 and paid strict attention to bloodlines. When he had time, he inspected his kennels every night and morning and hunted three times a week.[21] To this day, packs function in the old style, although they do not live in luxury like those of medieval aristocrats. The Thornton Hill Hounds of Sperryville, Virginia, sleep on boards in a rough shed and are fed on fatty meat scraps and budget dry dog food. Although they are not pets or companions, their huntsman knows every one by sight and voice. They chase foxes three times a week during the hunting season, from August to March, and are exercised twice a week during the off season. Despite the absence of pampering, they seem content; or at least foxhunters believe they are: one enthusiastic hunter says, "If I got a second life and could choose how to live it, I'd live it as a hound."[22]

The aristocratic monopoly on many forms of hunting was enforced by law in England from the eleventh into the nineteenth century. King Canute forbade commoners to hunt most game animals or to keep greyhounds within ten miles of the forest unless they were hamstrung—that is, crippled by cutting the tendons of their hocks. Under the Anglo-Norman kings, the forest was

enlarged to vast hunting reserves, as much as a quarter of the land in England, where only the king and a favored few who possessed his license could
hunt. Although the law recognized that people who lived within forests had
to keep dogs to protect their houses and goods, any dog capable of killing
game—that is, mastiffs and all dogs too large to pass through a dog gauge—
would have to be lamed if they lived in or near the forest. The requirement of
hamstringing was later mitigated to cutting out the ball of the foot, and, under Henry II, to striking off three claws of the right forefoot (expedition);
but even so, the operation must have been painful and it disabled the dog
from running naturally. Mastiffs were regularly inspected to see that this operation was done, and anyone caught in the forest with an unexpedited
mastiff would be fined three shillings. Greyhounds and spaniels were not to
be kept in the forest at all, except for those licensed by the king.[23]

Scott presented the spirit, if not the letter, of the royal attitude when he
showed King Richard in *The Talisman* infuriated by hearing that a mere
knight in his camp was maintaining a hound without permission. The king's
Master of the Horse had to intercede to preserve Roswal from being expedi-
tated: "it were a sin to have maimed or harmed a thing so noble as this gentleman's dog. . . . A most perfect creature of heaven . . . of the noblest
Northern breed—deep in the chest, strong in the stern, black colour, and
brindled on the breast and leg . . . strength to pull down a bull—swiftness to
cote an antelope."[24]

The forest laws lapsed after the Restoration, but game laws benefiting the
landed gentry were strengthened. No one was allowed to hunt deer, hare, rabbits, or game birds unless he had a sufficient estate in land; the amounts required increased over the years. In 1603, the qualification to keep sporting
dogs was lands worth ten pounds a year or other property worth two hundred
pounds or the status of a knight's or esquire's son or higher. The Game Act of
1671 raised the landed property requirement to a hundred pounds a year and
excluded non-landowners; it also authorized all lords of manors to appoint
gamekeepers with the power to search for and seize all dogs, as well as guns
and nets, kept on the manor by unqualified persons. In 1693, a penalty was
imposed of a fine of five to twenty shillings per dog or committal to the
house of correction for ten days to one month, there to be whipped and kept

at hard labor; and in 1707, the penalties went up to a five-pound fine or imprisonment for three months. Property qualifications for hunters were dropped only in 1831.[25]

Sporting dogs belonging to people without the proper qualifications might be summarily hanged if they were suspected of killing game. In 1725, the Earl of Cardigan ordered every [hunting] dog on one of his Northamptonshire manors to be destroyed. A pathetic episode in Henry Fielding's *Joseph Andrews* dramatizes the power of a tyrannical lord of the manor to use the game laws to harass his poorer neighbors. A spiteful squire who "had killed all the dogs, and taken away all the guns in the neighbourhood" shot the pet of a small landowner's daughter, "swearing at the same time he would prosecute the master of him for keeping a spaniel; for that he had given notice he would not suffer one in the parish."[26] Whether he was legally entitled to do this or merely taking advantage of the power of wealth, he had a pretext in the game laws because even a toy spaniel is technically a sporting dog.

Although it was not illegal for unqualified persons to keep greyhounds, setters, spaniels, or lurchers as pets, the owner had to prove that his dogs were not used for hunting, and the usual presumption was that he kept them for this "ill purpose." One squire declared that among the "lower orders," "[hunting] dogs were only useful to poachers . . . no industrious man would wish to keep a dog." In fact, the lurcher, a crossbreed between a greyhound and a terrier or sheepdog, was developed in the 1600s as a poacher's dog and gets its name from the Romany word *lur,* thief. It is intelligent, speedy, and able to fight; it could even be trained to pretend it did not know its master if they were caught poaching. In the eyes of the privileged classes, it took on the furtive air of its criminal owner, with a "lurking, sly, and downward expression" in its eye, a sullen aspect, and "dark and cunning" habits. The lurchers who helped the poacher in his "nefarious and demoralizing nocturnal trade" were highly proficient sporting dogs. Hunting was a practical business for their owners, and lurchers brought in far more hares than aristocratic breeds acting under the proper rules.[27]

Even though hunting with hounds was restricted to the landed gentry and aristocracy, it was part of the culture of all classes in early modern England. John Milton mentioned "the hounds and horn" along with the cock's crow as conventional signs of morning in "L'Allegro." Repeated figures of speech in William Shakespeare's plays show that he expected his audience to understand technical terms such as "let slip the dogs of war" (*Julius Caesar* 3.1.273), hounds crying on a false trail (*Hamlet* 4.5.108–109), and even the elaborate "A hound that runs counter and yet draws dryfoot well" (a hound that follows the scent in the reverse direction, although he tracks well by mere scent of foot, describing a bailiff who caught the wrong man even though he pursues debtors keenly—*Comedy of Errors* 4.2.39).

Shakespeare's representations of hunting scenes show detailed knowledge. Theseus and the Amazon queen Hippolyta compare notes on the "music" of hounds they have heard, and Theseus boasts of his hounds, "bred out of the Spartan kind"—sandy-colored running hounds with loose skin, long "ears that sweep away the morning dew," and crook knees; slow, but with voices matched like bells (*Midsummer Night's Dream* 4.1.108–28). On returning from a hunt, the Lord in the Induction to *The Taming of the Shrew* immediately attends to the welfare of his hounds: he orders his Huntsman to tend one that has overtired herself, arrange a coupling between two others, and feed and look to them all. Lord and Huntsman argue, in technical terms, which hound is the best at picking up a lost scent. In *Venus and Adonis,* Venus learns through Adonis's hounds that his hunt has gone terribly wrong. She hears their "timorous yelping," which remains in one place because they are all hesitating to attack the boar that has gored their master: "They all strain courtesy who shall cope [leap on] him first."[28]

Fielding expected his readers to follow the details of a mock epic battle between Joseph and a pack of hounds in *Joseph Andrews*. When a worthless squire interrupted his hare hunting to set his pack on Parson Adams, Joseph rushed to the rescue; and Fielding describes the combatants as Homeric heroes: "A harder fate remained for thee, O Ringwood! Ringwood the best hound that ever pursued a hare, who never threw his tongue but where the scent was undoubtedly true; good at 'trailing,' and 'sure in a highway'; no 'babler,' no 'overrunner'; respected by the whole pack: for, whenever he opened, they knew the game was at hand. He fell by the stroke of Joseph." At length the huntsman called them off, wondering that "his master would encourage the dogs to hunt *Christians*; that it was the surest way to spoil them, to make them follow *vermin* instead of sticking to a hare."[29] (Ringwood never bayed but on a true scent and never overran the trail; hounds are carefully trained to pursue only the designated quarry.)

At least until the turn of the twentieth century, when there were about 230 packs of foxhounds hunting regularly in Great Britain, hunters were claiming that their sport developed courage and leadership in the ruling class. Rawdon Lee in 1906 maintained that "Our bravest soldiers have been foxhunters; our most successful men in almost every walk of commerce have had their characters moulded in the hunting field." Gordon Stables declared that hunting was good training for war and therefore equally heroic: "many a decisive battle has been won by generals, who first learned to perform deeds of derring-do while following the hounds." Such views have come increasingly under attack in recent years, under the influence of egalitarian feeling and concern for animals' rights. In November 2004, the British Parliament approved a ban on foxhunting, to take effect in February 2005. The ban was promoted by the Labor Party and fiercely opposed by Conservatives on the grounds that it would undermine a traditional way of life, despite the fact that only a few thousand people actually participate in the hunt.[30]

Generally in America, however, hunting signifies virility rather than upper-class status. There have never been class restrictions on hunting here, and the great hunters in our folk tradition are rugged frontiersmen like Daniel Boone and Natty Bumppo (of James Fenimore Cooper's *Leatherstocking Tales*). Theodore Roosevelt wrote, in a Foreword to *The Master of Game* that tacitly subverts its aristocratic assumptions, "The chase is the best of all national pastimes," developing for all men "self-reliance, resourcefulness in emergency, willingness to endure fatigue and hunger, and at need to face risk."[31] Hunting retains this symbolic importance in traditional rural American communities today, especially in the South. Hounds are judged by performance rather than purity of blood, and any member of the community may earn manly prestige through his expertise with hunting dogs.

William Faulkner's "The Bear" is the classic expression of the southern mystique of hunting. For season after season, the men of the community had been striving to find the superhound that could bring a mighty bear to bay and hold him long enough for a man to get there with a gun. Normally the hounds pursued their quarry with a "ringing chorus strong and fast on a free scent," but they went after Old Ben with a shrill anxious yapping that passed out of hearing very slowly because they were afraid to catch up with the bear. Finally a huge dog was trapped in the corncrib after killing Major de Spain's pony; he silently and tirelessly flung himself at the door, but the mixed-race huntsman Sam Fathers subdued him by starvation. Sam did not even attempt to tame him, but succeeded in convincing him that "the only way he can get out of that crib and stay out of it is to do what Sam or somebody tells him to do. He's the dog that's going to stop Old Ben and hold him. . . . His name is Lion." Lion was a ninety-pound mixture of mastiff, Airedale, and other breeds, with cold malignant yellow eyes. He despised the other hounds and most humans. His muscles "quivered to no touch since the heart which drove blood to them loved no man and no thing." His solid stance "inferred not only courage, and all else that went to make up the will and desire to pursue and kill, but endurance, the will and desire to endure beyond all imaginable limits of flesh in order to overtake and slay."

He led the pack against Old Ben, and the other hounds followed him without the usual "high thin note of hysteria" in their voices; but they would not back him when he stopped the bear, and Old Ben got away. The next time, when Lion jumped and held Old Ben, "the hounds went in, in a sort of desperate emulation"; but the men could not manage to shoot the bear and went home shamed before Lion. On the third hunt, Lion held the bear long enough for a man to stab him in the throat, but was disemboweled by the bear's claws. Many people attended the dog's funeral, where General Compson "spoke as he would have spoken over a man." Lion gets this respect because he quintessentially embodies a certain model of masculinity, admired though rarely achieved by men—heroic courage and endurance, supported by the will to exert power by destruction and by superiority to the social ties that are normally essential to dog and man. He is strong because he stands alone; he will not even acknowledge fellowship with others by giving voice.

Concentration upon the male values that all share brings about a sort of equality in the hunting camp—between whites of all classes and men of color, between men and dogs. "We were not men . . . while we were in camp: we were hunters, and Lion the best hunter of us all, and Major de Spain and Uncle Ike McCaslin next; and Lion did not talk as we talked, not because he could not but because he was the chief . . . just as he lived under the house, under the kitchen, not because he was a dog, an animal, but . . . [because]

godhead required that he live apart. Lion did not belong to Major de Spain at all but just happened to like him better than he did any of the rest of us, as a man might have."

Apart from the equality among the men and the even heavier insistence on masculine power in men and dogs, this is much like the medieval hunts, with men on horseback following hounds after a dangerous beast, which is regarded with awe. Like their medieval predecessors, the men value their dogs highly but will ruthlessly sacrifice them in the hunt. Two men risk their lives to save their dogs, but Major de Spain does not mind when Old Ben kills his dogs, for "We gambled the dogs against him; we gave each other warning."[32] The men are nothing but hunters during the hunt; the dogs are never anything but hunters.

Because hunting carries such strong symbolic implications of aristocracy and virility, popular literature on dogs focuses disproportionately on those who hunt. This emphasis has continued long past the time that most dog lovers were also hunters. In "Dumb-Bell's Check," John Taintor Foote regales his readers with a picture of leisured wealth, in which owners who breed dogs for field trials all maintain kennels with kennel servants. His tale turns on the weighty question of whether pointers or setters are better bird dogs. MacKinlay Kantor's much-reprinted "The Voice of Bugle Ann" speaks to readers who see foxhunting as really important and thrill to the bugling of a first-class foxhound. Dion Henderson describes the pointer Algonquin's love of hunting and field techniques in lingering detail before using him as a vehicle for teaching a boy about the basic things in life. The boy's grandfather and uncle take him out on the aged dog's final hunt in order to teach him the meaning of death. Algonquin stood "on his last point, and he knew how it was. I could tell from the way he stood that he was speaking to the birds for the last time now . . . he was pouring out the final eloquence of his genius, saying: *Fare thee well, little brothers; be thee beautiful for me one time more, and be at peace, for it is not thee who shall be slain today; put out the candles of thy alarm and look upon me one time more—thou shalt not see my like again, little brothers, not like me who loved thee. . . .*" Then Uncle Ovid shoots Algonquin on point.[33] Henderson's sentimental effusion makes explicit what is implicit in most hunters' accounts of their sport: the rituals of hunting transform death and killing into something beautiful.

Rick Bass's memoir *Colter: The True Story of the Best Dog I Ever Had*

(2000) shows that glorification of the hunt and the hunting dog is still a potent popular theme. Bass, like Faulkner, finds a uniquely close bond between man and dog engaged in single-minded pursuit of prey, a closer, less ambiguous bond than a man could have with another person or even a dog with whom he was not united on the hunt. There is the further gratification of directing a skilled animal that follows one's commands to the letter. It is not the pointer's finesse in finding and pointing a bird that Bass extols so much as its restraint of its natural impulses in obedience to human wishes—learning "to want something, but then, when the thing flies, to *not* want it" and to abstain from running after a bird unless ordered to, even a bird that it bumps into by accident or one that the man has shot. Moreover, the hunt intensifies man's experience of nature and makes him feel that he is filling the primevally basic human (that is, virile) role of hunter and watching the dog fulfill his (or rather, the artificially restricted hunting behavior bred and trained into him by man). Colter, a German shorthaired pointer, soon revealed himself as "a raging genius." In order to do justice to that genius as it deserved, Bass sent Colter away for two entire summers to a first-class trainer, painful as it was to part with him. "If he had been less of a dog I would have tried to train him myself," but Bass would have made mistakes and Colter "deserved better." Colter is ready to hunt his heart out for himself (not for his master), and since Bass feels the same way, he sees them not as "master and dog, but partners." Although he attended a shooting school "to try to become worthy of this dog," he never became good enough: "he, through diligent effort and prodigious talent and desire-to-please—call it love—produces a bird, or birds, for me, and I fire and miss, again and again and again. The guilt, the regret returns. None of us are worthy of our dogs. But we can try."[34] On the one hand, the dog and his skills are glorified beyond reason; on the other, the dog is reduced to a vehicle for the circumscribed skills of a pointer.

There seems to be no doubt that hunting dogs find their utmost fulfillment in hunting, the work that instinct, breeding, and training have qualified them to do. Hounds delight in exercising their incredible powers of scent by locating and following a trail. On the other hand, does not this overspecialization limit the potential of what a dog can be? "Hounds run and snuffle, snuffle and run, and do precious little else. Even the characteristic fidelity of dogs is attenuated," for they will "adopt new masters with much the ease other dogs show in adopting new foods." Despite extravagant praise of the foxhound as "the model of the canine race," it is a narrowly limited dog. Bred for endurance in the hunt and the ability to tolerate living in a kennel with other dogs, it is not suited to be a companion to its owner.[35]

It is also clear that hunters can bond with their dogs more intensely than most owners, and that they value them highly. Bass is totally convincing on his close friendship with Colter. But the fact that hunters are interested entirely in one aspect of their dogs can make them ruthless. *The Master of Game* extolled the understanding and worthiness of hounds and gave them a luxurious kennel, but he expected them to entertain him by flinging themselves at the tusks of a boar. A boar could kill over half the pack before it was subdued. Elliott Barker, the twentieth-century author of "My Dogs Had What It Takes," invites his readers to share in his joy when his dogs are lacerated while killing an old mother bobcat and her two half-grown kittens. Edwardes, the developer of Sealyham terriers, unhesitatingly shot dogs that failed to live up to his extravagant standards of courage. Greyhounds were routinely killed when age slowed them down. In William Hamilton's poem "The Last Dying Words of Bonny Heck," a greyhound complains that, though he coursed with distinction in his prime, he is now to be hanged only for being old and lame. Scott, a genuine dog lover as well as a sportsman, found his pleasure in coursing alloyed by "the necessity of dispatching the instruments and partakers of our amusements" when they lost their youthful vigor. Racing greyhounds fare no better today. Training of bird dogs—up into the nineteenth century called breaking—could be sickeningly cruel. The anonymous author of *An Essay on Shooting* recommended chaining a dog to a stake in the yard and beating it "excessively" to teach it not to chase furred game. Cruelty was compounded by deceit: a servant was to give the dog a series of sound beatings for an hour; then the master, who had remained out of sight, would go to the dog, caress it, release it, feed it, and bring it back to the field.[36]

Nonhunters can take satisfaction in the novel uses that have recently been found for the hunting dog's nose. Not only have dogs a sense of smell over a thousand times keener than ours, but they can make fine discriminations among odors.[37] Thus they can be trained to locate hidden drugs, explosives, termites, or mold in lumberyards. Drug-sniffing beagles and retrievers can

detect drugs through thickly sealed packets buried in strong-smelling substances like bath salts or located five to six stories up in a building (by pluck-
ing scents from its ventilation system). The Beagle Brigade of the USDA's
Animal and Plant Health Inspection Service patrols airports and international
postal depots for contraband fruit and meat. Wearing green vests and trained
to sit when they detect any banned food, the dogs have an accuracy rate of
more than 90 percent. Dogs can detect arson by smelling a trace of accelerant
on an object. They can inform farmers when their cows are in estrus. Dogs
work better than any machine because machines have to be specifically programmed, while "A dog responds outside the parameters. He smells it wherever it is and responds. Half the time we're not even in search mode when the
dog finds something," say Jeff Gabel and Carl Newcombe of the U.S. Cus-
toms training center.[38]

Field zoologists are making ingenious use of dogs' keen scent and innate
interest in what is scientifically known as scat in order to study elusive wide-
ranging animals. Scat reveals an animal's movements, range, and diet; and it
contains hormones that reveal its reproductive status and level of stress, as
well as DNA that can identify a particular individual. Dogs can locate scat far
more efficiently by scent than humans could by sight, especially when it has
been purposely hidden, as by mothers with cubs. Sam Wasser, a conservation
biologist, is using dogs to collect scat for two research projects on bears: one
seeking to establish that grizzly bears do indeed live in an area that is being
protected for them, and one comparing the stress levels of bears in Jasper National Park with those in an adjacent area disturbed by mining and logging.
Another research team is using scat dogs to study the endangered Amur
(Siberian) tiger population in Russian forests. They cannot send the dogs out
to find scat because the tigers would eat them, but they use the dogs to identify particular tigers by matching fresh samples with those in a reference collection from known tigers.[39]

5

Working Dogs

Dogs were prized as assistants in hunting, but they were essential, up until recent times, as guards for property and herders of livestock. No portrayals of working dogs survive from the medieval period, because the dogs had no prestige value and their owners were usually illiterate. But in *Ivanhoe*, Sir Walter Scott vividly re-created Fangs, who helped the thrall Gurth herd swine in the forest. Fangs was "a ragged, wolfish-looking dog, a sort of lurcher, half mastiff, half greyhound." The ruling class conceded that he was necessary, but as a large dog roaming forest land, he had been lamed by having three claws struck from his right forefoot and thus had been made unfit for his trade. He "ran limping about as if with the purpose of seconding his master in collecting the refractory grunters," but only scattered them. Still, when he finally got the herd together, Gurth praised him, and man and dog drove them home.

When Gurth was condemned for helping Ivanhoe, poor lame Fangs followed him, howling piteously, until Gurth's master, Cedric, frightened the dog off by throwing a javelin at him. "Gurth's heart swelled within him; for he felt this meditated slaughter of his faithful adherent in a degree much deeper than the harsh treatment he had himself received"; he would never forgive Cedric for striving "to kill before my face the only other living creature [besides Ivanhoe] that ever shewed me kindness." When Gurth was emancipated, Fangs shared his delight, jumping "upon him, to express his sympathy."[1] Scott finely portrayed the mutual love that must have existed between a poor man and his constant companion and helper, articulating what poor men themselves were not able to express until the nineteenth century. Fangs loved Gurth as if he were a lord instead of a thrall; Gurth loved a dog who had negligible worth according to conventional standards of the day.

Actually, however, there is some evidence that skilled working dogs were considered valuable. The ancient law codes of Wales, written down in the thirteenth century but attributed to Howel the Good in the tenth, provide a useful guide to the value placed on dogs through stipulating the fines to be paid for killing them. Dogs were valued according to their function, their fitness for work in terms of maturity and training, and the social station of their owners. As would be expected, hunting dogs were esteemed the highest. The king's buckhound, once trained, was assessed at one pound (240 pence), the same as a stallion. It was worth 120 pence untrained, 60 pence at a year old, 30 pence as a whelp in the kennel, and 15 pence from birth up until the time it opened its eyes. The king's spaniel was assessed the same as his buckhound; his greyhound, half as much at every stage. A nobleman's or free man's dogs were assessed at half as much as the king's, and a villein's at only fourpence.

A cur like Fangs was assessed at fourpence no matter whom it belonged to, but highly trained working dogs were rated highly. A villein's shepherd dog was assessed at 60 pence (the same as a nobleman's untrained buckhound) if the owner and one neighbor from each side could certify that it led the herd out in the morning, brought them home in the evening, and made three turns around them in the night. The working watchdog was respected to the extent that killing even "a dog accustomed to bite" on its own premises entailed a fine of twenty-four pence; however, if it bit someone further away from the house, nothing was due. Pet animals belonging to the king or queen were assessed at one pound, those of a nobleman or his wife at half that, and those of a villein at only a penny.[2]

The original livestock dogs were flock guards from mastiff stock, essential while wolves remained a significant threat to herds. These are the dogs described by Roman writers on agriculture, and they are used in wild, mountainous areas even today. Our present Great Pyrenees and komondor were developed as flock guards. These dogs have to be big, to discourage predators, and placid, so as not to disturb the sheep. They are kept juvenile—they look like big puppies—so as to inhibit any tendency to eye/stalk, chase, or bite their charges. To maximize their compatibility with the stock they guard, typically sheep, they are socialized to them rather than to humans or dogs; and, as a result of directly bonding with the sheep, they are able and willing to protect them without human direction.[3]

Darwin was fascinated when he saw such dogs for the first time in South America in 1833. Large flocks of sheep were guarded by one or two dogs without any human around. The puppies were suckled by a ewe and brought up with sheep, so they thought of the flock as their pack and defended it as other dogs defend their human family. When anyone approached the flock, the dog would advance, barking, and the sheep closed in behind it. The dog brought in the flock at a certain hour each evening and came to the house every day for food, but it skulked away from the house dogs. Once it reached the flock, however, it would turn and bark, and the house dogs would all flee. A single one of these flock guards could keep off a whole pack of hungry wild dogs, probably because they were intimidated by the sheepdog together with the flock, as if the dog were supported by others of its own kind. "The shepherd-dog ranks the sheep as its fellow-brethren, and thus gains confidence; and the wild dogs, though knowing that the individual sheep are not dogs, but are good to eat, yet partly consent to this view when seeing them in a flock with a shepherd-dog at their head."[4]

This ancient type of dog has found a new use in our western states, where coyotes and other predators destroy 10 percent of the sheep and calves. Guns, poison, traps, and fences are undesirable expedients and also not very effective. The Coppingers set up the Livestock Dog Project in the late 1970s to find out whether the problem could be solved by guardian dogs. They imported flock guards from remote areas where they still work, trained the puppies appropriately, and sent them off to ranches. On one ranch in Colorado, they report, two flock guards guard a thousand sheep; the losses to coyotes have been reduced from the usual more than a hundred, worth $10,000, to two.[5]

In areas where large predators were no longer a threat, however, it was more useful to have another type of dog, whose main job was to help shepherds control the flocks. Herding dogs were developed in the early Middle Ages, probably in northwestern Europe and probably by crossing northern dogs with sight hounds. They combined the northern dog's toughness and resistance to cold with the sight hound's speed, good vision, and alert readiness to chase running animals. Many herding dogs retain the erect or semi-erect ears and thick, medium-length coats of northern dogs. Herding dogs drive stock where they are to go by frightening them—either circling and staring at them, like collies, or nipping at their heels, like corgis. Of course, unlike sight hounds, herders must never chase to kill; they need to be aggressive enough to threaten or nip, but not to bite. While flock guards were preferably white, to blend in with sheep, dark-colored dogs were preferred for herding, to distinguish them from sheep and add to their visual dominance over them.[6]

The British shepherd dog was developed at least by the middle of the sixteenth century. Johannes Caius described it as medium-sized, since it no longer had to deal with wolves, and responsive to its master's commands by voice or hand signals. With his dog's help, a man could bring in straying sheep or move the flock in any direction, without himself moving. By 1801, the typical shepherd's dog looked like a border collie, although it was a few inches lower at the shoulder.[7] Collies, the herding dogs of Scotland, got their name from the dark sheep they herded, colleys. Only after Queen Victoria loved them on sight and started them on their career as pets and show dogs did the rough collie develop its larger size, elegant narrow head, luxuriant silky coat, and long, slim legs.

Their new aristocratic owners took pride in the distinction between these new collies and their working ancestors. The dog had become worthy of his elegant new surroundings "despite his lowly origin," they congratulated themselves; and "constant association with his superiors has improved his disposition immensely." Still, as William Watson recognized, there is a loss when a working breed becomes a pet. He describes his highbred, majestic-looking collie running ahead of him on a walk:

His trick of doing nothing with an air,
His salon *manners and society smile,*

Were but skin-deep, factitious, and you saw
The bustling despot of the mountain flock,
The pastoral dog-of-all-work, underlie
The fashionable modern lady's pet,—
Industrial impulses bereft of scope,
Duty and discipline denied an aim,
Ancestral energy and strenuousness
In graceful trifling frittered all away.

Witness the depth of his concern which path they will take and his zeal in leading the way when, from pure indifference, they pick one over the other.[8]

Sheepherding was a major business in Britain until recent times. And it depended on dogs. According to the early-nineteenth-century writer James Hogg, who had started life as a shepherd, "A single shepherd and his dog will accomplish more in gathering a stock of sheep from a Highland farm, than twenty shepherds could without dogs . . . Without the shepherd's dog, the whole of the open mountainous land in Scotland would not be worth a sixpence. It would require more hands to manage a flock of sheep, gather them from the hills, force them into houses and folds, and drive them to market, than the profits of the whole stock would be capable of maintaining."[9]

The shepherd dog's job requires devotion, endurance, and great skill. While its wolf ancestors worked as a pack to herd a few prey animals, the dog must herd a whole flock of sheep by itself. It "must therefore work extremely hard to surround the 'prey,' rushing this way and that, trying to take up all the positions of the group of encircling wolves."[10] As it moves the flock, the dog must drive laggards from the back and then rush up to the front to restore order among the leaders, must round up strays and rescue any sheep that have slipped in a stream or got caught on a barbed-wire fence. It controls them by frightening them, but not too much—by stopping and fixing them with a steady stare, and by running around them rather than chasing them. Thus it can force sheep to leave the security of their flock without sending them into a panic, which would make them impossible to control. The dog has to recognize every individual of its flock, which may include hundreds.

One clever nineteenth-century dog helped his master steal sheep. Representing himself as a prospective buyer, the man would take his dog with him to look over a flock of several hundred and pick out the ten or twelve he wanted, secretly indicating these to the dog. Then he went away and sent the dog back alone that night to pick out the individual sheep he had pointed out, separate them from the flock, and drive them the ten or twelve miles to his master. The efforts of another devoted canine helper were less happily applied. A young thief selected some sheep belonging to his former master and set off for Edinburgh. But before he had got them quite off the farm, he thought better of the idea, sent them back up the hill, called off his dog, and rode away. After riding three miles, he heard many feet following him, and turned to find "his dog with the stolen drove, driving them at a furious rate to keep up with his master." Knowing it was now too late to get them away or back to their farm, the man "corrected his dog in great wrath, left the sheep once more, and taking his dog with him, rode off a second time. He had not ridden above a mile, till he perceived that his dog had again given him the slip; and suspecting for what purpose, he was terribly alarmed as well as chagrined; for the day-light approached, and he durst not make a noise calling the dog, for fear of alarming the neighborhood, in a place where both he and the dog were known. He resolved therefore to abandon the animal to himself, and take a road across the country which he was sure his dog did not know, and could not follow." He got safely to a farmhouse some distance away, but soon another man came to reassure him "that his dog had the sheep safe enough down at the Crooked Yett, and he need not hurry himself." Seeing no alternative, the thief collected the stolen drove and sold them, a felony that cost him his life.[11]

A folktale from Dorset, "Jack-with-the-Lantern," nicely conveys the partnership between shepherd and dog. Old Jacob and his old dog, Tan, were both wise and "a wonder with the sheep." But the farmer decided they needed helpers and hired "a lad and his clever young bitch that had quite a name down the valley for being real lively at their work." They proudly showed Old Jacob and Tan how fast they could round up the sheep—and reduced them to panic. Jacob showed the newcomers how to manage by sending Tan in to get a ewe from the middle of the flock, which the sheep tolerated because he was quiet with them. Nevertheless, the boy "thought Old Jacob silly slow, didn't handle

Tan with whistling, didn't do anything but speak a word or two to Tan who was slow and steady too, and far too old, and ought to be shot . . . he never raced and chased and made the sheep move any faster than a good even walk." Fan, the bitch, did begin to learn from copying Tan, but the boy continued to excite her to rush the sheep, and he was her master. One snowy night, the boy and Fan came in with the flock—but without three pregnant ewes. Jacob sent them back after them, with Tan to help them. But they got hopelessly lost, and Tan lay down and refused to move, even though the boy struck him on the muzzle with his crook. The boy and Fan stumbled about, "boy crying and Fan whimpering, without a notion where they was" till Farmer and his dog Lass found them. Tan, with Lass's help, had already brought in the three missing ewes, despite being hampered by his sore muzzle. Old Jacob gave the boy "a smart dozen with the strap" to punish him for laying hand on another man's dog and then sent him and Fan to eat their porridge.[12]

James Hogg's collie "was always my companion. I conversed with him the whole day—I shared every meal with him, and my plaid in time of a shower; the consequence was, that I generally had the best dog in all the country. The first remarkable one that I had was named 'Sirrah.' He was beyond all comparison the best dog I ever saw. He was of a surly, unsociable temper—disdained all flattery, and refused to be caressed; but his attention to his master's commands and interests never will again be equaled by any of the canine race." Hogg bought him, in a sorry state, from a drover who had abused him. "I thought I discovered a sort of sullen intelligence in his face, notwithstanding his dejected and forlorn situation. . . . He was scarcely then a year old, and knew so little of herding that he had never turned sheep in his life; but as soon as he discovered that it was his duty to do so, and that it obliged me, I can never forget with what anxiety and eagerness he learned his different evolutions. He would try every way deliberately till he found out what I wanted him to do; and when once I made him to understand a direction, he never forgot or mistook it again. Well as I knew him, he very often astonished me, for when hard pressed in accomplishing the task he was put to, he had expedients of the moment that bespoke a great share of the reasoning faculty." Indeed, "I have hardly ever seen a shepherd's dog do anything without perceiving his reasons for it. . . . I have often amused myself in calculating what his motives were for such and such things, and I generally find them very cogent ones."

Late one night, when Hogg had a flock of seven hundred lambs just separated from their mothers, they panicked and scattered in three groups. Two human shepherds searched for hours and found none of them. Meanwhile, Sirrah had gathered them all into a ravine and was standing guard, unable to leave because he had no one to help him. "How he had got all the divisions collected in the dark is beyond my comprehension. The charge was left entirely to himself from midnight until the rising of the sun; and if all the shepherds in the Forest had been there to assist him, they could not have effected it with greater propriety. . . . I never felt so grateful to any creature below the sun as I did to 'Sirrah' that morning."

Like working dogs throughout history, however, Sirrah could not be kept when he was too old to manage his work. Hogg could not afford to maintain a dog in addition to the working collie he needed to help him, so he sold Sirrah to a young neighbor who had less for him to do. Sirrah went off willingly, for he expected to return to Hogg at night. "But when he found that he was abandoned by me, and doomed to be the slave of a stranger for whom he did not care, he would never again do another feasible turn." The young man kindly got his father to look after Sirrah, but the dog would regularly meet Hogg on the hill, without approaching close, and wistfully watch the young collie do his job. Knowing how grateful the old dog would have been for one kind word, Hogg still felt he must not encourage him, a withholding that caused him guilt until his dying day.

Hector, Sirrah's son and successor, had a more engaging personality but was a less competent herder. One whole night he sat in drenching rain guarding a flock of lambs in the fold, when any other collie would have discerned that they were safe enough without his attention. But he showed intelligence in other ways. Although he could not follow all the family conversation, "he rarely missed aught that was said about himself, the cat [with whom he was obsessed, though he never hurt her], or of a hunt." Once Hogg mentioned to his mother that he was going to Bowerhope for a fortnight, but would not take Hector because he constantly quarreled with the dogs there. The next morning Hector was not to be found until he appeared at Bowerhope, impatiently waiting for Hogg.

By the time Hector became too old for work, Hogg was sufficiently prosperous that he could keep him anyway and reassure him that he would never be cast off:

Although thy strength begins to fail,
Its best was spent in serving me;
An' can I grudge thy wee bit meal,
Some comfort in thy age to gie?

For mony a day, frae sun to sun,
We've toiled fu' hard wi'ane anither,
An' mony a thousand mile thou'st run,
To keep my thraward flock thegither.

Whenever Hogg is depressed by his mistakes or misfortunes, Hector pushes forward to share his grief, silently assuring him that, whatever happens, Hector will hold him dear.[13]

In the nineteenth century, dogs were still essential for bringing livestock into the city markets. Charles Dickens reported amusingly on the capable performance of the shaggy black-and-white dog (probably a border collie) of a drunken drover. Once in London, the drover headed for a pub, and the dog took "undivided charge" of the sheep. At length the drover emerged, "besmeared with red ochre and beer, and gave him wrong directions, which he calmly disregarded. He has taken the sheep entirely into his own hands, has merely remarked with respectful firmness, 'That instruction would place them under an omnibus; you had better confine your attention to yourself— you will want it all'; and has driven his charge away, with an intelligence of ears and tail, and a knowledge of business, that left his lout of a man very, very far behind."[14]

There is a deeply serious counterpart to this story in *Bleak House,* where the utterly ignorant street boy Jo is contrasted with a dog who is waiting for his master outside a butcher's shop after driving a flock of sheep into London. It is "a thoroughly vagabond dog, accustomed to low company and public-houses; . . . but an educated, improved, developed dog, who has been taught his duties, and knows how to discharge them. He and Jo listen to the music [of a street band], probably with much the same amount of animal sat-isfaction; likewise, as to awakened association, aspiration or regret, melan-choly or joyful reference to things beyond the senses, they are probably upon a par. But, otherwise, how far above the human listener is the brute!"[15] A shocking comparison, all the more shocking because it is true. Unlike the child, the dog has reason to be happy and self-respecting, has a secure and valued place in a family, has a useful function in society.

The ancient skills are still required on hill farms in Britain today, where sheep must be moved regularly and cannot be moved without dogs. The dog must gather the flock in the autumn and drive the ewes into pens for mating with various rams. After this, it drives them to hilltops for grazing, so they can work their way down as the weather becomes colder. Generally the sheep are left alone in the winter, though in storms the dogs must find sheep buried in snowdrifts. Lambing time in the spring is the busiest season, when preg-nant ewes and lambs must be gathered repeatedly for injections and proce-dures; they are hard to move and yet must be treated gently. The dog will also keep a lost or orphaned lamb with a ewe until she accepts it as her own. In the summer the dog has to herd the sheep into pens for shearing and dip-ping in insecticide solution, keeping a constant supply of sheep running through.

A trained shepherd dog will respond not only to ten or twelve spoken or whistled commands but also to arm signals, which are less disturbing to the flock and enable the shepherd to direct the dog from a distance; the dogs are trained to look back at the shepherd regularly and if necessary jump up on a rock to see him better. But although these dogs work closely with humans, they must not just blindly follow the shepherd's commands. Sometimes they must work on their own, out of his sight and hearing, using their own initia-tive to meet whatever circumstances come up. On one occasion, a ewe with a lamb split off from the main flock and refused to be moved, defying the dog by stamping her hooves. The dog solved the problem by separating several other sheep from the flock and bringing them over to her; she joined them without difficulty, and the dog moved them all back to the main flock.[16]

Collies can herd almost anything, so they have been adapted to novel uses. In the nineteenth century, they herded ostriches in Cape Colony, South

Africa. Two men on horseback with a dog could drive a troop of 100 to 150 full-grown birds better than six or eight men on horseback, for the dog could gather the ostriches into a meek cluster that would move ahead without fighting, while men acting without dogs would scatter them.[17] Nowadays, border collies make themselves useful driving Canada geese off golf courses.

Each region in medieval Europe developed local herding dogs to fill its needs. With the rise of nationalism in the nineteenth century, it became important to have a creditable sheep dog representing one's own nation. Noticing the popularity of Scotch collies at the end of the nineteenth century, German dog lovers turned their attention to their own shepherd dogs and developed their ideal by combining various local types. Max von Stephanitz and Artur Meyer got a strong body from one variety, prick ears from another, and so forth, and achieved the German shepherd in 1899.[18] As the demand for herding lessened, von Stephanitz promoted his dog for police and military work, where its intelligence, keen senses, strength, size, and trainability would be equally valuable. Unlike British herding dogs, it could be a serious watchdog.

Watchdogs were self-evidently essential for protecting houses and property before there was an effective police force; even the Plantagenet laws recognized that people living in the royal forests had to keep mastiffs. Typically, they were kept chained up all day, which increases aggressiveness in any dog, and were therefore called bandogs, that is, tied-up dogs; at night they would be let loose to patrol the grounds. Although this job might seem to require no more than size, ferocity, vigilance, and an active sense of territory, it required discernment as well. Taplin wrote in 1803 that "in timber-yards, coal-wharfs, large yards, and widely extended manufactories," the utility of the mastiff "exceeds conception. Whatever is submitted to his superintendence and protection may be considered safe from depredation." When they were let loose at night, the dogs never stopped patrolling the property, inspecting minutely until they were satisfied that everything was "in a state of perfect safety." Their barks could attract attention more effectively than a human watchman. Dogs can still protect premises better than a mechanical alarm system. The Dobermans that patrolled Macy's department store at night would find intruders, bark to alert their handler, and then hold the intruder in place. On command, they would jump for his gun arm and hold on indefinitely. They would also detect fire and smoke and, because of the instinctive canine wariness about anything out of normal routine, draw attention to open windows or overflowing water. One dog insisted that his handler keep checking a certain office; at length the man lifted the cover on a costly adding machine and found it was silently running and overheated.[19] Back in the sixteenth century, Caius claimed that some mastiffs would not only bark and howl to arouse the household in case of fire in the night, but would actually try to prevent fires: on seeing "fiery coales . . . skattered about the hearthe," they would rake them together with their paws, "musyng and studying fyrst with themselves howe it might conveniently be done."

Caius went on to repeat Columella's praise of mastiffs and added that they would not forsake their master alive or dead. Caius's contemporary William Harrison went even further in his "Description of England." Not only are mastiffs "the principal causes" of arresting thieves, but they usually do their job through precise discernment and quiet, forbearing firmness; in fact, they dislike violence. Though some "must be tied day and night, . . . some are so gentle they may go loose around the house and yard and children may ride on their backs. Some will attack anyone who touches their master or anyone of the household; some will let a stranger come into the house and walk around where he likes without following him, but will attack him if he touches anything." Harrison once had a mastiff who would not let anyone bring his weapon beyond the gate and would also intervene if Harrison beat any of his children by gently trying to take the rod out of his hand with its teeth or else by pulling their clothes back down over their bared flesh. By 1800, the mastiff was distinguished above all for sweet temper, generosity, and attachment. "His docility is perfect; the teasing of the smaller kinds will hardly provoke him to resent, and I have seen him hold down with his paw the Terrier or Cur that has bit him. In a family he will permit the children to play with him, and suffer all their little pranks without offence." Even when modern mastiffs are acting as watchdogs, they are apt to examine an intruder carefully rather than barking and to knock down and sit on someone who transgresses proper limits rather than attacking him.[20]

Two particularly benevolent mastiff types were developed in early modern times. The monks at the Hospice du Grand Saint Bernard in the Alps realized by the eighteenth century that their watchdogs could give them invaluable help in their work of rescuing travelers lost in the snow. The dogs' superior scent and sense of direction guided them better than humans over treacherous narrow trails covered by snow and enabled them to detect buried travelers. Their big bodies cleared pathways through the snow and provided body heat to keep exhausted travelers alive. The dogs worked in teams: after digging out the victim, one would lie down beside him or her, providing warmth and licking their face to revive them, while the other would return to the monastery for assistance.[21]

The original settlers on the coast of Newfoundland developed the Newfoundland dog to ease their hard lives by land and sea. Three or four Newfoundlands would draw a sledge loaded with two or three hundred pounds of wood from the interior to the seacoast, following their assigned route without the guidance of a human driver. Having delivered their load, they returned to their owner in the woods. They were even more useful to seamen. They would haul fishermen's catches to market and retrieve equipment lost overboard. They also retrieved drowning people from the water and saved others by pulling lines to sinking ships from shore. When high waves prevented a small boat from reaching the ship, a Newfoundland could pull a line along which people could be brought in with harness and pulley. Imported into Britain, Newfoundlands were used to pull carts or work wheels to draw water from deep wells, but they soon became extremely popular as pets.

Dogs have been vitally important as draft animals, in Europe as well as the snowy expanses of the Arctic. Through the nineteenth century, they provided essential help to peddlers and other small tradesmen. Dogs were cheaper to maintain than horses or donkeys and could be kept in the house; moreover, they could pull carts through narrow streets and guard merchandise in their masters' absence. Unfortunately, the Royal Society for the Prevention of Cruelty to Animals organized a campaign against using dogs for draft in England, regardless of the fact that many poor tradesmen, especially in cities, depended on them for their family's livelihood. Although some of the dogs were abused or overworked, most were cared for as well as a poor family's circumstances would permit, and were malnourished only if the humans were

as well. Most of them lived inside their owners' homes and so would naturally have been treated as companions as well as workers.

But in 1839 the use of cart dogs was made illegal in London. The produce
peddlers petitioned Parliament on the grounds that their kindness to their
dogs was well known and their trade would be ruined because they could not
afford to keep horses. An editorial writer in the *Times* demanded in 1843:
"What suddenly is to become of the canine labor which is to be thus dis-
placed from its legitimate channel? Are out-of-work mastiffs to crowd our
crossings and hang disconsolately about the corners of our butcher's shops,
like coachmen thrown out of employ by the railroads?" Or should we adopt
the more frightful alternative of killing them? "Why condemn to dissolute
idleness or indiscriminate extinction whole generations of respectable
quadrupeds?" But the RSPCA and the lawmakers persisted and extended the
ban throughout England. The result was the ruin of many poor people's
trade and the slaughter or abandonment of many thousands of dogs. Nevertheless, dog lovers such as the novelist Ouida congratulated their nation on
this overzealous reform. In her *Dog of Flanders,* she made clear that using
draft dogs was a practice of benighted foreign Roman Catholic countries:
"Patrasche came of a race which had toiled hard and cruelly from sire to son
in Flanders for many a century—slaves of slaves, dogs of the people, beasts
of the shafts and the harness, creatures that lived straining their sinews in the
gall of the cart, and died breaking their hearts on the flints of the streets."[22]
The kind old man who rescues Patrasche from death actually feels guilty
about letting him pull the milk cart, as if an old human were a more appropriate beast of burden than a strong young dog.

Butchers required dogs that were less skilled than shepherds' dogs, but
larger and fiercer. They were used to bully frightened cattle into submission
and had to be ready to face an aroused bull. Before long, people saw that this
useful work could be turned into a source of entertainment. In 1209,
William, Earl Warren had looked from the walls of his castle at Stamford and
seen a crowd of butchers' dogs pursuing a bull through the town. He found
the sight so amusing that he gave the butchers his castle meadow on condition
that they stage the same spectacle every year on a day six weeks before Christmas. From these informal beginnings, an organized show developed in which

a bull or bear would be tied to a stake and then dogs would be set on it, either in series or all together. The dogs would try to sink their teeth into the bull's sensitive muzzle so that the pain would immobilize him or cause him to lash about and become weakened.[23] They were often killed by a toss from the bull's horns, but any dog that was not badly injured when tossed was expected to go in to the bull again.

At first bulls were baited by the regular butchers' mastiffs. Then a special smaller and faster dog was developed, the better to run in under the bull's horns, with nostrils set far enough back that the dog could breathe while clinging fast to the bull's nose. This original bulldog looked something like the modern boxer. Sydenham Edwards's plate shows a sturdy, trim, functional animal with a stocky muscled body, reasonably straight legs of medium length, and a flat but not squashed muzzle; they weighed only about thirty-six pounds.

Bullbaiting was enjoyed by the best people in the sixteenth century, but by the later seventeenth, many recoiled from it. John Evelyn, forced to accompany some friends to the Southwark Bear-Garden, condemned the cock fighting, dog fighting, bear- and bullbaiting he saw there as "butcherly Sports, or rather barbarous cruelties: . . . One of the Bulls tossd a Dog full into a Ladys lap, as she sate in one of the boxes at a Considerable height from the *Arena*: There were two poore dogs killed . . . & I most heartily weary, of the rude & dirty passetime." In 1801, a preacher at Wokingham, where the annual bullbaiting was a great event, condemned the cruelty to both attackers and victim: "two useful animals, the bull, who propagates our food, and the faithful dog, who protects our property, to be thus tormented!" The bull is teased to madness by humans yelling at and prodding him, and then a dog is loosed on him. The dog is expected to keep up the attack until it gets a good hold on the bull's face or is incapacitated by being tossed and gored. Then another is sent in, followed by as many more as are necessary to bring him down, "amidst the shameless shouts of a shameful victory, where 500 greater brutes have brought a lesser to the ground." By this time, many members of the better classes considered baiting animals with dogs to be a "vicious pastime," "attended only by the lowest and most despicable part of the people."[24]

Nevertheless, aristocrats were still arguing in Parliament against bills to prohibit bullbaiting on the grounds that (like hunting) it inspired courage and fighting spirit. Because the bulldog would unflinchingly attack an animal much larger than itself and could not be forced by pain or exhaustion to let go once it had taken hold, it was widely admired for its courage, fortitude, and unshakable resolve. A writer in 1771 credited the bulldog with "a larger share of true genuine courage than any other animal in the world." Vero Shaw rejoiced that people at home and abroad recognized it as peculiarly English, for "bull-dog pluck and endurance are qualifications eagerly cherished by Englishmen of all classes." Artists such as Théodore Géricault, in his formidable *Bulldog*, and Paul Delaroche, in his quietly menacing and yet somehow debonair *Belcher*, emphasized the bulldog's impressive self-assurance, determination, and power. The hero of a series of thrillers starting in 1920— hefty and xenophobic, ugly but charming, apparently brainless but in fact capable of foiling master criminals—was called Bull-dog Drummond.[25]

Although dogs are no longer economically necessary as guards, herders, or draft animals, they continue to provide important help to humans in new ways. Huge armored mastiffs are no longer sent into direct combat, where they would not have horses to terrorize and in any case would promptly be demolished by guns. American military dogs are selected for intelligence, character, and keen senses and are trained to control their aggression: to charge at an enemy, sit quietly while their handler searches him, and attack without command only if he touches their handler. They are to go for the limbs rather than the throat, and they must back off on command.[26] In modern armies dogs are not mere killing machines, but provide many kinds of auxiliary support for soldiers.

In World War I, Red Cross dogs carrying medical supplies and bottles of water and spirits sought out wounded men on the field, ignoring the dead. If a man was still unable to make his way to the aid station, the dog would return to inform its handlers and lead them back to the spot. Larger ambulance dogs would pull the wounded on carts to the aid stations. They could go where motorized ambulances could not; they presented a smaller target than horses and could work without a man to direct them. Colette vividly evoked what they did for soldiers in "The Ambulance Dogs (Winter 1913–1914)."

She describes a training session in which the dogs' earnestness contrasts amusingly with the playfulness of the human trainers and pretend wounded, but goes on to imagine "the day when the game and the lesson will be in grim earnest, and when a hundred, a thousand men will lie on the snow feeling their warm blood growing cold. There they will wait, with night coming on, hoping to be found by that intelligent, four-footed member of the stretcher service, who is never afraid and never tired, and who sees and scents in the dark. There they wait while life drains away; and suddenly there is the dog's breath, his cool muzzle and his friendly tongue wiping away the blood and at the same time the tears of weakness. Help has come, and with it the warm tide of life returns."[27]

Messenger dogs, carrying dispatches in a little canister attached to their collar, could carry messages four or five times faster than the average soldier and were also harder to shoot because they presented a lower profile. They would resolutely find a way to pass through, over, or under barbed wire, fences, water, clouds of smoke, and enemy fire to complete their mission. Once French soldiers holding a small village near Verdun were encircled by superior German forces. With their telephone lines cut and their messenger pigeons dead, they had no way to convey their position to headquarters and get relief. The Germans placed artillery on a nearby hill and started to demolish the beleaguered French. Then they saw Satan, a mongrel wearing a gas mask and a pigeon carrier on each flank, running in a zigzag pattern to avoid enemy fire. Although they slowed him down with a couple of shots, he managed to reach the French line on three legs. By means of the pigeons, the French conveyed their position and that of the German artillery to their forces; soon long-range French guns were firing on the Germans, and the French were able to relieve the village.

The Americans were slow to grasp the potential of dogs in warfare and began using them in combat only in 1942. Since then, over 30,000 dogs, predominantly German shepherds and Dobermans, have served in the U.S. military; and they have been responsible for saving thousands of American lives. Chips, a German shepherd mix, landed with Patton's Seventh Army in Sicily on July 10, 1943. As he and his handler were approaching an apparently innocuous grass-covered hut, a machine gun opened fire. Immediately

Chips broke loose and ran to the hut, trailing his leash. "Moments later, the machine-gun fire stopped and an Italian soldier appeared with Chips slashing and biting at his arms and throat. Three soldiers followed with their arms raised in surrender." By himself, the dog had overpowered four armed men. Chips was awarded the Silver Star and the Purple Heart, for a wound in his scalp. Unfortunately, the national commander of the Military Order of the Purple Heart objected that giving a medal to a dog demeaned the men who had received it, and Chips's decorations were rescinded.

Dogs were particularly useful in the jungles of the Pacific front, where they alerted patrols to concealed enemy soldiers. In September and October of 1944, 250 patrols were sent out into the heavy jungle of Morotai Island, where one could see only one or two feet ahead. With the dogs' help, not one was ambushed. Scout dogs could alert our soldiers to the enemy at seventy or sometimes even two hundred yards, enabling them to surprise and kill their opponents rather than the other way around. Dogs were even more valuable in the guerrilla jungle warfare of the Vietnam War, where again they invariably sniffed out enemy troops in time to prevent an ambush. Dogs were also, for the first time, effectively used to detect mines and other buried weapons. Their complex physiological equipment can be far more effective than narrowly focused electronic or mechanical devices. Unlike traditional metal detectors, land mine dogs sniff exclusively for explosives, so they can detect plastic land mines and ignore miscellaneous pieces of metal.

Most of the World War II dogs, including Chips, were successfully retrained for civilian life, at army expense, and were placed in their original or other homes, often with their wartime handlers. Unfortunately, it was officially decided in 1945 that dogs cannot be safely demilitarized, so they must remain in military service for the rest of their lives. The dogs who saved the lives of up to 10,000 American soldiers in Vietnam were treated even more callously. Even though their handlers generally wanted to take them home, the army insisted on classifying them as "war equipment" that was to be "abandoned in place"—that is, abandoned in Vietnam to be killed, eaten, or left to starve.[28]

Dogs were first recruited for police work in the later nineteenth century, and by 1910 they were attached to police departments everywhere. Like military dogs, they support human officers in many ways. They search and patrol buildings and parks, help to control crowds, and trail, pursue, or attack suspects as necessary. They search areas for objects that could be clues and sniff for drugs and explosives. They are essential partners in search and rescue work, locating people who have got lost or are trapped under the rubble of fallen buildings. Marcia Koenig, a civilian volunteer, describes her partnership with her German shepherd mix, Bear. He "is the best search dog I've ever had and also the most difficult. I suspect the two go together. He is very assertive and tests me periodically to see if I'm willing to give up leadership of the pack to him. His assertiveness enables him to range farther than most dogs and to think for himself, not allowing me to call him off from a scent. My greatest satisfaction in working with Bear comes from the knowledge that our partnership is greater than either of our individual abilities. I decide how to cover our area, taking advantage of terrain and wind. Bear searches for the scent of a human being. We have been partners for so long now that I don't say much when we're on a search. He reads my body language to know where he is to go, and I read his to know what he's doing."[29]

Dogs have been helping blind people at least since the sixteenth century, and according to Montaigne, they helped judiciously even without the professional training they get today. The dogs not only knew to stop at the doors of people who habitually gave alms, but kept their charges clear of carts and coaches and walked in the ditch so their master could take a plain and even path beside it. They could tell that a path might be broad enough for them, but not for a blind man. Surely they could not conceive all this without reason, Montaigne concluded.[30] Systematic training for guide dogs began in eighteenth-century Europe, and the Viennese Institute of the Blind issued a manual in 1819 that explained how to train a dog to guide and avoid obstacles on specific routes. Training was further developed after World War I, when the German government decided to present each of their war-blinded veterans with a guide dog. Britain, the United States, and other countries developed programs on the German model.

Until the 1950s, the dogs' training was confined to simple tasks—leading along paths, negotiating obstacles, and stopping for traffic. Now they are taught to find their way into and out of shops, which they identify by name or smell, to locate crosswalks by sight, to find a seat on a railway platform, to distinguish by smell between the ladies' and the gentlemen's toilets. A dog who has always accompanied its male trainer to the men's room will soon learn to take its female blind owner to the ladies'. The dogs can judge obstacles so precisely that they prevent their owners from so much as brushing against anything, even if they were trained by a person of middle height and then placed with a very tall blind person. In one such case, the dog stopped in front of a shop awning covering the path, figured out the highest point in the bars that supported it, and guided her man under these high points. After learning to reliably follow commands, the dogs must make the added leap of judging when to disobey. One guide dog insisted on leaving the sidewalk over the protests of her master, who thought she was taking him across the road and out of their way. He yielded to her insistence, and when she brought him back onto the sidewalk without crossing the road, he understood that she was guiding him around ripped-up paving and apologized to her. The human and the dog form a partnership in which they must recognize each other's needs, adjust to each other's personalities, and put up with each other's off days or irritating characteristics. "We're with each other twenty-four hours a day and, as with any partnership, at times I bug her and she bugs me."[31]

Guide dogs give blind people security and a freedom they had never dreamed of having. One middle-aged woman, who had never "been out alone before in my life" before she got her dog, described their "holiday in North Wales. . . . We did enjoy our walks. . . . We traversed country roads and river paths and bridges. Although neither of us knew anything about this countryside we were never lost and were always home in time. To feel that I am free to take such walks alone is simply wonderful to me." Dogs help blind people avoid passivity, depression, or withdrawal by being always there and responsive to love, facilitating contact with other people, building self-esteem by giving independence, providing help without pity or patronage, and serving as a model of confidence and enthusiasm for life.[32]

In recent years, with the increasing recognition that disabled people wish to be as independent as possible, dogs have been helping people in imaginative new ways. Epileptics have a new freedom when they have service dogs to warn them of an imminent seizure long before there are visible symptoms. Instead of staying at home for fear of an attack, they can go about, confident the dog will sense it is coming—possibly by perceiving tiny behavioral changes—and will guide them to a safe and secluded place. After Jay Liesener snapped his neck in an accident when he was seventeen, he was humiliatingly dependent on human assistants. But now he has a black Labrador, Teddy, who is always with him and always eager to help him. One rainy day in a University of Maryland parking lot, before Liesener had Ted, he dropped the remote control to his van. He had to sit in his wheelchair in a downpour until someone came by to pick it up: "It was probably five minutes, but it felt like thirty." Another time he dropped his pencil when he was working on a paper, and he had to sit doing nothing for three hours until his attendant arrived. Ted, who has been with him for two years, has freed him from "having to worry about what's going to happen to me this day." Now Liesener can live alone as he works toward his Ph.D., with only brief morning and evening visits from a human helper.[33]

While everyone can benefit at some time from a dog's visible devotion, reliable companionship, attentive eye, and uncritical acceptance, these gifts can be all-important to people with major difficulties in relating to humans. Patients who distrust and fear other people can approach animals, who do not use words or evoke ambivalent feelings. Patients who seem hopelessly withdrawn can respond normally to a pet and then be able to communicate with other people. Animals can elicit affection and nurturing even in prisoners with long histories of violence toward humans. In inner-city Minneapolis in 1999, the American Humane Association organized a pilot program called Caring Connections that demonstrated with heartwarming success how humans in need and dogs in need can help each other. In this twelve-week dog training/humane education program, young people predisposed to emotional and behavioral problems were taught to train shelter dogs whose bad behavior or fearfulness made them unadoptable. They succeeded in improving the dogs' attitudes and behavior to the point that they could be placed in loving homes. Through relating to the dogs and successfully training them, the children developed increased self-confidence, self-esteem, and understanding of how their behavior affected others.[34]

For old people in nursing homes, pets can represent grandchildren who never visit and can bring back the happiness and normality of youth; animals, who do not recoil from the smells and debility of age, restore their "belief that their essential identity is unchanged." Dr. Jan Loney points out that "the staff that includes a canine therapist has at least one colleague who is without vanity and ambition, who has no 'pet' theories, who is utterly unconcerned with role or status, who is free of intellectual pretensions, who does not fear emotion, and who does not feel that he is being underpaid. In truth, an inspiration and a model for us all."[35]

Nevertheless, even as we recognize that therapy dogs can be more unselfish and more amiable than humans, and that their affection and sympathy can be invaluable to needy, lonely people, we can enjoy Mary Flanagan's satire on canine therapy in her story "Beyond Barking" (1994). Florence Fox, the central human character, is a difficult old lady in an impeccable luxury nursing home. She longs for the disreputable delights of her youth as a vaudeville entertainer. She detests the sweet, bland harmony of the home; most especially she detests its mascot, Deirdre, the amiable, complacent black Labrador retriever whom everyone loves. As Deirdre

> *ambled placidly along the corridor . . . Mr. Bigsby struggled past on his walking frame and stopped to stroke her head. She gave him a look that mixed affection, understanding, encouragement and humility, an all-purpose look that she'd entirely perfected. In a way it came naturally because of her breeding. But you had to work at these things too. Deirdre had a repertoire of expressions and bestowed each one according to what she deduced to be the requirements of the sufferer.*

But her next assignment

> *Florence Fox was a real challenge, even for a person who'd come tops at the training center. She hadn't yet discovered that magic look, the one that would at last elicit a positive response. Perhaps if she paraded around with her blanket between her teeth. That never failed to raise a laugh, even among the Terminals. It was worth a try. She congratulated herself on possessing infinite patience and, despite her exquisite sensibilities, a thick skin.*

So she pushed open the door and got a roll hurled at her head, but didn't flinch because she knew the woman's sight was failing.[36] No doubt Flanagan's imputation of smug officiousness to the dog is unfair, but it is a refreshing corrective to the common sentimental overestimation of canine goodness. Flanagan reminds us that Deirdre's friendly overtures are mechanical, produced by instinct and training rather than consciously willed benevolence. And irresistibly amiable as retrievers are, their confidence that they love everybody and everybody loves them can verge on fatuous complacency.

6

Pets in Early Modern Times

DESPITE THE AFFECTION that existed between many hunters and hounds, many shepherds and sheepdogs, the idea that a dog could be valuable simply as a companion was unfamiliar through the Middle Ages and much of the early modern period. As late as the mid-eighteenth century, Samuel Johnson listed only two roles for dogs in his *Dictionary*: "The larger sort are used as a guard; the less for sports." The only varieties he named are the mastiff, spaniel, bulldog, greyhound, hound, terrier, and cur. On the other hand, toy dogs, as well as other varieties, were being widely kept as pets from the seventeenth century on. A few aristocrats cherished them as small humans, the way fond owners may today; but most pet owners still regarded dogs as amiable domestic animals to be kept in their place. Although blood sports, casual cruelty, and uncontrolled vivisection were generally condoned, individuals began to protest against cruelty to animals.

The Christian churches had traditionally discouraged affectionate friendship with dogs on the grounds that God cared only for people, who have souls and moral sense, and created the other animals merely to serve us; consequently, we should think of dogs as practical helpers, not companions. To treat a soulless beast like a Christian blurred a divinely ordained distinction. Moreover, whatever tenderness one felt should be reserved for humans. John Bromyard, a Dominican preacher, classed lapdogs with prostitutes and entertainers as undeserving creatures who "get rich food and presents when they ask for them, while the poor go empty away." John Bunyan reproached his countrymen who "cannot go half a mile from home, but they must have dogs at their heels; but they can very willingly go half a score miles without the society of a Christian." A pious Elizabethan woman on her deathbed virtuously beat away her pet dog, saying to her husband, "You and I have offended God grievously in receiving many a time this bitch into our bed; we would have been loathe to have received a Christian soul . . . into our bed, and to have nourished him in our bosoms, and to have fed him at our table, as we have done this filthy cur many times. The Lord give us grace to repent it."[1]

Few poor people could afford to maintain an animal that did not earn its keep, and anyone who did could get into serious trouble; for conspicuous intimacy with an animal might lay her open to a charge of witchcraft. Since witches in Britain did their evil deeds with the help of a familiar, an evil spirit that took the form of an animal, fondling or talking to one was in itself a suspicious act. Familiars might be dogs, typically small mongrels of no apparent utility. In 1596, a woman was accused of getting even with a man who had offended her by sending her familiar in the form of a little spotted dog to afflict him with fits. The seventeenth-century witchfinder Matthew Hopkins listed one unfortunate woman's familiars as a fat spaniel without any legs at all and a greyhound with a head like an ox, as well as a kitten, a rabbit, and a polecat.[2]

During the English Civil War, Puritan opponents of the Royalist general Prince Rupert found grounds for suspicion in Rupert's attachment to his white poodle, Boye, who accompanied him everywhere. They were outraged when he had Boye sit by him during council meetings and turned aside to kiss the dog during debate. There had to be some reason why Rupert defeated them in battle and knew their secret plans. Obviously, Boye was Rupert's familiar, "whelp'd of a Malignant Water-witch" and endowed with supernatural powers by the Pope and the Devil. Thus Boye could make himself invisible, pass through the enemy lines, and report the information he had gathered to Rupert. Years later, Rupert's niece recalled that people in England had regarded him "as a great sorcerer, and thought the great black dog, which was his companion, was the devil."[3] Notice that the white poodle has turned into the sinister great black dog of folklore.

Aristocrats could afford to disregard the church's strictures on pets. Keep-

ing and tenderly loving little dogs was one of the foibles of Chaucer's worldly
Prioress. Like the Master of Game's hounds, they lived decidedly better than
contemporary peasants:

> *And she had little dogs she would be feeding*
> *With roasted flesh, or milk, or fine white bread.*
> *And bitterly she wept if one were dead*
> *Or someone took a stick and made it smart;*
> *She was all sentiment and tender heart.*

Any concern for poor or suffering people is conspicuously absent from the description. Two little dogs sample dishes on the table of a fifteenth-century
Duke of Berry, while a sleek white greyhound is fed by a kneeling servant on
the floor in front.[4] Renaissance portraits of aristocrats frequently include their
favorite dog, a hunting dog for a gentleman, a toy for a lady.

Not only Prince Rupert, who was a cousin of King Charles II, but the
whole Stuart family loved companion dogs. When John Evelyn went to see
Queen Mother Henrietta Maria in 1662, she "recounted to me many observ-
able stories of the Sagacity of some Dogs that she formerly had." He thought
Charles II was too fond of the crowd of little spaniels that followed him
about "& lie in his bed-Chamber, where often times he suffered the bitches
to puppy & give suck, which rendred it very offensive, & indeede made the
whole Court nasty & stinking."[5]

In 1608, Sir John Harington had regaled an earlier Stuart, Prince Henry,
son of James I, with the exploits of his clever poodle, Bungey. He wrote a letter telling the prince how Bungey solved a problem when the string fell off a
bundle of two bottles of sack that he was carrying to Harington's house: he
hid one bottle in the rushes and took the other in his mouth to the house, and
then returned for the first one. On another occasion, when Bungey was stolen
and taken to the Spanish ambassador's, Harington proved his ownership of
the dog by making him do tricks: Bungey brought him a pheasant from a
dish on the dinner table and then returned it on command to the same dish.
In short, Bungey excelled Argus and Tobit's dog in "good faith, clear wit, or
wonderful deedes." Harington doted on his dog like any Victorian and was

not embarrassed to display his feeling. He had included Bungey in his portrait on the title page of his translation of *Orlando Furioso,* although he was aware that some might ridicule him for it; he justified himself on the grounds that many wise and great men have valued animals, especially dogs.[6]

Poodles were originally one among various types of European water spaniels; they are still called *caniche,* duck dog, in French, and got their English name from German *pudeln,* to splash. But because they have remarkable intelligence, as well as the sporting dog's trainability, Harington and other owners began teaching them to do tricks rather than fetch birds; by the seventeenth century their main role was one of entertaining companion or performer. A miniature variety was developed by the eighteenth century. The poodle's utilitarian cut, naturally bushy hair in front to keep its chest warm with shaved hindquarters to minimize the quantity of wet hair when it retrieved in water, became decorative. Once poodles began to perform in circuses, their pom-poms might be clipped to match those of clowns. Or fashionable owners might display their taste and wealth by ridiculously elaborate designs, such as clipping the family coat of arms into the coat.[7] The same taste prevails today, as the American Kennel Club requires that adult poodles be shown in either of two fantastically unnatural cuts.

In the aristocratic coterie of Horace Walpole, the pampered pet dog was accorded quasi-human status as an important member of the household. "Sense and fidelity are wonderful recommendations," he said, "and when one meets with them, and can be confident that one is not imposed upon, I cannot think that the two additional legs are any drawback." Walpole, who hated hunting as "a persecution of animals" and even more as "an image of war," sold off the family greyhounds, foxhounds, and pointers. But he kept toy spaniels all his life, and his correspondence is filled with references to them and his friends' pets, all spoken of in the same terms as people. He assured his friend William Cole in 1769: "Your fellow-travellers, Rosette and I, got home safe, perfectly contented with our expedition, and wonderfully obliged to you. Pray receive our thanks and barkings." He sat up with Rosette night after night in her final illness; perhaps his correspondent will laugh at him, but "I cannot help it, I think of nothing else." After he accepted Tonton as a bequest from his friend Madame du Deffand, he wrote to another friend,

with Tonton sitting on his paper: "I have gotten a new idol, in a word, a successor to Rosette and almost as great a favourite. . . . I was going to say, it is
incredible how fond I am of it, but I have no occasion to brag of my dog-
manity." Another successor, Busy, was "never out of my lap. I have already, in
case of an accident, insured it a refuge from starvation and ill usage. It is the
least one can do for poor, harmless, shiftless, pampered animals that have
amused us and we have spoiled."[8]

Samuel Pepys agreed with Evelyn that King Charles overindulged his
dogs, reporting with disapproval that during a council meeting the king
played "with his dog all the while . . . not minding the business." Still,
Pepys's diary provides evidence that affection for pets was now usual in the
middle class. In 1660, his "wife's brother brought her a pretty black dog,
which I liked very well." Unfortunately, a problem developed: "So to bed,
where my wife and I had some high words upon my telling her that I would
fling the dog . . . out at the window if he pissed the house any more." Nevertheless, when the dog got lost during an outing to Woolwich, it "did not only
strike my wife into a great passion, but I must confess, myself also, more then
was becoming me"; happily, they found him. Pepys was even more attached
to their next dog, Fancy. Her lameness so distressed him that "it troubles me
to see her." When his father wrote him of her death in the country, big with
puppies, he mourned the loss of "one of my oldest acquaintances and servants." A friend gave his wife a replacement, "a mighty pretty spaniel-bich,
Flora, which she values mightily, and is pretty; but, as a newcomer, I cannot
be fond of her."[9]

Frances Burney d'Arblay described a harrowing experience that she and
her little dog, Diane, survived with each other's support. One day in 1817,
the two of them were exploring a tidal cave. D'Arblay became so engrossed
in collecting mineral specimens that she failed to notice the incoming tide,
and by the time Diane's piteous whines and tugs at her gown alerted her, their
exit route was covered by rough water. Woman and dog searched frantically
for an outlet at the top of the cave; Diane found a hole and happily barked
her success, but it was large enough only for her to get through. D'Arblay
tried to send her away, and, after some plaintive howling, the dog disappeared
to attend to her puppy at home. With the water rising, d'Arblay managed to

clamber up a high sharp rock and precariously perch there. "In this terrible state, painful, affrighting, dangerous, & more than all, solitary—who could paint the transport of my joy, when suddenly, re-entering by the aperture in the Rock through which she had quitted me, I perceived my dear little Diane! For an instant, I felt as if restored to safety—I no longer seemed abandoned." She tried to persuade the dog to come down to her, but Diane wagged her tail appeasingly and stood still, barking to induce her mistress to join her. But there was no way d'Arblay could pass through the opening. With much difficulty, she coaxed the dog to a point where she could hook her parasol handle through Diane's collar and help her to a niche nearby. "To have at my side my dear little faithful Diane was a comfort . . . which no one not planted, & for a term that seemed indefinite, in so unknown a solitude can conceive. What cries of joy the poor little thing uttered when thus safely lodged! & with what caressing tenderness I sought to make her sensible of my gratitude for her return." D'Arblay "might have been subdued by a situation so awful, at once, & so helpless" if she had not been required to actively sustain Diane. The dog, who had always dreaded water, was "taken with a shivering fit, so strong and powerful that it seemed to shake the Rock itself. . . . I could neither sit nor kneel to offer her any comfort, but I dropt down" in place "& I then stroked and caressed her, in as fondling a way as if she had been a Child, & I recovered her from her Ague fit by rubbing her head & back with my shawl, she then looked up at me somewhat composed, though still piteous & forlorn, & licked my Gloves with gratitude." It was many hours before they were found and rescued.[10]

Although any type of dog may be a pet, toy dogs, who could be nothing else, became increasingly popular. A little white fluffy dog that looks like a modern bichon appears in the late-fifteenth-century tapestry *The Lady and the Unicorn.* It may be directly descended from the ancient Maltese breed. Soon thereafter, we find small spotted spaniels with long ears, pointed noses, large eyes, and feathery tails, who look like the modern papillon. They were developed in France or Italy in the sixteenth century from the smallest puppies in litters of hunting spaniels. Venetian Renaissance painters were fond of both types and constantly included them in secular and religious paintings.

Vittore Carpaccio placed a bichon in St. Augustine's study, and Paolo Veronese showed Susannah's little dog barking bravely at the elders who threaten her. Pugs arrived in Europe in the seventeenth century, when Dutch traders brought them from the Far East. One saved the life of William of Orange by waking him when enemy Spanish soldiers were approaching his camp, and he introduced them to England when he became King William III. Toy dogs were valued then, as now, in proportion to their tiny size. The first contest among the king's sons in d'Aulnoy's "The White Cat" is to find the smallest dog. The elder sons brought the king "two such tiny, fragile dogs that they hardly dared to touch them," and the youngest brought an even smaller one.[11]

Despite their popularity, toy dogs were persistently disparaged, partly because of the lingering assumption that dogs ought to justify their existence by useful work. In the catalogue he made of English dogs in 1576, Caius grudgingly included "the Spaniel gentle, or the comforter" among aristocratic dogs; but he disdained it. "These dogges are little, pretty, proper, and fine, and sought for to satisfie the delicatenesse of daintie dames, and wanton womens wills, instruments of folly for them to play and dally withal, to trifle away the treasure of time, to withdraw their mindes from more commendable exercises, and to content their corrupted concupiscences with vaine disport." The smaller they are, the more delightful, "as more meete play fellows for mincing mistresses to beare in their bosoms, to keepe company withal in their chambers, to succour with sleepe in bed, and nourishe with meate at bourde, to lay in their lappes, and licke their lippes as they ryde in their wagons." These women "delight more in dogges that are destitute of reason, then they doe in children that are capeable of wisedome and judgement." Caius tried in vain to find any possible use for these dogs, but finally admitted that they serve to relieve pain in the stomach by being clasped to the affected part and warming it; moreover, disease goes from the person to the dog through the interchange of body heat.[12] Thus early, toy dogs are associated particularly with women—one reason they are so readily disparaged—and dark insinuations are made about their suspicious intimacy with female owners.

Even after it became usual to love dogs as companions, the lady's lapdog remained a stock example of canine uselessness and human dotage on an unworthy object. One of John Gay's *Fables* features a pampered toy spaniel, who

> *Ne'er felt correction's rigid hand;*
> *Indulg'd to disobey command,*
> *In pamper'd ease his hours were spent;*
> *He never knew what learning meant.*
> *Such forward airs, so pert, so smart,*
> *Were sure to win his lady's heart;*
> *Each little mischief gain'd him praise;*
> *How pretty were his fawning ways!*

Listing the dogs of Britain in his natural history, Oliver Goldsmith went out of his way to sneer at "a variety of lap-dogs, which, as they are perfectly useless, may be considered as unworthy of a name." He emphasized that they were foreign breeds (forgetting that some hunting and working dogs were also imported) and charged that "the more awkward or extraordinary these are, the more they are prized." Ralph Beilby described the comforter (meaning a papillon) as "a most elegant little animal . . . generally kept by the ladies as an attendant of the toilette or the drawing-room. It is very snappish, ill-natured, and noisy."[13]

In the nineteenth century, when appreciation of dogs was often taken as a measure of human worth, some noted authorities continued to separate toys from other dogs in order to deny them any valuable qualities and disparage the women who liked them. "In the whole catalogue of the canine-species," Taplin found "not one of less utility, or possessing less the powers of attraction than the pug-dog." Useless for sport or work, it serves only to accompany sedentary philosophers or console old maids. The delicate Italian greyhound is deficient in "spirit, sagacity, fortitude" and seems "only calculated to sooth the vanity, and indulge the frivolities of antiquated ladies."[14]

Youatt deigned to mention only one toy in his supposedly comprehensive *The Dog*: the flat-faced, long-haired shock dog, which he dismissed as "a useless little animal, seeming to possess no other quality than that of a faithful attachment to his mistress." W. H. Hudson sneered at "the purely woman's drawing-room pet dog" for its lack of the "true" dog's instinct of pugnacity, charging with blatant untruth that every small dog from the toy terriers to the Pomeranian has acquired "a white liver to please their owners' fantastic tastes." Judith Lytton, an aristocratic fancier of toy dogs, complained that the average Englishman took pride in "contempt of prettiness." Show judges might even refuse to look at toy spaniels, "saying they hated the useless little things." Albert Payson Terhune extravagantly admired all dogs except "lap dogs—those excuseless excuses for caninity which childless women overfeed and underexercise."[15]

Women who loved their little dogs were equally blamable whether they were foolishly trying to compensate for their lack of husbands and children or selfishly neglecting their obligations to their human family. Joseph Addison censured a woman for mourning her lapdog on the grounds that such fondness should be directed to "the proper Objects of Love, as Husbands or Children." Often this line of criticism was spiced with sexual insinuations. Philip Sidney complained that Stella prefers her little dog to him: she rebuffs her devoted human lover while hugging the dog and letting him kiss her. Belinda's pet dog, Shock, plays an important part in Alexander Pope's *The Rape of the Lock*. (Pope loved dogs and kept them all his life, but he preferred Great Danes.) Shock is an emblem of the triviality of Belinda and her circle, to whom losing one's husband and losing one's lapdog are equal disasters. But it is equally significant that he is the only creature that enjoys physical intimacy with her and enters her bed. His first appearance is realistic enough, but it is also sexually suggestive:

> *. . . Shock, who thought she slept too long,*
> *Leap'd up, and waked his mistress with his tongue.*

Belinda fondles Shock while she puts off the Baron, who would like to be in Shock's place. The poem suggests that it is time for Belinda to stop wasting her affections on Shock, yield graciously to the Baron, marry him, and become a mature woman who devotes herself to husband and children. This seems eminently reasonable, and yet, when we think of the subjugation that eighteenth-century marriage imposed on women, we can see the appeal of a dog, who offered love without domination. The dog provided love that bol-

stered a woman's ego instead of diminishing it. When a woman's dog re-
pelled a human suitor, it acted as her ally against the man who would dominate both of them. Perhaps Belinda rejects the Baron not from prudery, but
from a rational desire to retain her satisfying single life. And perhaps the
Baron resents the dog because he supports her resistance by providing physical and emotional satisfaction independent of any man.[16]

Coarser poets used lapdogs simply as tokens of female lust. Edward Ward
charged that a lady "Kindly rewards the little Four-legg'd Beau, / For secret
Service he performs below"; and Robert Gould, that women satisfy themselves in private with lapdogs as well as dildos: "Lap_ds! to whom they are
more kind and free, / Than they themselves to their own Husbands be." A
lady's lapdog is practically identified with her human lover in a truly nasty
poem by Emanuel Collins, "The Fatal Dream: or, The Unhappy Favourite.
An Elegy." Tysey is placed on his mistress's milk-white bosom as she lies
asleep in bed and wanders "southward to some warmer clime." Meanwhile
she is having a passionate dream of her lover that moves her to an orgasm in
which she suffocates the dog between her thighs.[17]

Painters from the sixteenth century on used lapdogs to heighten erotic titillation. Titian included them in four of his pictures of nude Venus, as well as
one of Danae receiving her lover as a shower of gold. He even gave a lapdog to
the huntress Diana when he represented her surprised in her bath by Actaeon.

Eighteenth-century French painters constantly used toy dogs to heighten
their erotic effects. In Watteau's *Lady at Her Toilet* (c. 1716–17), a lush
nude about to pull her chemise over her head is avidly watched by her
spaniel. Fragonard's *Young Girl Playing with a Dog* (c. 1770–75) shows a
girl in a hiked-up nightgown lying on a rumpled bed with naked legs raised
high, holding out a ring-shaped biscuit to the fluffy white dog who is bal-
anced on her knees, with its tail resting between her legs exactly where a human lover would like to be. In his more subtle *The Love Letter* (1770s), the
young woman who looks provocatively backward at us as she holds her letter is seconded by a fluffy white poodle who sits immediately behind her
and also engages our eye. Other artists used toy dogs to aid in moralizing
rather than titillation. Jan Steen included an eagerly capering toy spaniel in
his pictures of Bathsheba being propositioned by David, and he placed one
next to the sluttish young woman who sits on a rumpled bed, provocatively

pulling a stocking up one of her naked legs, in *The Morning Toilette* (c. 1665).

In his novel *Humphry Clinker*, Tobias Smollett used the attachment of the hero's old maid sister, Tabitha Bramble, to her dog, Chowder, to express his dislike for women as well as their pets. Tabitha's dotage on Chowder highlights the selfishness and folly that make her an irksome burden to her brother, Matthew, and the rest of her touring family. Although Chowder is not one of the usual toy breeds—indeed, he is described as "a filthy cur from Newfoundland"—he is small enough to ride on a woman's lap. He fits the stereotype in being snappish and malformed to male eyes. "One would imagine she had distinguished this beast with her favour on account of his ugliness and ill-nature, if it was not, indeed, an instinctive sympathy, between his disposition and her own," her smart nephew remarks. "Certain it is she caresses him without ceasing; and even harasses the family in the service of this cursed animal." Everyone except stupid Tabitha and her simple-minded maid regards Chowder as an encumbrance. Because Smollett disapproved of admitting a dog to human society, the right-thinking Matthew is "ashamed of his situation" when he must sit in a coach opposite Chowder, who sits on the maid's lap.

Smollett almost explicitly puts affection for a dog in its proper place in the climactic scene where Humphry, a destitute but worthy and obliging young man whom Matthew has charitably taken on as a servant, offends Tabitha by accidentally treading on Chowder and then, misinterpreting her agitated reaction, offering to kill him. She screams that she will not "be affronted by every mangy hound" that Matthew picks up on the highway and insists that Humphry must go. Matthew counters by insisting that Chowder must go; she, as a dependent sister, must meekly acquiesce. Smollett makes clear that this is the right outcome; her attachment to her dog is a selfish folly, not worthy of consideration. Its insignificance is demonstrated when, after finally catching a man, she shows herself to be "indifferent to Chowder."[18]

Frances Burney d'Arblay presented a similar character in Mrs. Ireton of her *Wanderer,* an odious rich woman who coarsely derided and berated all her dependents except the only two beings for whom she could feel affection—her "tiny old lap dog," Bijou, and her little nephew, "two almost equally indulged and spoiled animals." The two constantly set each other off, as the child kept teasing the dog and the dog kept snarling at the child.

Juliet, the heroine, had to wait on both of them; when she took Bijou out, she had to carry "him where the road was rough or miry, that he might not soil those paws," with which the lady of the mansion let him freely pull and scratch her clothes. Juliet was magnanimous enough, however, not to detest the two ill-behaved animals; for she recognized that the dog's snarling and snapping, like the child's wanton mischief, resulted from lack of education. Unlike Smollett, d'Arblay showed understanding of the dog and recognized that its misbehavior was the fault of the human who spoiled "a poor innocent little beast." She shifted the emphasis from canine obnoxiousness to human irresponsibility.

Moreover, later in the story, d'Arblay presented an amiable dog with the sympathetic appreciation that was to flower in the nineteenth-century novel. Juliet, now wandering alone through the countryside, was terrified when a huge watchdog sprang at her. She understood dogs, however, so instead of fleeing she faced him and extended a friendly hand. "The dog, caught by her confidence, made a grumbling but short resistance; and, having first fiercely, and next attentively, surveyed her, wagged his tail in sign of accommodation, and, gently advancing, stretched himself at her feet." When she later encountered the dog's loutish owners, who thought it would be fun to rape her, the dog defused the situation by exuberantly capering about between his new friend and his old ones. In the last pages of the novel, where every character is rewarded according to his or her deserts, the dog is not forgotten; Juliet's husband bought him and made him his "inseparable companion."[19]

It is a measure of the new appreciation for dogs as a species—all dogs, not just aristocratic hounds—that the greatest naturalist of the eighteenth-century seized the opportunity to eulogize them in his *Natural History*. "The dog," Buffon declared, "independently of his beauty and shape, of his liveliness, strength, speed, has preeminently every inner quality that can attract human esteem." The fierce predatory canine nature

> *yields in the domestic dog to the gentlest feelings, to the pleasure of affectionate attachment and the desire to please; he comes, creeping, to place at his master's feet his courage, his strength, his talents; he awaits his orders in order to obey them; he looks to him, questions him, beseeches him; a glance*

is enough to convey his master's will; without having the light of reason like
man, he has all the warmth of feeling; he has more fidelity, constancy in his
affections than man; no ambition, no self-interest, no desire of vengeance,
no fear except that of displeasing; he is all zeal, all eagerness and all obedi-
ence; more mindful of kind deeds than of injuries, he submits and forgets
the latter, or remembers them only in order to be more affectionate; far from
becoming angry or running away, he voluntarily exposes himself to more in-
jury; he licks the hand that has just beaten him; he opposes only by lamenta-
tion, and finally disarms by his patience and submission.

The dog is not only receptive to education, but even conforms himself to
the emotions, the manners, all the habits of those who rule him; he takes his
tone from the household where he lives; like other servants, he is disdainful
in grand households and clownish in the country: always assiduous for his
master and obliging only to his friends, he pays no attention to anyone else.

We can understand the importance of dogs if we imagine what our life would
be like if they had never existed. How could man, without the help of the dog,
have conquered and enslaved the other domestic animals or destroyed harmful
wild beasts? "Thus the first art of man was the education of the dog, and the
result of this art was the conquest and the peaceful possession of the earth."[20]

We have to applaud Buffon's appreciation of the dog's perceptiveness, eagerness to please, invaluable help in human activities, fidelity, and willingness to overlook injuries. On the other hand, he sees the dog exclusively in
terms of its usefulness to man and glories in its excessive submissiveness.
Buffon's views quickly passed into Britain. Oliver Goldsmith repeated them
almost verbatim in his *History of the Earth and Animated Nature.* Even owners who were very fond of their dogs generally accepted Buffon's view of
them as agreeable subordinates, on a totally different level from humans.
Anna Laetitia Barbauld's "To a Dog" illustrates the real but measured affection of her time:

Dear faithful object of my tender care,
Whom but my partial eyes none fancy fair;
May I unblamed display thy social mirth,
Thy modest virtues, and domestic worth.

Thou silent, humble flatterer, yet sincere,
More swayed by love than interest or fear;
Solely to please thy most ambitious view,
As lovers fond, and more than lovers true.
Who can resist those dumb beseeching eyes,
Where genuine eloquence persuasive lies?

Thou safe companion, and almost a friend.[21]

She appreciates her dog's gaiety, its flattery without ulterior motive, its eagerness to please, its faithfulness, its expressiveness; but she sharply differentiates it from the human: it is *almost* a friend. She seems to be taking care to avoid overstating the dog's virtues or giving it more emotional importance than is fitting.

Possibly she was influenced by the moral views of edifying writers for children such as Sarah Kirby Trimmer, who severely spelled out the proper limits to our regard for dogs. Trimmer condemned cruelty to dogs (and other animals), but warned against overvaluing them. A lady's exclusive fondness for her lapdog is pronounced "more than ridiculous . . . it is really sinful." Dogs, says the moral arbiter Mrs. Benson, "are in general so very social, grateful, and pleasing, that they seem formed to be the humble-companions of mankind; and if kept in proper order, may be familiarized with safety; but then they should be well educated, and taught to know their distance."[22]

Eighteenth-century novelists occasionally introduced dogs into their work, but kept them in their place. They did not, like their Victorian successors, enter the minds of their canine characters or endow them with interesting, vividly defined personalities. Even the well-meaning watchdog in d'Arblay's *Wanderer* is there to further the plot. The dog in Daniel Defoe's *Robinson Crusoe* provides the shipwrecked hero with vitally important companionship for sixteen years, but even so, he is not specifically characterized. In normal social settings, dogs are merely accessories that reveal a bit about the human characters. Shallow gentlemen in Jane Austen are distinguished by their sleek sporting dogs (Sir John Middleton and Willoughby in *Sense and Sensibility*). The character of the brainless and lethargic Lady Bertram in *Mansfield Park* is neatly defined by the pug who constantly sits by her on the sofa, for whom she cares more than for any human creature. It is as fashionable, useless, and inert as she is.

Although a dog is the nominal hero of Francis Coventry's *History of Pompey the Little: or, The Life and Adventures of a Lap-Dog,* he is not seriously portrayed as a character. Coventry's book is based on the ubiquity and importance of toy dogs in eighteenth-century fashionable circles, but his interest is in satirizing people; the dog is hardly more personalized than the gold coins that served an analogous function as they passed from person to person in other fictions. Pompey, whose heroic name makes him ridiculous from the beginning, is a vehicle for satire on contemporary fashionable life, from aristocrats through social-climbing bourgeois; he has no importance in himself. Even when he is on the scene, the author is concerned with the behavior of the people he meets, which only occasionally involves how they treat him.

Pompey, a black-and-white Bolognese bichon, was born to Phyllis, dog of the foremost courtesan in Bologna. When her English lover Hillario moved on, she gave him Pompey in return for a gold watch. Back in London, licentious Lady Tempest insisted that Hillario give Pompey to her, to which he agreed on condition that he might visit him at any hour in his new home. Lady Tempest's natural love of dogs has been confirmed by her husband's loathing for them; as a result, Pompey joined a household including an Italian greyhound, a pug, two King Charles spaniels, a harlequin greyhound, a spotted Great Dane, and a bulldog. Pompey soon became the canine equivalent of a man of fashion: he accompanied his mistress to parties and masquerades, became a critic of opera, "soon established an Acquaintance and Friendship with all the Dogs of Quality, and of course affected a most hearty Contempt for all of inferior Station . . . he . . . had seldom less than two or three Amours on his Hands at a time with *Bitches of the highest Fashion.*"

After two happy years with Lady Tempest, dining on partridges and ragouts and caressed by all his mistress's fashionable visitors, he got lost in the park. He was picked up by a little girl and suffered from the attentions of a houseful of unsupervised children, suffering first "the Barbarity of their Kindness," and then, when they quickly tired of him, the worse torments of their mischief. Rescued by their prudish old aunt, he was thrown out for urinating on a pious book.[23] Taken to Cambridge, he narrowly escaped a vivisectionist who planned to cut him open to satisfy his curiosity about peristaltic motion. The book ends with a mock eulogy of Pompey that points to the similarity of courtiers and lapdogs. Despite placing his hero in a dog's situations and giving him a few doggy actions, Coventry makes no serious attempt to convey the thoughts, feelings, or point of view of a dog. Pompey's feelings about his human owners are never developed, nor are his perils and sufferings presented seriously.

Edward Augustus Kendall's *Keeper's Travels in Search of His Master* (1798), in contrast, is genuinely concerned with its canine hero and with promoting kindness to animals. But the novel is overshadowed by its moral, applicable alike to Keeper and the children who read his story: "one dereliction from the path of right; one moment's inattention to . . . virtue, though trivial and harmless in itself, may expose us to the whole train of vices and sorrows." Keeper's dereliction is his failure to pay constant attention to his master: he got lost on market day because he became so engrossed in a basket of chickens that he forgot his duty of keeping an eye on him. The man moved on, and Keeper was unable to track him. Totally dependent on his master for food, comfort, and approval, Keeper was desolate. He set off for home, but on the way some wagoners hit him, simply because they had whips in their hands, he was helpless, and the low and ignorant like to exercise power. A servant threw a pail of water on him and a stagecoach guard shot him, just for the fun of emptying the pail and using the gun. He was rescued by kind people, who agreed that bad treatment of dogs reveals bad character in humans. They treated him well, but Keeper "did not forget the master who had formerly cherished him, and whom he had lost through his own negligence and inattention."[24] Finally he succeeded in finding his master, and they had a mutually ecstatic reunion. The author and all the decent characters like and sympathize with Keeper, but his duties as a subject being are relentlessly emphasized, and there is no attempt to get inside his consciousness.

Condemnation of cruelty to animals was a new development in the eighteenth century, reflecting people's increasing attachment to their companion animals and related also to the relatively secular atmosphere of the period and the high value it placed on sympathetic feeling. Traditionally, the Christian churches did not concern themselves with our obligations to animals. St.

Thomas Aquinas codified the Roman Catholic position in his *Summa Theo-logica*, where he argued (with striking irrelevance) that we have no obligation to extend charity to "irrational animals" because we can have no fellowship with creatures that lack free will, cannot participate in a society "regulated by reason," and cannot attain everlasting life. The dominion that God gave man over the animals signifies not only that he may use them for his own benefit but also that he may treat them in any way he likes. This attitude persisted for a shockingly long time. Even in the mid-nineteenth century, Pope Pius IX re-fused to permit a Society for the Prevention of Cruelty to Animals to be es-tablished in Rome lest it would mistakenly suggest that humans have duties to animals.[25]

In the seventeenth century, René Descartes systematized Aquinas's position to make it even more heartless. He located all thinking and feeling in the im-mortal soul; this must be an exclusive possession of humans, because the only sure evidence of soul or reason is the capacity of speech, which of course the other animals lack (unless we accept Montaigne's sympathetic interpretation: "How many waies speake we unto our Dogges, and they seeme to understand and answer us?"). It followed that only humans could have thoughts or feel-ings. Although "it is difficult to rid ourselves" of the opinion that the brute beasts "feel as we do," we must be logical and see that they are nothing more than machines, who may go through the motions of suffering but cannot ac-tually be feeling pain. Descartes' disciple Malebranche sneered that to believe in a dog's love for his master "is to humanize him, and to make of your dog a little man with big ears and four paws." He is said to have wantonly kicked a pregnant bitch that rolled at his feet and, when his friend expressed pity, coldly exclaimed, "Don't you know that that creature does not feel anything?"[26]

To make things worse, Descartes' view predominated at just the time that scientists were becoming interested in anatomy and physiology. The physi-cian Galen had dissected dogs in Roman times, but the New Science of the seventeenth century inspired experimentation on an unprecedented scale. Dogs are plentiful, docile, and a convenient size—and if one can cut them open in the serene knowledge that they only *seem* to be feeling pain, they are ideal subjects for experimentation. So alien substances were injected into dogs' veins to test Harvey's new theory of the circulation of the blood. Or blood was transfused from dog to dog in hopes of working out a way to replace a sick person's blood with healthy blood. Some experiments were necessary, of course, to understand physiology and develop new medical treatments. But all too many were repeated for the amusement of spectators or performed simply to find out what would happen.

Robert Boyle described an experiment, witnessed by several Oxford physicians and virtuosi, in which a dog's paws were tied to the four corners of a table and Christopher Wren inserted a narrow pipe into the vein of its hind leg and poured in a solution of opium and white wine. Released, the dog began to stagger around, as the blood circulated to its brain. Everyone present began to offer bets that it would die. But Boyle wanted to keep it alive for further observation, and managed to do so by having it whipped up and down the garden until its brain cleared. Although Pepys was attached to his spaniels and very distressed to see a child maltreat a little dog, he reported several vivisections on dogs with unfeeling interest. An acquaintance told him of "a pretty experiment" done that night at Gresham College on a mastiff and a spaniel, in which the blood of one dog was let out "(till he died)" into the body of the other, while the second dog's own blood was let out on the other side; the second dog survived, at least temporarily. "This did give occasion to many pretty wishes, as of the blood of a Quaker to be let into an Archbishop, and such like."[27]

Evelyn also observed vivisections of dogs, but he was upset by one designed to find out how long a dog could live without functioning lungs: "the poore curr, kept long alive after the *Thorax* was open, by blowing with bellows into his lungs, and that long after his heart was out, & the lungs both gashed & pierced, his eyes quick all the while: This was an experiment of more cruelty than pleased me." In the eighteenth century, a few people began to criticize the whole idea of vivisection. Alexander Pope doubted the benevolence of the esteemed Dr. Stephen Hales because " 'he has his hands so much imbrued in blood.'—'What, he cuts up rats?'—'Ay, and dogs too!' (With what emphasis and concern he spoke it!) 'Indeed, he commits most of these barbarities with the thought of being of use to man; but how do we know that we have a right to kill creatures that we are so little above as dogs, for our curiosity, or even for some use to us?' "[28]

Johnson denounced those who torture animals in the name of scientific inquiry as "wretches . . . whose favourite amusement is to nail dogs to tables and open them alive; to try how long life may be continued in various degrees of mutilation, or with the excision or laceration of the vital parts; to examine whether burning irons are felt more acutely by the bone or tendon; and whether the more lasting agonies are produced by poison forced into the mouth or injected into the veins." Although he is aware of the alleged justification for such practices, he asserts that, "by knives, fire, and poison, knowledge is not always sought, and is very seldom attained. The experiments that have been tried, are tried again; he that burned an animal with irons yesterday, will be willing to amuse himself with burning another tomorrow." Even if dissections of living animals increase our knowledge of physiology, "he surely buys knowledge dear, who learns the use of the lacteals at the expense of his humanity."[29]

An increasing number of people rejected the Cartesian view of animals. Voltaire poured scorn on the idea that they are "machines deprived of knowledge and feeling." These can be conveyed without speech, as a person's feelings can be evident from his expression and behavior; consider a "dog who has lost his master, who has searched for him with mournful cries in every path, who comes home agitated . . . who at last finds his beloved master in his study, and shows him his joy by the tenderness of his cries, by his leaps, by his caresses." And yet "Barbarians seize this dog . . . nail him to a table and dissect him alive to show the mesenteric veins. You discover in him all the same organs of feeling that you possess. Answer me, mechanist, has nature arranged all the springs of feeling in this animal in order that he should not feel?"[30]

The secular utilitarian Jeremy Bentham presented the first systematic argument for just treatment of animals in 1780 by cutting right through the scholastic rationalizations that divided humans with rights and feelings from animals without them. We cannot trace an "insuperable line" based on reason or speech, because "a full-grown horse or dog is beyond comparison a more rational, as well as a more conversable animal, than an infant of a day, or a week, or even a month, old." And even if the case were otherwise, "the question is not, Can they *reason*? nor, Can they *talk*? but, Can they *suffer*?"[31]

Probably the most influential of these eighteenth-century protests was

William Hogarth's series of popular prints *The Four Stages of Cruelty* (1751), issued "in hopes of preventing in some degree that cruel treatment of poor Animals which makes the streets of London more disagreeable to the human mind, than anything what ever."[32] He demonstrated the point, confirmed by modern studies, that cruelty to dogs (and cats and birds) leads inevitably to cruelty to people. Plate 1 shows young Tom Nero shoving an arrow up a bull-dog's anus; Plate 3 shows him arrested for murdering his pregnant mistress; the last plate shows his executed body being dissected. His heart has dropped to the floor, and in a neat reversal of the usual situation of humans profiting from the dissection of a dog, a starving dog is eating it.

7

Dogs in the Nineteenth Century

AROUND THE TURN of the nineteenth century, a warm attitude toward dogs spread through all classes of society. Although dogs continued to perform essential economic functions, they were now thought of primarily as companions. It became generally acceptable to express deep affection for one's dog and to glorify the virtues of the whole species, sometimes with a sentimentality that would have been dismissed as absurd in earlier periods. There was an endless appetite for pictures of dogs, anecdotes about dogs, and shows of performing dogs. Dogs were accepted as beloved members of the family, whose doings were reported along with the rest of the domestic news. For the first time, dogs appeared as individualized characters in memoirs and fiction.

Robert Southey's "On the Death of a Favorite Old Spaniel" (1796) illustrates the new nonutilitarian view of dogs. Phillis's sight and hearing were dim; she was certainly no use in the field or, one might argue, anywhere else. So while Southey was away, leaving no one to plead "For the old age of brute fidelity," she was drowned. This was the traditional practice for superannuated dogs, yet Southey protests it as he would similar treatment of a person. "The warm Sun / Might still have cheer'd thy slumbers; thou didst love / To lick the hand that fed thee," he tells her. Had he been home, he would have pleaded earnestly for her, for he remembers her companionship in his boyhood.

. . . I have beguiled
Often the melancholy hours at school,
Sour'd by some little tyrant, with the thought
Of distant home, and I remember'd then
Thy faithful fondness.

Still, though he deplores her execution, he consoles himself with the assurance that she has gone to a better world:

Where the proud bipeds, who would confine
Infinite Goodness *to the little bounds*
Of their own charity, may envy thee.

Robert's sister Caroline expressed the same consideration for an aging canine companion. In "Conte à Mon Chien" she invites her old dog to rest his head on her knee and tell her what is troubling him. She realizes he is jealous of the cat—how silly of him!

Can "auld acquaintance be forgot,"
And love, and worth, and faith like thine?

What though I smooth her velvet fur,
Whose mottled hues so finely blend?
What though I coax and fondle her?
*She's but a favourite—*thou *my friend.*

Though his nose is white and his hearing dulled, she loves him more "for every sign / That tells how long we've lived together." His ear is still keen to hear *her* voice and *her* step. She assures him that they will share "good and evil, joy and pain . . . until our journey's end" and that he will never be "mercifully" put down:

Their mercy shall not end thy "pain,"
As they are pleased brute age to call.

Finally she consoles him by telling him about a dog who remained faithful to her imprisoned royalist master during the French Revolution.[1]

Queen Victoria set the example for an animal-loving nation. Pet dogs, whom she cared for personally, had sustained her during her difficult childhood. When the Society for the Prevention of Cruelty to Animals was on the brink of collapsing for lack of funds, Princess Victoria and her mother saved it by becoming its patrons. In 1840, Victoria permitted the society to call itself royal, and she publicly supported it in every way she could. She was a patron of the Home for Lost and Starving Dogs at Battersea. She regularly kept eighty or more dogs of many breeds in the kennels at Windsor and often fed them herself, two at a time. Her favorite artist was the animal painter Edwin Landseer, and she commissioned many portraits of her favorite dogs. Occasionally she would exhibit some of them at the newly established Crufts Show. Several breeds became popular as a result of her interest, such as dachshunds after her marriage to a German prince, collies after she fell in love with the breed on a trip to Scotland, and Pekingese after British soldiers presented her with one they had taken while looting the Summer Palace in Peking during the Boxer Rebellion in 1860. (Victoria appropriately named her Lootie.) She never allowed one of her dogs to be killed, and she forbade the docking of tails or the cropping of ears.

Victoria transmitted her love of dogs to her descendants. Her son Edward VII actively supported the RSPCA and the Battersea Home, and he was accompanied everywhere by his cherished and spoiled terriers. Once, visiting a heavily bombed area in London during World War II, Princess Elizabeth (the present queen) found a woman crying because her terrified terrier refused to come out from under a heap of rubble. "Perhaps I can help," she said. "I am rather good with dogs." And, with great patience, she succeeded in talking the dog out.[2]

Several working breeds became pets at this period, most notably the Newfoundland. In Burns's dialogue "The Twa Dogs," a Newfoundland speaks for the gentry and a collie (modeled on Burns's own dog) for the peasants. Owners became concerned about maintaining the purity of the Newfoundland's blood lines: "Uncontaminated by the blood of any inferior race," he is majestic and at the same time seems "to be the friend of every individual, without displaying the least tendency to animosity with any part of the creation." Although the dogs were no longer used for serious work, they delighted in doing little errands of carrying and retrieving that their owners equally delighted in assigning them.[3]

Byron's passionate tribute to the character of his Newfoundland, Boatswain, contrasts strikingly with Barbauld's measured praise of her dog. Byron did not find his dog almost equal to a human; he found him better than most. His epitaph on Boatswain praises him as "one / Who possessed Beauty / Without Vanity, / Strength without Insolence, / Courage without Ferocity, / And all the Virtues of Man / Without his Vices." (Admittedly, Byron's praise of the dog was intensified by his zest for cynical misanthropy.) His inscription on Boatswain's handsome marble monument proclaims that he deserved it more than many humans who get memorialized:

> . . . *the poor dog in life the firmest friend,*
> *The first to welcome, foremost to defend,*
> *Whose honest heart is still his master's own,*
> *Who labours, fights, lives, breathes for him alone,*
> *Unhonour'd falls, unnoticed all his worth,*
> *Denied in heaven the soul he held on earth,*
> *While man, vain insect! Hopes to be forgiv'n,*
> *And claims himself a sole exclusive heaven.*
>
> *To mark a friend's remains these stones arise;*
> *I never knew but one,—and here he lies.*

The poet wished to be buried in a vault near Boatswain's monument, although he lost the opportunity when Newstead Abbey was sold.[4]

No praise was too high for these dogs: a correspondent to a sporting magazine declared that "the great, the good, the self-sacrificing belongs to the Newfoundland." Lord Eldon wrote that his Caesar's vigilance was "the safeguard of Encombe House" and his "talents and manners" were "the amusement and delight / Of those who resorted to it." The Earl of Dudley had his Newfoundland Bashaw immortalized in an elaborate statue that reproduced the dog's black-and-white coat with pieces of black-and-white marble painstakingly fitted together (1832–34). The animal is represented with his foot on the neck of a snake poised to strike, recalling images of the Blessed Virgin Mary treading underfoot the snake of sin.

The dog fancier Gordon Stables explained that in training the sagacious Newfoundland, you must "never change the tone of your voice, or make use of jargon or dog-English. Speak to the dog as you would to any other rational being." If you want him to carry home your purchases from a shop, point out to him what you have paid for and "then walk out, but don't look over your shoulder to see if he is bringing your parcel—such a want of confidence is an insult to a well-bred dog, for the Newfoundland dog is as certain as sunrise, and will part with his life sooner than with anything you have given into his charge." The same conscientiousness, however, can sometimes make a dog over-enthusiastic about his work. Once Stables's Newfoundland discovered seven or eight large rafters floating on a pond and insisted on bringing them one by one to shore. This took him half an hour, "during which time I had the option of either cooling my heels in waiting or walking on without him—'Nero' didn't care which; he had his work to do, and did it. When he had arranged all the rafters in a line to his entire satisfaction, he shook himself and came on."[5]

In *Peter Pan,* J. M. Barrie cleverly used the Newfoundland's methodical conscientiousness to parody the estimable but limited virtues of the traditional nanny. Nana, nursemaid of the Darling children, is a perfect model of the smugly reliable human servant, keeping strictly to old-fashioned ways because no other possibilities had ever entered her mind. She was drawn from the Barrie family's Luath (as well as his previous dog Porthos, a Saint Bernard). Catherine Crowe featured the dog's benevolence in "The Dutch Officer's Story" (1859), where the regimental Newfoundland comes back from the dead to rouse sentries sleeping on duty and thus saves them from being caught and punished (though he is less assiduous when they are sleeping because they are drunk). A large, warm, placid Newfoundland adds to the atmosphere of secure, prosperous well-being in Pierre-Auguste Renoir's picture of *Madame Georges Charpentier and Her Children* (1878). Reposing in the foreground, with a child sitting on its back, the dog seems to provide a foundation for the family. Dogs contributed to an atmosphere of wholesome domesticity in scenes from humble to the highest life. In Thomas Hovenden's *Breaking Home Ties*, a large house dog forms part of the sympathetic family that is sending an apprehensive young farm boy into the world. And when Landseer represented the royal family as a domestic model for the nation in *Windsor Castle in Modern Times* (1841–45), he surrounded them with dogs. Edgar Degas used the same symbolism in reverse form when he emphasized the mutual alienation of *The Bellelli Family* (1858–60) by pointedly includ- ing their dog walking out of the picture: we see only its rear half.

Taplin recapitulated Buffon's eulogy of the dog in his *Sportsman's Cabinet*, but he adopted an even higher and more emotional tone. "Every expressive gesture" of the dog "demonstrates the strongly implanted seeds of sagacity." "With the utmost humility in his manner, and penetrative property in his eye, he approaches his master at every interval of possibility, and submissively obtruding himself upon his attention, endeavours to demonstrate the powers he possesses, and only waits his master's orders to bring them into use. The moment he has obtained the attention thus solicited, he watches every look and action, that he may the better conceive the intents and suggestions, or an- ticipate the wishes of his master, to execute whose commands seems the sole and absolute happiness of his life."[6]

Later eulogies of the dog emphasize its superlative love more than its obe- dience. When the owner of a dog shot for trespassing sued for damages in 1870, his lawyer, George Graham Vest, rightly perceived that he should focus not on the facts of the case but on the enormity of killing so noble an animal. A man's best friend may turn against him, he exhorted the jury; his son or daughter may prove ungrateful. Indeed:

The one absolutely unselfish friend that a man can have in this selfish world, the one that never deserts him, the one that never proves ungrateful or treacherous, is his dog.

A man's dog stands by him in prosperity and in poverty, in health and in sickness. He will sleep on the cold ground where the wintry winds blow and the snow drives fiercely, if only he may be near his master's side. He will kiss the hand that has no food to offer, he will lick the sores and wounds that come in encounters with the roughness of the world. . . .

And when the last scene of all comes, and death takes the master in its embrace, and his body is laid away in the cold ground, no matter if all other friends pursue their way, there by the graveside will the noble dog be found,

his head between his paws, his eyes sad, but open in alert watchfulness,
faithful and true, even in death.[7]

Of course, the jury was melted and awarded the bereaved dog owner twice
the damages he had requested.

Queen Victoria and many other pious dog lovers expressed confidence that
their beloved pets would be with them in heaven. Anna Hempstead Branch assured her dog, "If there is no God for thee / Then there is no God for me," and
(disregarding the single-minded voracity of dogs and their instinctive compul-
sion to submit to their leader) praised it for sharing its "frugal fare" with the
poor and taking "Angry words for sweet love's sake." Delabere Blaine, an early
veterinarian who justified the importance of his work by extolling canine virtue,
could find nothing "noble, generous, or amiable in man, which may not be
found in the dog also." Dogs' fidelity is incorruptible, invulnerable to any bribe
whatsoever. The fact that a bitch may sometimes be unhappy to stay with her
puppies if it means separation from her master proves that she has "moral principle" conflicting with her instinct, and principle is evidence of high intellect.
Ouida, author of the classic *A Dog of Flanders*, explained that great men always
have dogs because "they find the world so full of parasites, toadies, liars, fawn-
ers, hypocrites; the incorruptible candor, loyalty and honor of the dog are like
so much water in a barren place to a thirsty traveler." It follows that people must
value dogs if they value virtue. Anyone who does not love dogs, Philip Hamerton declared, must be "utterly dead to all the better feelings of our nature."[8]

Although Darwin and earlier naturalists were well aware of the kinship
between dogs and wolves, many nineteenth-century authorities refused to acknowledge any connection. Taplin admitted that they look somewhat alike,
but insisted that their nature was wholly different. Youatt declared that the
dog's sagacity and faithfulness, evident from the dawn of history, prove that
he could not have descended from an "inferior and comparatively worthless
animal" such as a wolf, but must have been created "expressly to administer
to our comforts and to our pleasure."[9]

H. D. Richardson agreed, and went on to speculate that the dog did not
even have to be domesticated, for it is "far more reasonable to suppose, that a
benevolent Deity . . . formed the dog for the express purpose of being the
ever faithful, constant friend and companion of man, and one who would re-

main his friend after the unhappy Fall should have deprived him of the services and society of other animals." In a comparison that reveals the kinship people feel with dogs, George Jesse insisted that "The dog is no more a wolf than man is an orang: structure of frame in both cases brings them near to each other, but constitution of mind puts them far asunder." The idea that dogs evolved from wolves evokes the even more distressing idea that humans evolved from lower primates.[10]

Only in recent decades, when we no longer require the dog to be a model of nobility and are more appreciative of wildness, have we been willing not only to recognize its descent from the wolf but to see the similarities between the animals. Zoologists point out that they show almost identical patterns of social behavior, body language, and vocalization; that working dogs use elements of lupine hunting patterns; and that wolves, like dogs, are capable of love, loyalty, and play. Now certain nature enthusiasts actually idealize the wolf and denigrate the dog as its degenerate descendant.[11]

The nineteenth-century public had an insatiable appetite for anecdotes illustrating the moral and intellectual virtues of dogs. George R. Jesse filled the pages of his scholarly *Researches into the History of the British Dog* with anecdotes illustrating its faithfulness, sagacity, love, vigilance, and compassion. Joseph Taylor's *The General Character of the Dog: Illustrated by a Variety of Original and Interesting Anecdotes of That Beautiful and Useful Animal* is a collection of tributes and anecdotes designed to stop people from abusing "kind creatures, which Divine Providence has been pleased to make subservient to us," who are necessary "for our assistance, and amusement, and very frequently our preservation." His seventy-one anecdotes reiterate the familiar themes of the dog who brings his master's murderer to justice, the dog who ingeniously gets help to save his master's life, the dog who alerts his master to a crime plotted by someone he trusted, the dog who was faithful until his master's death and then pined away on his grave. They are distinguished from earlier versions by intensified pathos.

Taylor added heartrending embellishments to a story he found in Aelian of a merchant who forgot to pick up his bag of money by the roadside and disregarded his dog's attempts to remind him. Unable to carry the bag himself, the dog barked and howled to get his master's attention and finally bit the heels of his horse. The merchant concluded he must be mad and, very regretfully, shot him. Then the man saw that his bag was missing and, like Gelert's master, immediately realized his error: "Wretch that I am! I alone am to blame! I could not comprehend the admonition which my innocent and most faithful friend gave me, and I have sacrificed him for his zeal." He followed the dog by its blood trail and found it guarding the abandoned bag. "His heart was ready to bleed; he cursed himself in the madness of despair. The poor Dog, unable to follow his dear, but cruel master, had determined to consecrate his last moments to his service. He had crawled, all bloody as he was, to the forgotten bag, and, in the agonies of death, he lay watching beside it. When he saw his master, he still testified his joy by the wagging of his tail—he could do no more—he tried to rise, but his strength was gone. The vital tide was ebbing fast; even the caresses of his master could not prolong his fate." He died licking his master's hand in token of forgiveness.

In another heartwarming anecdote, a dog has been living for eleven years in a small cave near the churchyard where his master lies buried, shunning "all canine as well as human intercourse" and emerging only to visit the grave and, every two or three days, to eat. He stays "no longer than just to eat the morsel sufficient to keep alive the lamp of life; which he probably takes, because he would not wish to shorten his sorrows over the sacred dust, of which he is now the generous sentinel. He is a steady martyr to his fidelity."[12] Taylor's book was so successful that he followed it with *Canine Gratitude* in 1806 and *Four-Footed Friends* in 1828.

The shaggy terrier Greyfriars Bobby was a real dog who was turned into a culture hero of canine fidelity. He was the helper of a market policeman in Edinburgh, and after his master died and was buried in Greyfriars Churchyard, he did not seek a new home, but stayed around the churchyard for fourteen years, living on handouts from the local publicans and shopkeepers. Journalists heard about him and wrote increasingly detailed and sentimental versions of his story. They turned his actual master into an appealing shepherd called Old Jock, who died after bringing him to the big city and was buried there. Then they related in detail Bobby's inconsolable grief, his steadfast refusal of comfortable new homes, his resolution to remain with his old master in the cold churchyard and subsist on scraps obtained in hasty forays outside. He became so famous for his fidelity that an English philanthropist erected a life-size bronze statue to him in 1873, and "American Lovers of 'Bobby'" added a marker on his master's grave. Pilgrims still flock to see these memorials. However, in actuality, it is only old dogs who, like old people, cannot get over a friend's death. Since Bobby was young enough to adjust to a new master, it seems likely that he simply enjoyed living on his own and being fed and petted by all the neighborhood dog lovers.[13]

Many magazines filled their pages with doggy anecdotes, obviously responding to a public interested in dogs and eager to admire them. *The Spectator* regularly published letters from readers illustrating the affection and moral virtues, but especially the intelligence of dogs. A doctor wrote in 1875 about a ferocious-looking bulldog who came many times to his office to watch his master's arm being treated; a few weeks later, it brought a dog with a broken front leg to the doctor's doorstep. A dog in Scotland hung around a baker's shop begging for halfpennies; when the writer gave him one, he went into the shop, put his forepaws on the counter, and held out the halfpenny. After rejecting a bun, he exchanged his coin for a piece of shortbread (1877). In 1885, a group of children were playing on a pier and one fell in. Just in time, a Newfoundland rushed over and rescued the child, and was rewarded with as many sweets as he could eat. The next day he joined the children playing on the pier, but they only patted him. So he crept up behind a child standing near the edge, pushed him into the water, and "then sprang in after him, and gravely brought him to shore." As the writer drily comments, intelligence, canine as well as human, may well conflict with the absolute disinterestedness that sentimentalists attribute to dogs.[14]

Scientific study of animals often seems to dry up people's feeling for them, but Charles Darwin observed his dogs with loving sensitivity and concluded that such observation should convince anyone "that animals can reason." Moreover, since they refrain from stealing food even when their masters are absent, they must "possess something very like a conscience." (This can be traced to the social necessities of the wolf pack, where the animals must be faithful to each other and obedient to their leader.) Finally, the "drooping ears, hanging lips, flexuous body, and wagging tail" of a dog greeting his beloved master are every bit as expressive as "the beaming eyes and smiling cheeks of a man when he meets an old friend."[15]

Nineteenth-century audiences, predictably, loved animal acts. Performing dogs have always been appealing, though Caius in the sixteenth century pronounced them disreputable, like human entertainers. The low comedian in Shakespeare's acting company worked with a dog, and accordingly two scenes in *The Two Gentlemen of Verona* feature a loutish servant remonstrating with his ill-conditioned cur, Crab. In the early eighteenth century, a company of dancing poodles was introduced at Southwark Fair and subsequently delighted the aristocracy, including Queen Anne.

Of course people can delight in performing dogs without necessarily caring about animals. Sometimes trick dogs were driven unmercifully by greedy owners, like the pathetic troupe described by Dickens in *The Old Curiosity Shop*. "Four very dismal dogs," dressed in little gaudy coats soaked with the rain, entered the poor rustic inn where Nell and her grandfather were staying. They were "headed by an old bandy dog of particularly mournful aspect, who stopping when the last of his followers had got as far as the door, erected himself upon his hind legs and looked round at his companions, who immediately stood upon their hind legs, in a grave and melancholy row." When dinner was served, the dogs "watched with terrible eagerness" and stood on their hind legs. Nell was about to give them some morsels, but Jerry, their master, stopped her. The old lead dog "lost a half-penny to-day. *He* goes without his supper." "The unfortunate creature dropped upon his fore-legs directly, wagged his tail, and looked imploringly at his master." But Jerry forced him to play the barrel organ all through the meal. He ordered the others to stand upright in a row, allowing no one to move until he called its name and threw it a morsel. "Meanwhile the dog in disgrace ground hard at the organ, sometimes in quick time, sometimes in slow, but never leaving off for an instant. When the knives and forks rattled very much, or any of his fellows got an unusually large piece of fat, he accompanied the music with a short howl, but he immediately checked it on his master looking round, and applied himself with increased diligence to the Old Hundredth."[16]

Happily, not all performing dogs were so severely disciplined. Dickens also described a Newfoundland "who has greatly distinguished himself in the minor drama." He did well in his first scene, when "He had merely to bark, run on, and jump through an inn window, after a comic fugitive." But in his last and greatest scene, he had to track a murderer into a forest and fly at him when he found him:

> *It was a hot night, and he came into the forest . . . in the sweetest temper, at a*
> *very deliberate trot, not in the least excited; trotted to the foot-lights . . . and*
> *there sat down, panting and amiably surveying the audience, with his tail*
> *beating on the boards, like a Dutch clock. Meanwhile the murderer, impa-*
> *tient to receive his doom, was audibly calling . . . "CO-O-OME here!" . . .*
> *when [the dog] was in course of time persuaded to trot up and rend the mur-*
> *derer limb from limb, he made it . . . a little too obvious that he worked out*
> *that awful retribution by licking butter of[f] his blood-stained hands.*[17]

Hamerton tells the story of a wonderful performing poodle, Blanche, who spelled out *fromage* by picking out cards with the letters on them; translated *Pferd,* written in Gothic script on a slate, to *cheval* and then to *horse*; and given the intentionally misspelled *meson,* corrected it to *maison.* Although Hamerton recognized that her performance was beyond canine comprehension, he could not detect evidence that the trainer was signaling to the dog. Clearly she was responding to "a system of signaling which the intelligence of the human spectators was not keen enough to discover." He later got the trainer to admit that there was a secret, but not to explain what it was. Hamerton wondered whether the accomplished dog was overstressed, but she may well have enjoyed the work and the praise she got for it. As a circus trainer points out, "Applaud a dog, pet him, make much of him, and his ego swells before your eyes same as his stomach does after a fine full meal."[18]

Visual artists responded to the public's warmer feelings for dogs by producing more pictures of them and investing their subjects with greater human interest. Most earlier dog portraits, such as Desportes' and Oudry's royal hunting dogs and Stubbs's foxhounds, represented rich men's status symbols, valued for their structural beauty and prowess as hunters. Now artists set out to evoke the personalities of their canine subjects. Théodore Géricault's *Bulldog* (c. 1815) engages the viewer's interest and respect as a forceful man would. Édouard Manet's Japanese spaniel Tama enchants with his vivid personality.

Dogs were anthropomorphized by being placed in contexts that evoke human feelings. When Jean-Baptiste Oudry painted a nondescript dog with her family in a barn, *Bitch-Hound Nursing Her Puppies* (1752), he gave her a painfully alert expression and lit her face with heavenly light, so that we think of a devoted poor human mother who loves her children and worries about their security. Robert Alexander's *The Happy Mother* (1887), a picture of a working-class collie also raising her puppies in a barn, calls attention by its title to the feelings that canine mothers share with humans. In this case the mother is comfortable and secure as well as loving, despite the evident poverty; motherhood is presented the way sentimental Victorians liked to see it—as undiluted happiness.

Sir Edwin Landseer, who specialized in dogs, was probably the most wealthy and popular British painter of his time. He portrayed almost every breed with superb realism, demonstrating their beauty and indicating the sagacity, courage, and devotion that the Victorians wanted to see in dogs. His dogs are subtly or blatantly infused with human feelings, and his subjects are edifying or genially amusing. *The Old Shepherd's Chief Mourner* (1837) shows a nondescript collie all alone, sitting with its chin pressed onto the shepherd's coffin; and it genuinely touches the heart. *Alpine Mastiffs Reanimating a Distressed Traveller* (1820) portrays two huge, noble Saint Bernards solicitously tending an almost dead man in the snow. One has a little cask around its neck, apparently the first appearance of the famous brandy cask that legend now attaches to these dogs.

Landseer often heightened the pathos or humor of his subjects by giving them anthropomorphic titles. A well-observed, entirely realistic picture of a plump bulldog proudly sitting in his master's cart to guard it, while four hungry street curs look up wistfully, becomes a commentary on human class distinctions when it is entitled *Jack in Office*. In the phenomenally popular *Dignity and Impudence* (1839), we see a large, quiet, solemn-looking hound in a doorway, while a white terrier's little prick-eared head with black eyes and nose pokes forward beside him. The pose is natural, although the dogs really do appear to express the qualities imputed to them. On the other hand, *Laying Down the Law* (1840) is cheapened by its blatant contrivance. A large, formally clipped white poodle is posed to suggest a bewigged judge with one forepaw on an open book, while seven other dogs surround it, including a small one gazing up like a sycophantic human hanger-on. Even here, however, the dogs are realistically painted. It is the placement of the poodle rather than its form or pose that makes it obtrusively anthropomorphic.

Francis Barraud's painting of his fox terrier, Nipper, attentively cocking his head in front of the horn of an old-fashioned phonograph started as a realistic picture of Nipper investigating the sound of a voice coming from a mysterious source. But when Barraud named it *His Master's Voice* (1899), it became a picture of canine devotion. After it was adopted as an advertisement for RCA Victor, Nipper's natural curiosity became known worldwide as an emblem of canine fidelity (to represent the fidelity of RCA in reproducing music and in serving its customers).

Fortunately, the Victorians' warm sentimental feelings for animals were given practical expression. Cruel practices did not, of course, cease with the beginning of the nineteenth century. Villagers still enjoyed their traditional pastime of catching a stray dog and drowning it as slowly as possible, so as to prolong the fun. Thomas Hardy's heartbreaking poem "The Mongrel" exposes the utter callousness of some humans toward companions who are merely dogs. Faced with the need of paying a tax on his dog, a man decided to get rid of him, because he regarded the animal as a piece of worthless property rather than as a sensitive being and a trusting friend. Too obtuse to feel guilty over this betrayal, he made a joke of it by playfully throwing a stick into the harbor for the dog to fetch, knowing the tide would carry him away. The dog leapt in "with ardent pride" but soon was struggling desperately; still, all the while he looked hopefully toward "the man he held as a god enshrined," confident "That his owner would save him by and by," never suspecting that the man intentionally sent him in to be drowned:

> *Till the effort not to drift from shore*
> *Of his little legs grew slower and slower,*
> *And, the tide still outing with brookless power,*
>   *Outward the dog, too went.*

Only just before he went down did he awaken to the man's treachery.[19] Reason, which is supposed to mark our moral superiority to the other animals, has been used to calculate the monetary value of a loving friend and to outsmart him by double dealing. This poem evokes more intense feeling than earlier protests against cruelty because Hardy enters the dog's mind as if he were human.

By the nineteenth century, indignation at callousness to animals was no longer confined to a few sensitive individuals, but extended to the general public. Cropping pieces off dogs came to be recognized as an abuse and was opposed by many people besides Queen Victoria. Hamerton inveighed: "The ignorant and stupid mutilation of dogs by cutting their ears and tail . . . is barbarous in the last degree, because it spoils their instruments of expression. It is like cutting out the tongue of a human being. There is a poor dog near me whose tail has been amputated at the very root, and the consequence is that he cannot tell me the half of what he thinks." (The contemporary dog psychologist Stanley Coren confirms this with the example of a crop-eared boxer who got into trouble with other dogs because he was unable to communicate his peaceful intentions by appropriate ear signals.) After Victoria's son Edward VII publicly denounced the cropping of dogs' ears, the British Kennel Club ruled that no dog born after March 31, 1895, could win a prize at any of its shows if it was cropped, and the practice ceased in England.[20] Unfortunately, the American Kennel Club continues to require that certain breeds must be cropped for showing.

Humane feelings were institutionalized in laws and organizations. The Battersea Home for Lost and Starving Dogs, the first institution of its kind, was established in 1860. The Society for the Prevention of Cruelty to Animals had been founded in 1824 and was sustained by the patronage of Princess, then Queen, Victoria from 1835. Its first goals were abolishing bullbaiting and dogfighting, and in 1835, it pushed through Parliament a prohibition of these sports, the first law in Britain for the protection of animals.[21]

The RSPCA prosecuted the lower-class pastimes of bullbaiting and dogfighting (as well as poor tradesmen's use of draft dogs) with more zeal than it opposed the excesses of the vivisectionists, because scientists were a highly respected class in Victorian society. Nevertheless, cruel experiments aroused more widespread and intense indignation among the general public, especially when the victims were dogs, than would have been thinkable in earlier centuries. The morality of doing experiments on animals was debated in the newspapers, and popular authors published antivivisectionist works. In 1875, an English physician, George Hoggan, worked for four months in the laboratory of the eminent French physiologist Claude Bernard, a latter-day Cartesian who self-righteously insisted that the vivisector maintain a dispassionate attitude, because a howling, struggling dog was no more than a machine and it was mawkishly sentimental to place its pain before the advancement of science. Hoggan wrote a famous letter to the *Morning Post* in which he declared that, although he had seen dreadful things during three military campaigns,

> *the saddest sight I ever witnessed was when the dogs were brought up from the cellar to the laboratory for sacrifice. Instead of appearing pleased with the change from darkness to light, they seemed seized with horror as soon as they smelt the air of the place, divining apparently their approaching fate. They would make friendly advances to each of the three or four persons present, and, as far as eyes, ears, and tail could make a mute appeal for mercy eloquent, they tried it in vain. Even when roughly grasped and thrown on the torture-trough, a low complaining whine at such treatment would be all the protest made, and they would continue to lick the hand that bound them till their mouths were fixed in the gag, and they could only flap their tails in the trough as the last means of exciting compassion.*

Similar procedures were publicly performed in Britain. Two women medical students revealed that they saw a dog cut open in the physiology laboratory of University College, London, that must have been the subject of a previous experiment because it already had an unhealed wound in its side; this violated a law that forbid reviving a vivisected animal from one experiment in order to use it for another. The *Times* dismissed their testimony as mischievous, but the Liberal, working-class *Daily News* insisted that, even if "man has the right to make use of animals for experimentation in the means of alleviating human suffering and saving life . . . surely there must be some limit to this right," especially in the case of the dog, which so trusts and worships man: "Does not this overwhelming trust—this absolute confidence that glistens in the dog's eye—lay upon us some obligation?" Jesse condemned the vivisector as the worst of all abusers of dogs. How appalling to inflict on "this innocent, noble, and most sensitive creature hideous and lengthened tortures" that our law has not imposed on the vilest felon. "What is a dog that he should meet with less consideration than his owner? Has he less sensitiveness or less virtue? Neither. In the former he is on a level at least with his master. . . . In the latter, how far beyond compare his superior!"[22]

Leading Victorian authors articulated the popular outrage at scientists who disregarded animal suffering in order to satisfy their intellectual curiosity. Wilkie Collins wrote an entire novel to discredit vivisectionists: *Heart and Science: A Story of the Present Time*. Collins did not dwell on the gruesome details of experiments on animals, believing it would be more effective to expose the motives of the experimenters, who hardened their hearts so they could pursue knowledge without feeling guilt. The villain is Dr. Benjulia, a brilliant neurologist who maintained a locked laboratory full of suffering animal subjects. He did not even claim that he sacrificed them to promote human welfare through medical progress, but brazenly declared that he worked only for knowledge that would bring him fame and superiority over other men. The ignorant mob might roar against cruelty, but to an enlightened scientist, "Knowledge sanctifies cruelty." When the hero (who was properly fond of dogs and cats) forestalled his great discovery, Benjulia was reduced to despair, released those of his animal subjects still able to move, and then burned himself up in his laboratory. "The last of the liberated creatures" was "a large dog, limping as if one of its legs was injured. It stopped as it passed the master, and tried to fawn on him. He threatened it with his hand. 'Be off with you, like the rest!' he said. The dog slowly crossed the flow of light and was swallowed up in darkness."[23]

Poets drew a poignant contrast between the insignificant cash value of a typical canine experimental subject and the spiritual or emotional worth of a dog. In Robert Browning's "Tray," a scientist observes a stray dog rescue a beggar child from drowning and wonders idly what motivated it, so he sends his servant to catch or purchase it:

> *By vivisection, at expense*
> *Of half-an-hour and eighteenpence,*
> *How brain secretes dog's soul, we'll see!*

Edmund Vance Cook's poem "Rags" is more moving because the situation it describes is more believable. A veteran was sustained through the war by Rags, a cheerful, lively cur who attached himself to his regiment, but then was lost. The man is now a medical student; and he sees Rags split open on a vivisection table.[24] The contrast between the dog as a loved and rightly valued companion and as an expendable stray brute may be sentimental, but it hits hard.

Unfortunately, unnecessary and unfeeling experiments are still being performed on animals today, although they are subject to more regulation. Richard Adams's *Plague Dogs* opens in a huge laboratory where animals are subjected to experiments that are neither restrained by kindness nor rationally justified by utility. And, he specifies, they are all based on fact. In the opening scene, two scientists watch a large black mongrel swimming in a tank, deciding whether "it" is close enough to death by drowning to be taken out. Their objective is to find out whether the hope of being pulled out will extend "its" efforts to keep afloat, and how long. He is not to be dragged out until he "definitely sinks and stops moving." In the same experiment performed on rats, some swam much longer than others before they died. The scientists are gratified to measure that the dog has kept going "2 hours 20 minutes, 53⅔ seconds . . . about 6½ minutes longer than Wednesday's test." This regular increase produces an interesting straight incline on a graph, "although obviously we must reach a diminution somewhere. There must come a point where the additional endurance induced by the dog's expectation of removal is counterbalanced by the limits of its physical capacity." At this point, of course, "it" will drown.[25]

The great practical legacy of nineteenth-century dog lovers has been a general revulsion against cruelty to animals and belief that they deserve consideration. The great imaginative legacy has been the rich collection of portraits of dogs, both real and fictitious, created by the many distinguished writers who loved them.

Dogs were so important in the life of Walter Scott that he could hardly help putting them into his work. His historical novels brought to life the aristocrat's noble hound companion and the swineherd's loyal working cur. The foxhunting terriers of Dandie Dinmont in *Guy Mannering*—"auld Pepper and auld Mustard, and young Pepper and young Mustard, and little Pepper and little Mustard," so called to indicate their color and their generation— made such an impression on the public that they gave his name to the type, now a modern breed.

According to his biographer J. G. Lockhart, Scott always talked to his bull
terrier Camp "as if he understood what was said—and the animal certainly
did understand not a little of it; it seemed as if he perfectly comprehended
that his master considered him as a sensible and steady friend." When Washington Irving visited Abbotsford in summer 1817, Scott came out to greet
him with a crowd of dogs. When they went out for a walk,

> *every dog in the establishment turned out to attend us. There was the old
> staghound, Maida . . . a noble animal, and Hamlet, the black greyhound,
> a wild thoughtless youngster . . . and Finette, a beautiful setter . . . the par-
> lour favourite. When in front of the house, we were joined by a superannu-
> ated greyhound, who came from the kitchen wagging his tail; and was
> cheered by Scott as an old friend and comrade. In our walks, he would fre-
> quently pause in conversation, to notice his dogs, and speak to them as if ra-
> tional companions,*

as, indeed, they appeared to have become through "their close intimacy
with him." Maida, a Scottish deerhound, had arrived in 1816. As the favorite dog of a famous man, Maida became so weary of being painted "that
whenever he sees brushes & a pallet he gets up and leaves the room." When
Scott had to leave Abbotsford because of his enormous business debts, he
grieved particularly for the dogs who would wait for him in vain. "It is
foolish—but the thoughts of parting from these dumb creatures have
moved me more than any of the painful reflections I have put down—poor
things, I must get them kind masters. . . . I must end this, or else I shall
lose the tone of mind with which men should bear distress. I find my dogs'
feet on my knees—I hear them whining and seeking me everywhere—this
is nonsense—but it is what they would do could they know how things
are."[26]

The Brontës loved animals and used them in their novels as measures of
human character. Elizabeth Gaskell, Charlotte's biographer, described Charlotte's feeling for animals as "affection," Emily's as "passion." "The helpless-
ness of an animal was its passport to Charlotte's heart; the fierce, wild
intractability of its nature was what often recommended it to Emily." Emily's

beloved bulldog, Keeper, was so ferocious that no one dared strike him. He insisted on stretching himself on the fine white bedspreads, and Emily finally promised that the next time he did so, she would punish him so he would never offend again. So when the indignant housekeeper reported that Keeper was lying on the best bed, Emily went up and dragged him down the stairs, heavily resisting and growling. Realizing that if she took her eyes off him she would lose her dominance and he might attack her, she had no opportunity to get a stick and had to beat him over the eyes with her fist until he was half blind and stupefied. After this she nursed and comforted him, and he not only reformed but "loved her dearly ever after. He walked first among the mourners to her funeral; he slept moaning for nights at the door of her empty room."[27] Emily's sensitive drawing of Keeper shows a mixed breed with elements of bullmastiff and bull terrier.

The heroine of *Shirley*, Charlotte's idealized portrait of Emily, has a strong, ugly dog named Tartar, modeled on Keeper. She fearlessly intervenes to defend him in an unequal fight and, though a rich woman, personally attends to his needs. Although he has been "obstinately insensible" to everyone except his mistress, Tartar immediately fixes his affection on Louis Moore, following him around and even giving him precedence over Shirley. Tartar's true canine instinct supposedly leads him to recognize the new head of the family; Charlotte must have hoped that this canine tribute would make her flat human character seem more worthy of the noble heroine she was to bestow on him. Charlotte drew from life the episode in which Shirley demonstrates her heroic nature with her reaction to the bite of an apparently rabid dog. Emily had once been bitten by "a strange dog running past, with hanging head and lolling tongue," and then, "with noble presence of mind," gone into the kitchen, taken up a red-hot iron, and seared the bitten place; she told "no one until the danger was well-nigh over, for fear of the terrors that might beset their weaker minds."[28] (It was believed at the time that rabies could be prevented in humans by cutting out or cauterizing the bitten part.)

The Earnshaws at Wuthering Heights live comfortably with their rough, tough dogs, the sort that Emily Brontë found most congenial. The urban intruder Lockwood's inability to deal with them is one of many signs of his inadequacy. Sentimentally determined to see dogs as loving pets, he attempts to caress a "canine mother" even as she is sneaking up to nip his legs. Left alone with three large, grim, watchful dogs, he indulges himself in making faces at them, without apprehending that this will arouse them to fury. (He should, of course, have been aware that dogs are very sensitive to body language.) The gentle, well-behaved Lintons reveal a moral limitation in their lack of proper feeling for their dogs. On their first appearance, the two Linton children have almost pulled a little dog in two as they struggled who should hold it, and Isabella Linton persists in eloping with Heathcliff after watching him hang her pet spaniel.

Dickens enjoyed playing with the mastiff-type watchdogs he kept at Gadshill, as well as his daughter's Pomeranian, Mrs. Bouncer. He often brought dogs into his novels and generally used them to highlight the characters of their owners. In *Oliver Twist*, Bill Sikes's constant companion, the bulldog Bull's-eye, is as surly and ferocious as his master. When Sikes relieves his fears of arrest by kicking the dog, Bull's-eye sinks his teeth in his leg. On the other hand, he so appreciates a rare indication of approval from his master, evoked by his evident willingness to attach himself to Oliver's throat, that he is actually moved to wag his tail. When Sikes is running for his life, the dog rightly suspects that Sikes intends to kill him and, failing to appease Sikes, runs away; but the dog later rejoins him and dies missing a jump to his shoulders. Bull's-eye is vicious and wary, but indissolubly attached to his master; Sikes is slightly humanized by his grudging pride in and affection for his dog.

Hugh of the Maypole and his dog form a more sympathetic pair in *Barnaby Rudge*. The wild ostler and rebel is followed by a dog as rough, sullen, and unprepossessing as himself. The dog both reflects his master and brings out his latent humanity, causing us to pity a criminal who is more sinned against than sinning. On his way to execution, Hugh asks if "any person here has a fancy for a dog; and . . . means to use him well. There's one, belongs to me . . . and it wouldn't be easy to find a better. He'll whine at first, but he'll soon get over that,— You wonder that I think about a dog just now. . . . If any man deserved it of me half as well, I'd think of *him*."[29]

In *David Copperfield*, Dora's toy spaniel, Jip, is as pretty, spoiled, and useless as his mistress. Like Dora, he can do nothing but parlor tricks, and he cannot even do them competently. Dora is sweeter than her eighteenth-century coquette predecessors, but her lapdog is equally undisciplined, walking around on the dinner table, "putting his foot in the salt or the melted butter," and barking and running at their guest's plate "with such undaunted pertinacity, that he . . . engrossed the conversation."[30] Jip accentuates Dora's childishness, as when she reacts to David's news that he has become poor by wailing that the dog cannot be deprived of his daily mutton chop, or to his attempt to impress her with her responsibilities in managing their household by putting up the dog's face for him to kiss. David is irritated by the dog's inadequacy long before he awakens to Dora's.

Elizabeth Barrett's life was transformed by her spaniel, Flush, a vibrant little personality who cheerfully kept her company in her sickroom. (It was at this period that the cocker spaniel's affection and eagerness to oblige made it even more desirable as a pet than as a hunter's assistant.) Barrett appreciated his willingness to stay with an invalid in a darkened room when he could have been tracking hares through a sunny meadow; because he loves her so, she will give him "more love . . . Than dogs often take of men." She constantly reported details of his life and feelings in her letters to Robert Browning during their courtship in 1846. Despite their mutual devotion, she was aware of Flush's foibles and his willfulness. He "has a very good, stout vainglory . . . and, although perfectly fond of me, has no idea whatever of being ruled over by me! He had his foot pinched in shutting the cab-door, & though he cried piteously & held it up, looking straight to me for sympathy, no sooner had he touched the grass than he began to run without a thought of it. Flush always makes the most of his misfortunes—he is of the Byronic school—il se pose en victime." After he bit Browning in a fit of jealousy, he "came up stairs with a good deal of shame in the bearing of his ears, & straight to me—no indeed! I would not speak to him. So he lay down on the floor at my feet looking from under his eyebrows at me—I did not forgive him till nearly 8 o'clock however." Then, having "spoken to me (in the Flush language) & . . . examined your chair, he suddenly fell into a rapture and reminded me that the cakes you left, were on the table."[31]

Prickly Jane Welsh Carlyle was almost embarrassed by her intense feeling for Nero, a small black-and-white Maltese mix that she was given in 1849, about whom she made "more fuss . . . than beseems a sensible woman." "The pleasantest fact of my life for a good while," she wrote to a friend, "is, that I have got a beautiful little dog . . . I like him better . . . than I should choose to show publicly . . . When I say I am well," she went on, "it means also Nero is well: he is part and parcel of myself . . . night and day he never leaves me, and it is something, I can tell you, to have such a bit of live cheerfulness always beside me." At first she feared that her husband would find the dog annoying and insist on getting rid of him, but Nero won him over by his doggy obliviousness to bad temper or dislike. When Thomas Carlyle "comes down gloomy in the morning, or comes in weary from his walk, the infatuated little beast dances round him on its hind legs as I ought to do and can't: and he feels flattered and surprised by such unwonted capers to his honour and glory." Note her quiet wit in drawing a connection between the dog's natural behavior and what was inappropriately expected of amiable Victorian wives.

Jane was devastated when she had to have Nero euthanized after he was run over by a cart: "the grief his death has caused me has been wonderful even to myself. His patience and gentleness and loving struggle to do all his bits of duties under his painful illness up to the last hour of his life was very strange and touching to see, and had so endeared him to everybody in the house, that I was happily spared all reproaches for wasting so much feeling on a dog. Mr. C. couldn't have reproached me, for he himself was in tears at the poor little thing's end; and his own heart was (as he phrased it) 'unexpectedly and distractedly torn to pieces with it.'" She wrote gratefully to the doctor who had euthanized Nero: "Oh, don't think me absurd, you, for caring so much about a dog? Nobody but myself can have any idea what that little creature has been in my life. My inseparable companion during eleven years, ever doing his little best to keep me from feeling sad and lonely. Docile, affectionate, loyal up to his last hour. When weak and full of pain, he offered himself to go out with me, seeing my bonnet on; and came panting to welcome me on my return, and the reward I gave him—the only reward I could or ought to give him, to such a pass had things come, was, ten minutes after, to give him up to be poisoned."[32]

Harriet Beecher Stowe's family had "a warm side towards everything that goes upon four paws . . . we have been always kept in confusion and under the paw . . . of some honest four-footed tyrant, who would go beyond his privilege and overrun the whole house." The first was Carlo, a big tawny mastiff who started life as a watchdog living in a kennel, where "Nobody petted him, or stroked his rough hide, or said, 'Poor dog!' to him." Consequently he kept running away to the Stowe children, "who told him stories, gave him half of their own supper, and took him to bed with them sociably." Finally his old lady owner let him go to them. He would sometimes tiptoe into Professor Stowe's study "and sit quietly down by him when he was busy over his Greek and Latin books, waiting for a word or two of praise or encouragement. If none came, he would lay his rough horny paw on his knee, and look in his face with such an honest, imploring expression, that the professor was forced to break off to say, 'Why, Carlo, you poor, good, honest fellow, — did he want to be talked to? — so he did. Well, he shall be talked to; — he's a nice, good dog; — and during all these praises Carlo's transports and the thumps of his rough tail are not to be described."[33]

Dogs were so much a part of Stowe's life that she naturally fitted them into her great indictment of slavery, *Uncle Tom's Cabin*. The murder of George's dog stands out among many harrowing examples of cruelty. Eliza gave her husband, George, a little dog that was his only comfort in his life under a mean-minded master: "He has slept with me nights, and followed me around days, and kind o' looked at me as if he understood how I felt. Well, the other day I was just feeding him with a few old scraps I picked up by the kitchen door, and Mas'r came along, and said I was feeding him up at his expense, and that he couldn't afford to have every nigger keeping his dog, and ordered me to tie a stone to his neck and throw him in the pond." He refused and was flogged and then had to watch while Mas'r and his son threw Carlo in and "pelted the poor drowning creature with stones. Poor thing! He looked at me so mournful, as if he wondered why I didn't save him." As a slave, George hadn't even the right to feed a dog or save a friend. The decent natural dog had no comprehension of evil human social distinctions. Like the dog, George was a sentient creature who could be tormented at will because he was regarded as property.

Bruno, the Shelbys' Newfoundland, typifies the benevolent atmosphere of that plantation: he is the friend of everyone there, white and black. There is a droll moment when Haley, the slave dealer who is going to pursue Eliza, asks one of Shelby's slaves whether his master keeps dogs—meaning of course the savage hounds used to catch fugitive slaves. "Heaps on 'em," the man replies with feigned ingenuousness, and calls over the lumbering Newfoundland.[34]

George Eliot particularly welcomed the pug dog that filled "the void left by false and narrow-hearted friends" who abandoned her for living unmarried with George Lewes. "He is without envy, hatred, or malice . . . he will betray no secrets, and feel neither pain at my success nor pleasure in my chagrin." Moreover, "his physiognomy . . . is expressive, full of gentleness and affection, and radiant with intelligence when there is a savoury morsel in question."[35]

Her novels constantly reflect her sympathy for dogs. In a priceless scene in *The Mill on the Floss*, she used the natural behavior of the Tulliver terrier, Yap, to highlight human pretensions and self-righteousness. The children Maggie and Tom have a single jam puff, which Tom has not succeeded in dividing evenly; and each wants the better part. However, neither can admit this; for Maggie wants desperately to be a properly self-sacrificing female and to please Tom, and Tom is determined to be a chivalrous male and indulge the weaker sex. To maintain absolute fairness, he orders her to choose with her eyes shut, but he lets his bitterness appear when she chances on the better piece. She offers him her piece; he refuses to accept it, but accuses her of greed for eating it. Meanwhile Yap had "been looking on while the eatables vanished, with an agitation of his ears and feelings which could hardly have been without bitterness. Yet the excellent dog accepted Tom's attention with as much alacrity as if he had been treated quite generously."[36] Only the dog has the honesty to reveal the appetite that they all share. And yet he can cheerfully forget his disappointment, while the two more complicated human hypocrites go on to nurse their imaginary grievances.

Many of Eliot's amiable characters demonstrate consideration for dogs. When Adam Bede was so annoyed by his mother's nagging that he would not eat the supper she had lovingly prepared, she called his Old English sheepdog, Gyp, who "was watching his master with wrinkled brow and ears erect, puzzled at this unusual course of things." Though he knew she was inviting him to supper, he felt he should not leave Adam and so remained seated, with eyes fixed "anxiously on his master. Adam noticed Gyp's mental conflict, and though his anger had made him less tender than usual to his mother, it did not prevent him from caring as much as usual for his dog. We are apt to be kinder to the brutes that love us than to the women that love us. Is it because the brutes are dumb?" Probably so—dogs do not irritate us with silly or tactless talk, as humans constantly do. Moreover, they offer uncomplicated sympathy that does not provoke conflict or ambivalence. So Adam sent the dog off to eat, "and Gyp, apparently satisfied that duty and pleasure were one," followed Adam's mother into the house. Furnishing a comic parallel to this harmonious pair, the eccentric misogynist Bartle Massey has a turnspit dog that he rescued from drowning by boys. How disgusted he was to find that she was female and, besides, about to present him with a litter of puppies. Nevertheless, he takes good care of the family, all the while railing against her female weaknesses. A small but significant virtue of Dorothea Brooke, the noble hero of *Middlemarch*, is her dependable attentiveness "to the feelings of dogs"; if she cannot respond to their advances, she declines them with politeness.[37]

The heedless, perverse heroines of Rhoda Broughton, a popular sensational novelist who specialized in the misadventures of erring women, are consistently made more sympathetic by their love of dogs. Jock, a wirehaired fox terrier in *A Waif's Progress*, brings out hidden good qualities in the two principal female characters. Affection for Jock is the only soft spot in his forbidding, rigidly principled mistress, Camilla Tancred; and the mutual affection between Jock and the calculating waif, Bonnybell Ransome, indicates her basic kindness, despite her want of tenderness and principle. Jock is the only character in the book who can draw out spontaneous joy and affection from Bonnybell.

Broughton constantly noted the presence of dogs in her scenes of everyday life, and her precise observations of their behavior adds lively humor and realism to human dramas that are often far-fetched, insubstantial, and doleful. A sheepdog lies on the dining room rug, "licking his chops every now and then when he sees some morsel more tempting than ordinary conveyed to another mouth than his"; three pugs realizing they are being left at home form "a little dismal row" and send "reproachful yaps through the uprights of the balcony" as they watch their mistress go downstairs; and a jealous pug squeezes "herself under a piece of furniture . . . from beneath which there is now nothing visible of her but a small spiteful face, full of mortification and ire . . . she firmly resists all Belinda's blandishing inducements to her to come forth, though the agitated beat of her tail upon the floor proves that she is not wholly unmoved by them."[38]

Although dogs are no longer so constantly present in fiction, contemporary novelists sometimes introduce them in the Victorian manner: to highlight aspects of their human characters' personality or situation. However, these portrayals are generally less joyful and positive than those of their nineteenth-century predecessors, perhaps because we have become more ambivalent about dogs and about life in general. In Graham Greene's *The Human Factor*, the boxer Buller is the perfect dog for Maurice Castle, a seedy, joyless secret service agent who spies for the Russians from a sense of obligation and is effectual neither as British agent nor as Communist spy. Buller, too, is a failure. Castle got him to make his wife feel safe, but the dog fawned on everybody. Instead of giving pleasure, as a dog is expected to do, Buller was a burden and an irritation, especially to Castle, whom he loved best of all. "The square black muzzle of Buller pushed the door fully open, and then he launched his body like a sack of potatoes at Castle's fly. Castle fended him off. . . . A long ribbon of spittle descended Castle's trouser leg." Then the dog settled down to lick "his private parts with the gusto of an alderman drinking soup." It was typical of Buller to lick "with undiscriminating affection" the trouser bottoms of the South African policeman who had persecuted Castle and his wife, and typical of the man to praise this "fidelity."[39] On the other hand, Buller was murderous to cats, on one occasion killing a leashed cat that accompanied its family on a picnic. He is a realistic composite of distasteful canine characteristics, whose mindless friendliness to all humans is a travesty of traditional canine love.

When Castle had to flee to the USSR, Buller presented the last unsolved problem, because he could not go with Castle's wife to stay with his mother, who had a cherished Burmese cat. The dog had to be shot, lest, left alone in the house, he would bark constantly and alert the neighbors. Castle shot him—fatally, he believed. But we find out later that the dog was only wounded and had whined in agony for hours until the police came and finished the job. One more failure for Castle. Annoying as he was, Buller did not deserve to suffer, nor did Castle mean him to. Like his master, the dog meant well and did the best he could, but his best was not good enough; he, too, ended in meaningless defeat.

A far more sympathetic dog suffers innocently amid the human complications of William Maxwell's *So Long, See You Tomorrow*. In this bleak story of two farm families destroyed by the adulterous passion between one of the men and his neighbor's wife, the two men were not guilty enough to deserve their deaths by murder and suicide; but the suffering of two other parties, the murderer's teenage son and Trixie, the shepherd dog who loved him, is more affecting because they were completely innocent—the dog even more than the boy, because she understood less than he and so suffered even more. When the adulterous wife took her boys into town, leaving the dog with her husband, Trixie waited every day at the school bus stop, lest the boy might come and not find her there, even though she knew she would be beaten for failing to round up the cattle. She was distressed when the deserted father auctioned off the furniture, unable to understand why she was not allowed to drive off the intruders taking away the family property. When he left her tied to a tree for the next tenant, who failed to arrive for two days, "She waited a long long time, trying not to worry. Trying to be good—trying to be especially good, and telling herself that they had only gone in to town and were coming right back, even though it was perfectly obvious that this wasn't true. . . . Eventually, in spite of her, howls broke out." When the new owner set her to herding the cows, she kept running off to town in hopes of finding her family. In the end she was chloroformed because she had become useless as a worker. Maxwell's editor wanted him to remove the dog from the story, on the grounds that he made her puzzlement and misery unrealistically articulate.[40] But she brings needed warmth into a chilly, understated book, as Maxwell enters her mind to express her simple affections and good intentions in a world swirling with complicated, equivocal human feelings. Because her motives are realistic and she is destroyed not by cruelty but by the simple callousness of humans too preoccupied with their own feelings to think about a dog's, the effect is not sentimental.

The fact that Alison Lurie's Fido in *Foreign Affairs* is imaginary does not make him any less vivid and true to doggy nature. Fido is the faithful companion of Vinnie Miner, Lurie's perceptive and unlovable protagonist, in her frequent periods of self-pity. Fido is unattractive and annoying, but Vinnie cannot drive him away any more than she can give up the masochistic gratification of feeling sorry for herself. Wallowing in self-pity instead of striving for constructive change can be as comforting as accepting warm uncritical sympathy from a dog. Besides, dogs are chronically prone to self-pity themselves. As the book opens, Vinnie is boarding an airplane for England, upset by a hostile review and "followed by an invisible dog." It "is her familiar demon or demon familiar, known to her privately as Fido and representing self-pity. She visualizes him as a medium-sized dirty-white long-haired mutt, mainly Welsh terrier: sometimes trailing her silently, at other times whining and panting and nipping at her heels; when bolder, dashing around in circles trying to trip her up, or at least get her to stoop down so that he may rush at her, knock her to the ground, and cover her with sloppy kisses." When she has to admit to herself that she could gain nothing by responding to the critical attack, "Fido, who has been standing with his forepaws on her knees, whining hopefully, now scrambles onto her lap." No wonder she feels queasy, "whines Fido: this public sneer will be in her life forever, part of her shabby history of losses and failures." After five months of successful research and an unexpectedly satisfying love affair, she tries to dismiss Fido; but her insistence that she is "perfectly fine . . . not a bit sorry for myself" sounds hollow even to her, and as she boards her plane home, she "sees Fido standing by the wall . . . looking up at her with anxious devotion and wagging his feathery white tail. 'Well, all right,' she says to him. 'Come along, then.' "[41]

1. Bas-relief of wild asses being hunted by hounds, seventh century BCE

2. Roman marble statue of a pair of dogs, possibly second century BCE

3. Pisanello, *The Vision of St. Eustace,* 1440

4. Vittore Carpaccio, *The Vision of St. Augustine*, 1502

5. Paolo Veronese, *Feast in the House of Simon*, 1560

6. Le Nain Brothers, *The Supper at Emmaus*, 1645

7. Jacob Jordaens, *The Bean King*, 1640-45 or circa 1655

8. Jan Steen, *The World Upside Down*, 1663

9. Pierre-Auguste Renoir, *Madame Georges Charpentier and Her Children,* 1878

10. Tiziano Vecelli, *Danae,* 1553-54

11. Jean-Honoré Fragonard,
The Love Letter, 1770s

12. Jan van Eyck,
The Arnolfini Portrait, 1434

13. Tiziano Vecelli, *Captain with a Cupid and a Dog,* circa 1552

14. Anthony Van Dyck, *James Stuart, Duke of Richmond and Lennox,* 1634

15. William Hogarth,
A Painter and His Pug, 1745

16. Anthony Van Dyck, *Children of Charles I,* 1637

17. Diego Velázquez,
Infante Felipe Próspero,
1659

18. Édouard Manet,
*Tama, the Japanese
Dog,* circa 1875

19. Théodore Géricault, *Bulldog*, circa 1815

20. Rosa Bonheur, *"Barbaro" After the Hunt*, undated (mid-nineteenth century)

21. Alexandre-François Desportes, *Dog Guarding Game,* 1724

22. Constant Troyon,
Hound Pointing, 1860.

23. Frans Snyders, *Wild Boar Hunt,* mid-seventeeth century

24. Thomas Gainsborough, *Pomeranian Bitch and Pup,* 1777

25. Jean-Baptiste Oudry, *Bitch-Hound Nursing Her Puppies*, 1752.
Musée de la Chasse et de la Nature, Paris. Dépôt du musée du Louvre

26. Robert Alexander, *The Happy Mother*, 1887

27. Sir Edwin Landseer, *A Jack in Office,* before 1833

28. Susan Meddaugh,
illustration from
Martha and Skits,
2000

29. Rufino Tamayo, *Animals*, 1941

30. J. M. W. Turner, *Dawn After the Wreck,* circa 1841

8

How Dogs Are Classified

AS NINETEENTH-CENTURY owners came to value dogs more and to see them more as companions than as specialized workers, they developed a new interest in their dogs' purity of ancestry and appearance. It was no longer vital for a Newfoundland to retrieve fishermen's equipment or drowning people from rough seas; it was important for it to look handsome and impressive and have an amiable disposition. The modern conception of breeds developed only in the nineteenth century, together with the belief that purebred dogs excel others in courage and other virtues.

The first systematic classification of English dogs, written by Johannes Caius as a contribution to the natural history encyclopedia compiled by his friend Konrad Gesner in the mid-sixteenth century, is based on the functions performed by the different varieties, rather than their appearance. It reflects the general assumption of his time that the most valuable and interesting dogs were those used by the aristocracy in hunting. His first group, "the gentle kinde, serving the game," included by far the most breeds: harriers (all the smaller scent hounds), terriers, bloodhounds, gazehounds, greyhounds ("the best" hounds), lymers, and tumblers, as well as spaniels, setters, and water spaniels. The mysterious tumbler, which cannot be identified today, was supposed to have hunted by "deceit and guile," like a cat, rather than by straightforward pursuit, like a proper dog. It looked like a mongrel greyhound and was far more efficient, taking as many rabbits in a day as a horse could carry. Perhaps it was a lurcher and took its shifty character from the cunning poacher who used it. Despite that character, Caius let its function, hunting, outweigh its sneaky plebeian ways and classed it among "gentle" dogs. He also admitted a toy dog, "the Spaniel gentle" or *Melitaus* (dog from Malta), on the grounds that its owners belonged to the upper class.

Caius's second group was "a homely kind, apt for sundry necessary uses," which included the shepherd dog and the mastiff or bandog. Lastly, there was "a currishe kinde, meete for many toyes"—miscellaneous mongrels, defined as such by function more than ancestry. This group included turnspits, dancing and trick dogs (taught by "theyr vagabundicall masters"), and those that had no use at all except barking at strangers.[1]

Two hundred years later, Buffon attempted to classify dogs scientifically on the basis of ancestry and environmental influences, although he could not resist opening his article in *Natural History* with a long emotional eulogy on the dog's devotion to his master and general virtue (as he used his article on cats to denigrate them). Theorizing that the relationship between people and dogs began with the dog's role in domesticating livestock, he concluded that the shepherd dog—the one programmed to watch over herds—must be the original form. "This dog is the true dog of Nature; the one she has given us for the greatest usefulness; the one that fits the best with the general order of living beings." Buffon's theory is too vague to be arguable, however, because his physical description of this dog is sufficiently elastic to include many sorts of large mongrels. Plate X in his book represents a nondescript shaggy black cur with prick ears that could pass for a lurcher as well as a shepherd dog. Even if dogs of similar appearance may be found among every group that keeps dogs, they are not necessarily herders.

Buffon believed that all "races" (varieties) of dog developed from the shepherd dog under the influence primarily of climate but also of training and of crossing between races. In temperate climates and among fully civilized Europeans, it produced the mastiff, the beagle (and other scent hounds), and the matin (a tall, rangy sheepdog with short rough hair). The semi-erect ears and "bloodthirsty nature" of the matin and the mastiff reveal their kinship with the shepherd dog, while "The beagle is the one of the three that is most removed from it; the long ears, entirely hanging, the sweetness, the docility, and, if one may say it, the timidity of this dog, are so many proofs of the great degeneration, or, if you wish, of the great perfection produced by a lengthy domestication, together with a careful, consistent education." Transported into rigorous northern climes, the shepherd dog produced the northern breeds, similar in form, with erect ears, thick long hair, a savage air, and a tendency to howl rather than bark.[2]

Beilby and Bewick's *General History of Quadrupeds* gives a good picture of English dogdom at the end of the eighteenth century. They start with the shepherd's dog, depicted as a border collie, and the larger, fiercer cur dog—smooth-haired and with a naturally short tail—who was used to drive cattle. The Greenland dog, an accurately drawn husky, represents the several northern breeds. They proceed to three mastiff breeds: the bulldog, which looked like a modern boxer, a modern-looking mastiff, and the bandog, a lighter, less powerful, and more active watchdog. The Newfoundland, oddly, appears among the sporting breeds; it was lighter and less shaggy than today's dog and was still occasionally used as a sporting retriever.

Hunting breeds, as usual, get disproportionate attention, comprising twenty of the thirty types listed. They include the greyhound, the beagle, the harrier, and the foxhound, all depicted much like the modern breeds. The Dalmatian is of hound stock, although it was used "as an elegant attendant on a carriage." The large, tediously painstaking Old English hound with wonderful scenting powers was dying out; its relative the bloodhound (or sleuthhound) was used to track wounded deer or deer-stealers, but not other criminals. Bird dogs include the heavy Spanish pointer, a modern-looking English setter, the large rough water dog and the large and small water spaniels (evidently workingman's and sportsman's versions of the same dog), and the springer and cocker spaniels, listed as one breed; the dog pictured looks like a modern springer and has an undocked tail. Bewick had evidently never seen an Irish wolfhound, for he drew it like a Great Dane. He listed the Scottish deerhound, the gazehound, the lymer, and the tumbler on the basis of other authors, without, evidently, knowing quite what they were. The lurcher is represented by a clumsy picture and hostile description befitting its low associations. Bewick distinguishes two kinds of terrier, a rough-haired, low-slung dog soon to be named the Dandie Dinmont terrier, and a smooth, more handsome, but less hardy dog that must have been the now extinct black-and-tan terrier, ancestor of several modern breeds. Toy dogs include miniaturized spaniels, the profusely haired shock dog (probably a Maltese), the comforter (pictured as a papillon), and the pug.

Although dog fanciers take pride in the antiquity of their favorite breeds, it is only canine types such as greyhounds, mastiffs, and bichons that can be traced back for many centuries; breeds in the modern sense have existed only for the past 150 years or so, when varieties of dog loosely defined by their function became breeds precisely defined by their appearance. Collies were originally dogs who herded sheep and were judged on how well they did their job. "Their untutored masters saw no need for pedigrees, if indeed they were capable of keeping stud books." But in 1886 a standard was formulated to specify that their heads must be wedge-shaped with the right degree of taper from ears to nose, their ears carried about three quarters erect, and their eyes almond-shaped and of medium size. Fanciers agreed that certain physical characteristics were intrinsically attractive, expressed the function that the dog was designed to perform, or distinguished it from other breeds; and breeders strove to fix and accentuate these distinguishing characteristics. Kennel clubs were organized to recognize the breeds officially and monitor their purity by keeping records of pedigrees in stud books. For the only way to make sure that any canine union produced pups of a predictable appearance was to know the ancestry of dog and bitch, both of whom had to be of the same breed and of unmixed ancestry since the time that breed was officially recognized. The British Kennel Club issued its first stud book in 1874; it included the pedigrees of 4,027 dogs divided into 40 breeds and varieties.[3] In effect, then, a breed was a group of dogs recognized by a kennel club.

This shift in emphasis from proven competence to purity of blood was rationalized on the grounds that purebred dogs performed better than random breds. Henry William Herbert, an Englishman who moved to America, described pure-blooded pointers

tearing their way through cat-briar brakes, literally bleeding at every pore, and whimpering with pain, while great, coarse-bred, hairy brutes of six times their apparent frame, and capacities of endurance, slunk away like curs, as they were, unable to face the thorns. . . . In every animal, from the man, in whom I believe it tells *the most, down to the bullock and the Berk-shire hog, I am an implicit believer in the efficacy of blood and breeding to develop all qualities, especially courage to do, and courage to bear—as well as to produce the highest and most delicate nervous organization; and I would as willingly have a cur in my shooting kennel, as a mule in my rac-ing stable, if I had one.*

Accordingly, in "any well-kept kennels a chance litter" from a setter and a pointer would be drowned, for "*Only* a pure-bred setter can do the work."[4] Herbert's association of moral superiority with upper-class status is typical of his time and class, and like many self-proclaimed dog lovers, he defines ca-nine nobility as willingness to suffer to gratify human whims.

Such snobbish sentiments were widespread because they appealed even more to the middle than to the upper class. Those who aspired to gentility but could not be aristocrats by birth gained surrogate aristocracy by keeping dogs of high lineage. Gordon Stables was gratified to report that by the end of the nineteenth century, "the number of curs and mongrels has sensibly di-minished on our streets, the number of good dogs has greatly increased, and every one who possesses a well-bred member of the canine race seems to take an honest pride in the possession thereof." He believed that the dog fancy promoted better treatment of dogs by creating measurable standards of ca-nine excellence and encouraging the reproduction of purebreds who had ob-vious monetary value.[5]

Unfortunately, this attitude led to disvaluing dogs that did not meet ken-nel club standards, regardless of any fine qualities they might have. Stables sniffed that "Nobody now who is anybody can afford to be followed about by a mongrel dog" and declared that "the value of a mongrel" was "just a trifle less than the price of a rope you would purchase to hang him." George Tay-lor rejoiced that the public was becoming aware of "the evil of harboring mongrels, and the advantage of keeping animals of distinct race," the only kind "worth caring for and making friends of." Keeping mongrels as pets is like planting weeds in a window box. " 'Beware the mongrel,' is a good rule for dog lovers." In the early twentieth century, the dog expert Edward Ash was amused by the ignorance of his gamekeeper, who could not see why Ash refused to mate his purebred terrier bitch to a dog "of questionable parentage," even though he looked like the bitch and "was famed as a rat-killer." Edwin Megargee, a noted breeder of Scotties, painter of purebreds, and dog show judge, pronounced that "Well-bred dogs will give their all of affection and loyalty in the face of death itself. To me a purebred animal seems proud of its lineage. I have never known a purebred dog to be a snake or a coward when put to the test."[6]

Although bald assertions of the moral superiority of aristocrats (canine or human) are rarely heard today, authorities in the dog fancy remain convinced of the essential importance of pure bloodlines. Roger Caras, who did a lot for dogs both as a writer and as president of the ASPCA, nevertheless accepted uncritically the contention that winning prizes at shows is the best measure of canine quality. Although mongrels from shelters "can make super pets," neither they nor even pet-quality purebreds "should ever be allowed to reproduce. There is no rational argument for breeding dogs whose genes are not needed to improve the genetic package of its breed." Without a smile or doubt, he described his comically low-slung basset hound as "a classically beautiful animal." He looked forward to the day when the Australian cattle dog, a highly effective working dog of nondescript appearance, will "be as refined as . . . the collie."[7]

It did not take long for the new emphasis on the distinguishing physical characteristics of purebreds to produce ludicrous exaggerations. A *Punch* cartoon, "Dog Fashions for 1889," depicts a lady leading two crocodile-length dachshunds, accompanied by a Yorkshire terrier with huge ears and a long hairy body suggesting a caterpillar, a microscopic Chihuahua, a wolfhound the size of a pony, a tubular pug, and a grinning bulldog all fangs and tongue. A few contemporary authorities did deplore the new overemphasis on appearance: Nathaniel Southgate Shaler declared that breeding for "trifling and often injurious features of shape," rather than mental characteristics and the ability to do useful jobs, degrades a noble animal; and already in 1911 the aristocratic breeder Judith Lytton complained that toy spaniels had "some very grave defects," because breeders ignored soundness in favor of beauty.[8]

Unfortunately, however, the *Punch* cartoon would still be appropriate today and could include more breeds. The job of the basset hound was to track game slowly through dense cover, so it was bred for short legs, a long nose, and long drooping ears that sweep up scents from the ground and muffle hearing so it will not be distracted by sounds. It is depicted in Buffon as a long, low-slung, but not distorted hound. The dog fancy has proudly extended its ears, lengthened its body, and shortened its legs to the point that its penis practically drags on the ground. These extreme features have made it liable to ear infections and structural problems in its back and hips.

The standards of excellence set for every breed, which are defined by the breed club, overemphasize physical appearance, specifying in minute detail the required shape of the head, color of the coat, color of the eyes and nose, and so forth. A dog is evaluated in terms of its conformity to this abstract ideal. This is measured on a scale of a hundred points, of which at least ninety are divided among the parts of the dog's body. Standards may stipulate that character is "the more important side of a dog" and usually include some statement about the desired mental and temperamental characteristics. But these inner qualities are assumed from details of the dog's appearance. The smooth coat and assured stance of the Doberman pinscher convey that it "is an honest dog, uncamouflaged by superfluous coat or the wiles of the artful conditioner," that it is "a blue-blooded animal, or aristocrat," and that it "looks upon the stranger boldly and judges him with unerring instinct." Most standards require that a dog must look as if it is able to do the job for which it was bred, a point on which commentators at the Westminster Dog Show constantly insist. But in America, unlike several European countries, there is no requirement that it actually do that job. The standard for the flat-coated retriever explicitly claims to be determined not by fashion but by sportsmen interested only in the dog's working abilities, yet it disqualifies yellow- and cream-colored dogs, as well as those deviating by more than an inch from the preferred height, on the grounds that any such deviation "should be considered not practical for the types of work for which the Flat-Coat was developed."[9]

The increased preoccupation with distinguishing each type of dog by its proper appearance led naturally to a proliferation of breeds. At the beginning of the nineteenth century, every region of the British Isles had developed some type of terrier, bred for proficiency in unearthing foxes (by the upper class) or in catching rats (by the working class); but they were classified only as rough or smooth. From the various terriers prevalent in different localities, people formed distinguishing breed standards and then developed dogs to match them. Because cairn terriers are typically dark, breeders routinely killed all white puppies in their litters. Then a Scots family decided to start collecting them and formed a new breed, the West Highland white terrier. (Presumably dark-colored puppies in West Highland white litters are now destroyed.) The breeds have become more and more specialized, so that, according to an authority writing in 1957, "no show champion of twenty years ago—certainly in the terriers, and in most other breeds as well—would stand a chance today."[10]

Originally, spaniels were classified by function as land and water spaniels. Springer and cocker spaniels were sometimes found in the same litter, but in 1892 they were separated into two breeds. Some years later, a rich fancier named Geraldine Rockefeller Dodge felt it was necessary to separate the English from the American cocker spaniel, on the grounds that confusion between them "militated against the best interests of both varieties." Generations of interbreeding made this task very difficult, but after an exhaustive pedigree search directed by Dodge, the pure English lines of descent were separated out so that the English cocker could be recognized as a separate breed by the American Kennel Club in 1946. The American cocker has longer hair on ears and body and has almost lost the ability to hunt.[11]

In addition to insisting that the physical characteristics they exquisitely develop in their dogs reflect equally fine inner qualities, dog fanciers like to trace their breeds back to antiquity. The ancestors of Central European mastiff breeds like the rottweiler may perhaps have followed the Roman legions over the Alps, but those ancient drover dogs were not in any meaningful sense rottweilers. The Pekingese has not been pampered by Chinese emperors ever since the eighth century, as its devotees claim, although fluffy, flat-faced miniature dogs are recorded in China from even earlier times. Writings from the sixth century BCE refer to dogs so small that they fit under the table, which in traditional China was only eight inches off the floor, and described them as "square" or "short" and having short muzzles. But dogs definitely recognizable as Pekingese first appear in a late-eighteenth-century silk scroll painting. The modern Pekingese was developed in the nineteenth century under the supervision of the Dowager Empress Tzu Hsi, who prescribed a heavy neck ruff, bent forelegs, and golden color. The dogs' features were further exaggerated after they were introduced in the West in 1860, so that they now have flatter faces, shorter legs, and more hair.

Irish wolfhounds figured heroically in ancient Irish literature, and in the seventeenth century the poet Katherine Philips praised one (which she called an "Irish Greyhound") for uniting courage with gentle manners; but they died out in the eighteenth century when there were no wolves left for them to hunt. A nineteenth-century army officer resolved to revive, or re-create, this emblem of nationalist pride. He set out to find surviving Irish wolfhounds, but despite official claims to the contrary, there is no evidence that he succeeded. What is known is that he matched Scottish deerhounds with other breeds until he got what he thought reproduced the original dog and then wrote a breed standard which conscientious breeders try to match. The present Irish wolfhound splendidly fits the image we can create from ancient Irish literature, but there is no evidence that it looks like its medieval predecessors. It is also so large that its heart becomes overstrained, shortening its life expectancy to about seven years (as opposed to over thirteen for the average mixed breed).

When bullbaiting was outlawed in England in 1835, the agile, muscular, aggressive bulldog, a symbol of British pluck, no longer had a function. Fanciers who could not endure "the passing of so fine a breed" set out to re-create it in an innocuous form. Since they had to eliminate the animal's defining characteristic of belligerence, they bred to accentuate physical characteristics that supposedly suggest the strength, tenacity, and courage of the traditional bulldog. The resulting animal has a large square head, a disproportionately broad chest, and short, thick crooked legs, designed to create an impression of solidity. The flattened nose of the old bulldog has been exaggerated by preventing the nasal bones from growing properly, so that the normal-sized lower jaw protrudes grotesquely, upper and lower teeth do not come close to meeting, the mouth does not close, and the dog drools constantly. Because its legs extend beside, rather than under, its rib cage, it has trouble walking. It also has serious difficulties with breathing, chewing, mating, and delivering puppies. Its life expectancy is seven to nine years. A dog with a function worthy of respect (however distasteful to modern sensibilities) has become "a dysfunctional lapdog." The breeders did achieve a sweet disposition: already by 1911, a typical bulldog was "wistful to be noticed by anyone—effusively grateful for every word or pat, an ever-ready wagger and nuzzler."[12]

Of course, most breeds have not been so drastically turned from their original purpose, and most breeders have a responsible concern for health and temperament as well as appearance. Nevertheless, there are intrinsic dangers in breeding for the show ring. Characteristics such as a naturally pricked ear take on a disproportionate importance, so they are pursued without sufficient regard for other qualities. A fashionable trait such as merle (speckled blue-gray) coloring may be cultivated even though it is genetically linked with partial blindness and deafness. Inbreeding, which is the only way to fix desired traits, can lead to the spread of harmful recessive genes. The gene pool, already limited by the requirement that sire and dam must be registered members of the breed in question, becomes further reduced as breeds are subdivided—say, from cocker spaniels to American cocker spaniels to cockers of the different color varieties. A prize dog will be sought for as a stud even though he may be carrying a bad recessive gene. He will be bred to several hundred bitches, and the recessive gene will spread among his descendants, who will be mated with each other, so that the defect will become endemic in the population. "Thus current dog breeding practices can be described as an ideal system for the spread and preservation of injurious recessive genes."[13]

In 1980, Robert Schaible, a geneticist at the University of Indiana School of Medicine, bred out the Dalmatian's chronic problems of deafness, skin defects, urinary stones, and epilepsy by crossing a Dalmatian with a pointer (a closely related breed) and then breeding back to Dalmatians. After five generations—ten years—the crossbreeds were indistinguishable from purebred Dalmatians; and the AKC approved registering them as such. But they reneged under pressure from the Dalmatian Club of America, which "objected that the purity of the breed was being compromised."[14]

Another problem develops when a breed suddenly becomes popular: opportunists will move in to produce profitable puppies as fast as possible, regardless of their quality. The popularity of German shepherds, for example, has impaired the wonderful working dog perfected by von Stephanitz. They quickly became popular in the United States when American soldiers brought them home after World War I, and became even more popular after Rin Tin Tin, the original canine movie star, made his first feature-length picture in 1926. In the mid-1920s, a third of all registered dogs were German shepherds. At that point, irresponsible breeders began to mass-produce dogs without regard to character, so that nervousness and snapping became common problems. They are sufficiently common that the authors of the standard find it necessary to warn that a German shepherd in the show ring "must not be timid, shrinking behind its master or handler," or "nervous, looking about or upward with anxious expression," or attempt to bite the judge.

Meanwhile, even top breeders have been striving to "improve" the dog's gait from a "naturally easy trot" to a movement that has the appearance of being effortless: "his structure has been modified to increase the power, elasticity and length of his gait . . . the dog seems to glide forward without visible effort," as if "suspended . . . from the firm beam of his back." Supposedly the dog's "structure has been developed to meet the requirements of its work"— but no one asks what was wrong with its gait when in the old days it expertly herded sheep. Once it had a straight back like other sheepdogs; now its hindquarters slope down markedly. The best in breed at the 2003 Westminster Show ran with hindquarters strangely lowered; posed in his official stance, his tail actually touched the ground. The low, tapering hindquarters also predispose the breed to hip dysplasia. In Operation Desert Storm, the army turned to Belgian Malinois, who are very similar to German shepherds and free of their genetic defects.[15]

The worst result of the pressure to meet demand for purebred dogs of popular breeds is puppy mills, where dogs are relentlessly bred to produce the maximum number of puppies, without the least regard for their welfare or possible hereditary defects. The puppies are then taken too young from their mothers and transported in airplane cargo holds to pet shops interested only in selling them for profit. Caras, representing the dog fancy, did condemn puppy mills, but more for their disregard for bloodlines than their abuse of dogs; and he absolved the AKC from any responsibility for them. However, they could not function without its sanction, since dogs cannot be sold as purebreds without registration papers from the AKC. Because the AKC accepts registrations by mail for any puppies whose sire and dam are AKC registered, it needs to know nothing about possible defects in the puppies or possibly appalling conditions in the places where they are bred.[16]

Susan Conant, author of mystery stories featuring a dog writer detective and her two malamutes, is sympathetic to the dog fancy. Her novels display respect for responsible breeders and exhaustive knowledge of the dog world, and her detective competes in AKC obedience trials. Nevertheless, in *Bloodlines,* Conant denounces the AKC's passivity in regard to puppy mills. Dogs are abused in order to mass-produce puppies, pet shops sell the unsound and unsocialized products, and the AKC enables them to operate by issuing breed papers without investigation or discrimination to anyone who pays its fees. There are thousands of puppy mills in the United States, she reports; "pet shops sell about half a million dogs a year, and when you buy a puppy from a pet shop, all you do is perpetuate the suffering of the breeding animals." The climax of the book is the detective's surreptitious visit to a puppy mill, where she finds a starving pregnant golden retriever, barely able to drag herself to her feet, shut up in a shed full of feces that "she'd pitifully tried to confine to one end of the shed"; a male malamute chained outside without shelter, driven by abuse to aggressiveness; and a Norwegian elkhound bitch nursing three puppies "in a space that would have cramped a chihuahua" with a wire floor for droppings to drop through. "She was preparing the merchandise for the clean fiberglass cages of Puppy Luv [a pet store] . . . customers *see* the puppies. But who sees a puppy mill brood bitch? Who even imagines her?"[17]

The new class of owners who took pride in the appearance of their carefully bred dogs naturally wanted to show them off competitively. The first formal dog show in England, held at Newcastle in 1859, was limited to bird dogs. It was promoted by a local sporting gun maker, who offered his guns as prizes; and the entrants were twenty-three pointers and twenty-seven setters. Later the shows were broadened to include other types of dog, which were lumped together as nonsporting breeds. Ultimately, as more and more breeds were added, they had to be placed in classes. A dog show of 1863, including twelve hundred dogs of fifty-four breeds, was said to have "very fairly represented all the varieties now in England." There were nine types of terrier, three types of setter, and the Clumber as well as the springer/cocker spaniel. Two types of retriever were included, as well as the Saint Bernard, the French poodle, and foreign dogs such as the elkhound, the "Australian dog," and a pariah dog from India. The lurcher was too low to appear in a show; the turnspit had disappeared, as well as the Irish wolfhound.

Crufts, the first major British dog show, was established in 1886. In 2001, it drew 20,780 dog entries and 88,000 people. Its American counterpart, the Westminster Kennel Club show, began in New York in 1877, with 1,201 dogs entered; and it has been held every year since. In 2004, 2,500 dogs were entered, representing 162 breeds.

Advocates of dog showing, such as Caras, maintain that the sport promotes respect for dogs and improvement of their quality. It is certainly true that prize dogs are highly valued and carefully looked after, and that they can be extremely beautiful themselves, as well as setting standards that others can aim for. On the other hand, the dogs must make sacrifices for their owners to compete in AKC-sponsored shows. The cocker spaniel's pretty feathered tail is docked; the Doberman's is cut almost to its rump, and its naturally lop ears are cropped to make them prick up in a fierce manner. Grooming for the show ring can be an irksome trial. A wirehaired terrier's naturally long, untidy coat must be carefully stripped to produce the right hard-wire texture and give the dog a neat shape; this means pulling out every dead hair, one by one, from all parts of its body. A professional fox terrier breeder describes the process, with much feeling for human inconvenience but none for canine pain: "A large part of the hair" is wrenched from the dog's body "by main force—a proceeding not without peril when the hair on the tenderer portions of his stomach is attacked. A conscientious dog plucker will spend six or eight hours on the initial grooming of a wire-haired terrier."[18]

Some show dogs live in their owners' homes as companions and members of the family, but others have no life outside the show circuit and little connection with their owners except to aggrandize their egos and incomes. Such dogs spend their lives in shows or traveling between them, in the company of whatever professional handler can best ensure their winning. It is the handler who presents the dog in shows and is responsible for keeping it in top condition through diet and exercise. If one handler does not achieve a satisfactory number of prizes, the dog is shipped off to another one, most likely a stranger.

Jane and Michael Stern describe this life in *Dog Eat Dog: A Very Human*

Book About Dogs and Dog Shows, which examines Mimi Einstein's kennel of prizewinning bullmastiffs. Bullmastiffs were developed in the later nineteenth century for catching poachers on the estates of the landed gentry. Because the mastiff was too slow and not sufficiently aggressive to catch these lawbreakers and the bulldog was too ready to mangle them, gamekeepers crossed the breeds to produce an agile dog strong enough to throw a man to the ground, but pacific enough to hold him without doing bodily harm. The breed continues, even though its function has disappeared. Many of Einstein's dogs live in kennels when they are not on the show circuit and have no close human ties. When one of her 160-pound bullmastiffs was admitted to a house for the first time, he peed on the furniture, knocked over a coffee table covered with china, and ripped up pillows—charging around so fast that he could not be stopped. He "had no idea what a home was, having lived his life in kennel runs and [traveling] crates."

At the annual American Bullmastiff Association specialty show, held on a treeless field in Rhode Island on an oppressively hot, humid day in July, fourteen bullmastiffs had to run around the show ring in the sun until the judge could make her decision. With their shortened muzzles, bullmastiffs have even more difficulty with heat than most dogs. After the judging, supporters cooled them with blocks of ice, spray bottles of cold water, and chilled blankets. But one competitor failed to respond: he staggered, his eyes went out of focus, and he seemed about to drop from heatstroke. Everyone gathered to hold frozen washcloths to his belly and ice cubes to his testicles and rectum, and finally he was able to walk to his air-conditioned van. There is a curious discrepancy between the effort expended to revive the dog and the indifference to his welfare that placed him at risk in the first place. Einstein entrusts her dogs to handlers who are not scrupulous about the techniques they use to impress the judge, such as provoking a dog into alertness by yanking on its choke collar or shouting in its face. Yet she will not sell a puppy without a searching interview with the prospective buyer. Her goal is not profit, for, despite high puppy prices and stud fees, top breeders seldom do better than break even. It is "the perfection of the breed."[19]

The movie *Best in Show* (2000) hilariously lampoons the follies of dog showing, but at the same time it portrays a warm bond between owners and valued dogs. The five doting owners competing for Best in Show at Westminster are a South Carolinian yokel with his bloodhound, two gay men with their shih tzu, a rich blonde and a lesbian trainer with their elegant white poodle, a trailer-trash couple with their Norwich terrier, and two yuppie lawyers with their Weimaraner, Beatrice. Their dogs, each the winner of its group, illustrate the absurdities produced by human manipulation of the natural dog: the drooling, flabby-lipped, dangling-eared bloodhound; the beribboned shih tzu barely visible under its hair; the grotesquely clipped poodle; the tense Weimaraner. Only the homely little Norwich terrier, who will be the winner, looks healthy and undistorted. All the owners attach absurd importance to winning and fuss over their dogs continually to achieve that end. And yet it is manifest that they love their dogs as companions, whether they win or not; and all (with the exception of poor Beatrice, made neurotic by her owners) are happy with each other.

One of the oddities of the dog fancy is the kennel clubs' arrangement of breeds. The American Kennel Club distributes the unmistakably distinctive northern dogs among four of its seven groups: Norwegian elkhounds among hounds; akitas, Samoyeds, and sled dogs (malamutes and Siberian huskies) among working dogs; Pomeranians among toys; and the American Eskimo, chow chow, Finnish spitz, keeshond, schipperke, and Shiba Inu among nonsporting dogs. The nonsporting group, which also includes bichons frises, bulldogs, Dalmatians, and poodles, has in fact no unifying characteristic. The term derives its only meaning from the historical fact that early dog shows featured sporting dogs and relegated all other breeds to a nonsporting category.

In 1948, Clifford Hubbard divided dogs into (1) the greyhound group (sight hounds, including the Italian greyhound), (2) the spitz group (northern dogs, including the Pomeranian), (3) the mastiff group (the French and English bulldogs and the pug, as well as large mastiff types); (4) the sheepdog group (corgis as well as collies), (5) the spaniel group (bird dogs and toy spaniels), (6) the hound group (scent hounds), and (7) the terrier group (including toy terriers as well as larger ones and the poodle).[20] Bruce Fogle offers a modified version in his *New Encyclopedia of the Dog*: (1) primitive dogs (such as the dingo, Ibizan hound, and basenji), (2) sight hounds, (3) spitz-type dogs, (4) scent hounds, (5) gun (bird or sporting) dogs, (6) terriers, (7) livestock and guarding dogs (herding dogs and mastiffs), and (8) companion dogs (toys and various larger dogs).

Even the most logical classifications, however, reveal that it is impossible to fit all breeds neatly into categories. While there is justification for incorporating the toy breeds into the groups from which they were developed, as Hubbard does, it seems incongruous to class a pug with a mastiff. Fogle's eighth group is too miscellaneous to be useful. Some breeds would fit equally well into two categories: the dachshund, for example, has both scent hound and terrier characteristics. Louis Doberman, aiming to create an ideal dog in the late nineteenth century, combined German terriers (pinschers) for agility with shepherd dogs and rottweilers for strength and guarding ability. Manchester terrier and greyhound were later added to the mix, so that breeds from four major groups contributed to the Doberman.

In 1986, cocker spaniels were the most popular breed in America, as measured by the number of them registered with the AKC, followed by poodles, Labrador retrievers, golden retrievers, German shepherds, chow chows, beagles, miniature schnauzers, dachshunds, and Shetland sheepdogs. The list has remained fairly constant through 2004, the last year for which statistics are available. Cockers continued to head the list until 1989 and remained among the top ten until 1998, when they dropped to thirteenth place. Poodles, Labrador and golden retrievers, German shepherds, beagles, and dachshunds continue to place in the top ten every year. Rottweilers appeared in seventh place in 1988, had moved to second place from 1992 through 1997, but dropped to eleventh in 2000 and sixteenth in 2004: people were attracted by the idea of a powerful guard dog, but lost enthusiasm when they realized that these strong, dominant animals could prove dangerous. Dalmatians and Pomeranians each appeared among the top ten for a few years, though Dalmatians have now dropped to eightieth place. Yorkshire terriers have been among the top ten from 1995, Chihuahuas from 1998, boxers from 1999, and shih tzus from 2000. The Labrador retriever moved into first place in 1991 and remained there. As of 2004, Labrador retrievers were the most popular breed, with almost three times as many registrations as the runners-up, golden retrievers; these were followed by German shepherds, beagles, Yorkshire terriers, dachshunds, boxers, poodles, shih tzus, and Chihuahuas.[21]

9

———

Dogs Used as Surrogates
for Humans

THE INCREASING WARMTH of our feelings for dogs since the nineteenth century has intensified our tendency to project human qualities
onto these animals who are so close to us and to find in them the virtues and
feelings we long for in our own lives. Proud owners of pedigreed dogs see in
them the honor and chivalry that are supposed to characterize human aristocrats. Fiction writers use dogs to act out simplistic plots that call forth pleasurable emotions in readers or confirm their wishful view of the world.
Canine characters are easier to manipulate than humans because their minds
and life situations are simpler, and it is more plausible to project thoughts and
feelings onto characters that cannot speak for themselves. Love of dogs
prompts writers to make them into junior people who express the writers'
own prejudices as well as values. As most nineteenth-century authorities on
dogs were upper-class men, they projected onto canine characters their valua-
tion of their own nation over others, of upper- over lower-class people, and
of men over women.

Anglo-Saxon dogs were supposed to be superior to those of other nations,
just as pedigreed dogs were superior to mongrels. Taplin claimed that British
dogs of all types "are generally admitted superior to the production of every
other" country: British foxhounds excel all others in speed and perseverance,
British setters in sagacity, British bulldogs in invincible and vindictive ardor,
and so forth. An article in the *Times* of February 29, 1864, dilated on "the

difference of the Irish from the English dog. In England—a comparatively honest and justice-loving land—the canine race bark at the thief; but in the sister isle they give warning of the approach of the police! . . . The number of worthless dogs in Ireland is prodigious, one or more of them being kept at every cabin. . . . Being half-starved at home, since the failure of the potatoes, they go prowling over the country at night in search of food," killing sheep. Besides warning night-prowling criminals by barking at the constabulary patrol, they assist in poaching: "their owners overrun the country hunting game, especially during the hours of worship on Sunday."[1]

The contrast was even more marked when the alien dogs belonged to another race, such as American Indians. According to Dr. B. S. Barton, Indian dogs "have less fidelity and will steal from their masters" and in general are "much more imperfect" animals even than European mongrels. Mrs. R. Lee claimed that white people's dogs would easily hunt down and kill Indians' dogs but would then plunge into water as soon as possible "to rid themselves of the contamination caused by such contact." At the same time, Indians were blamed for treating these undeserving animals cruelly, although in fact they might be kind or cruel just as whites might. Nathaniel Southgate Shaler, a scientist at Harvard, was so convinced that "the dog of the savage is in all countries much like his master—a creature with few arts and unaccustomed to subdue his rude native impulses," that he ignorantly denied that it was used in hunting.[2] Actually, dogs such as the basenjis of Central Africa compare favorably with our own "civilized" hounds and bird dogs.

In Edward Peple's story "Feud to the Death," the superiority of Anglo-Saxon to Mexican is demonstrated in the conflict between Joe and Tonque, the dogs of the cowboy Chip Moseby and the mixed-race camp cook, Greaser Sam. When Chip brought Joe to the camp, Tonque bullied him and nipped him in tender spots. Good manners prevented Joe from resisting, for his master had not given him permission and "somewhere through the mongrel's many breeds ran the blood of a gentleman dog." (Even in America the canine hero has to be a gentleman, regardless of his ancestry, and he shows his gentlemanly virtue by improbably extreme obedience to his master's wishes.) Only when provoked by Greaser Sam's gibes at Joe's cowardice did Chip set up a fight between the two dogs, in which Joe of course routed the Mexican dog.[3]

Gentlemen's dogs were supposed to recognize upper-class superiority as surely as their masters did. Where Buffon accurately noted that dogs follow their masters' attitudes toward people, Taplin endowed his dog with the ability to discriminate "at first sight, between the higher classes and the lower orders of society . . . the former he receives at the door, and conducts to the family-parlor . . . with the politesse of a courtier; the latter he keeps at a proper distance, with the stern look and rigid eye of a sheriff's-officer." Observing his retriever strike up an acquaintance with a ratcatcher and his dog and then cut his new friends when his master appeared, the zoologist George Romanes concluded that dogs understood "the idea of caste."[4]

The pointer hero of Roy Norton's story "Bill" is a natural racist. Having somehow become stranded among Alaskan Indians, he is overjoyed to be found by two white men: " 'I've had a devil of a time here in this strong-smelling Indian village,' Bill said by way of conversation, 'and am mighty glad you came along. I'm hungry to talk to, and be with, my own people again.' " After Bill is lamed in a dog fight, his new white owners leave him for the winter with a half-caste missionary, who must have been "a good man . . . because Bill forgave that half-strain of Indian blood and took to him." "Dog and half-breed, both were gentlemen." Nevertheless, Bill wondered pathetically when his white masters left, "What have I done? Haven't I always tried to do the square thing? Aren't we pardners? Did I ever show the white feather?"[5] The dog is recognized as an equal partner because he is virile, gentlemanly, and (symbolically) white.

Robert Michael Ballantyne's *The Dog Crusoe,* a standard boy's adventure tale that centers on the bond between a superdog and a manly man, is imbued with the conventional prejudices of its time, especially derisive hostility toward Indians, who are generally referred to as savages. As a pup, Crusoe was seized by a squaw, smashed with a stick, and held, still living, over a fire to singe off his hair before being thrown into a pot to be cooked. He was saved in the nick of time by Dick, a manly young hunter who recognized him as a white leader's dog. When Crusoe grew up, he "learned to treat the eccentricities of Indians and their curs with dignified contempt." Crusoe is a typical idealized Victorian dog: a sagacious Newfoundland, of a breed whose love for its master "is beyond calculation or expression." He is not only an expert retriever and gundog, but can also dig like a terrier and run like a husky. He can find a half-tamed mustang among a herd of wild ones, seize its trailing halter, and lead it, bucking and galloping, back to Dick. At first Crusoe communicates with eyes, tail, and ears *as if* he were speaking, but then "He said to Dick as plain as dog could say it, slowly and emphatically: 'That's my opinion precisely, Dick. You're the dearest, most beloved, jolliest fellow that ever walked on two legs, you are; and whatever's your opinion is mine, no matter *how* absurd it may be.' "[6] The man and the miracle dog validate each other's worth.

The association of dogs with men, developed when hunting was glorified as the highest calling of dogs and a particularly noble one for (male) humans, has persisted long after hunting ceased to be a major preoccupation even of men. Victorian authorities continued to proclaim dogs' affinity with manly men, despite the fact that Queen Victoria herself set the tone for dog-loving British society. Men were supposed to be more capable of appreciating the dog's courage and readiness to follow a strong leader, while women small-mindedly resented its disruption of domestic order and cleanliness. Hamerton contrasts the impeccably graceful cat, the woman's favorite, with the boisterous dog, whose carelessness about noise and dirt repels women, but whose magnanimous and heroic qualities win "the serious sympathies of noble and generous-hearted men." When Max Beerbohm's irresistible belle Zuleika Dobson paused to caress a big bulldog, she did so merely to arouse envy in the man who loved her. "Of course," she "did not care for dogs. One has never known a good man to whom dogs are not dear"; but the only "woman who is really kind to dogs is . . . one who has failed to inspire sympathy in men. For the attractive woman, dogs are mere dumb and restless brutes—possibly dangerous, certainly soulless."[7]

Captain, the large sporting dog who narrates Julia Maitland's popular children's book *Cat and Dog; or Memoirs of Puss and the Captain*, embodies the superiority of male virtues, in contrast to the gentle, graceful, modest femininity of Puss. He fights with and defeats a mastiff who flew at her, presumably motivated chiefly by the male dog's drive to protect his turf and property; but the episode impels her to acknowledge his superiority: "I am content to shun danger and avoid blame; but it is your nature to meet danger and to court praise. . . . It is a capital thing that there should be such as you, able and willing to defend the weak, and to stand up for the right without fear of consequences. It is your proper part, and I am truly grateful to you for acting it so nobly as you did yesterday."[8]

An anthology of 1946, mistitled *All the Best Dog Poems,* is filled with verses on the theme that boys (not girls) want and need dogs, which their mothers consider dirty and generally undesirable. In Edgar A. Guest's contribution, "The Joy of a Dog," Ma says a dog is "too much care" and "will scatter germs an' hair," while Pa rejoices: "it's a sign he's growin' up / When he is longin' for a pup."[9] Boy-dog memoirs are a classic form, while the equally strong bond that girls can form with dogs goes uncelebrated.

Men continue to assert their particular bond with dogs and use it to confirm their superior strength of character. Traditional greeting cards into the 1970s represented men and boys with dogs to suggest reliability, enterprise, or healthy activity. Girls and women appeared with kittens to suggest prettiness, sweetness, and caprice. James Thurber envisioned the human-canine bond as arising between dog and man, even though by his own account his mother was the particular protector and lover of dogs in his family. "When the first man brought the first dog to his cave (no doubt over and above his wife's protests), there began an association by which Man has enormously profited." Ted Patrick contented himself with pointing out that everyone he knows who has a really good relationship with dogs has "large, confident, strong hands and a soft, controlled, nonshrill voice." If a dog "senses strength in a person's hands, he realizes that person's control over him and ability to help him, and thus respects him." Unless a woman can somehow modulate her shrill voice and give authority to her delicate little hands, she will tend "to be at a disadvantage with dogs, except small dogs."[10]

Only toy dogs were supposed to be compatible with women, and accordingly they were disparaged, even denied the status of real dogs. Captain A. H. Trapman extolled all dogs—except for "petty . . . mean, selfish and jealous" lapdogs, pampered by fashionable ladies who share the same contemptible qualities. The better type of dog finds women uncongenial. When the master of an upstanding collie was killed in the war, his flighty, selfish widow took over the dog and spoiled him into an "oversized lapdog." He became greedy, selfish, bad-tempered, and jealous. But when an old friend of his late master showed him the dead man's cigarette case, "the dog hung his head low, then, in an apparent agony of remorse, he lifted up his nose to the ceiling and howled as if his heart would break." From then on, he would have nothing to do with his mistress, and three days later he was found drowned in a lake. Probably "remorse and shame were strong enough still to make him prefer suicide to the pampered life of the pet of a woman of no account, and whom he well knew to be of no account."[11]

Hugh Walpole's "The Whistle" takes its point from the assumed natural connection between superior dogs and virile men. Charlie brings home a magnificent Alsatian, to whom his spoiled little wife takes an immediate dislike. He puts the dog in the care of Blake, their strong, silent chauffeur, who finds in the dog "all the things that he admired—loyalty, strength, courage, self-reliance, fidelity, comradeship, and, above all, sobriety of speech and behavior." The Alsatian finds at last the master he has been seeking in Blake, and Blake finds the comrade he has been needing in the dog; theirs is manifestly the only good relationship in the household. Blake, Charlie, and the Alsatian form an alliance from which their wives and the women's Sealyham terrier are excluded. It is broken when the Sealyham attacks the Alsatian, who inadvertently bites Blake when he tries to separate them, and Charlie's wife seizes this pretext to insist that the Alsatian is dangerous and must go. Two fine masculine lives are wasted because of an upper-class woman's silly pettiness and her husband's weakness.[12]

Robert Louis Stevenson claimed that the stock manly virtues can be found in their purest form only among dogs and schoolboys: "I have known dogs, and I have known school heroes that, set aside the fur, could hardly have been told apart, and if we desire to understand the chivalry of old, we must turn to the school playfields or the dungheap where the dogs are trooping."[13] This is certainly true in fiction, if not in life. Often canine characters are made to serve as models for human masculinity, displaying courage and chivalry more unequivocally than men generally do. The simpler characters and simpler situations of dogs make these models more plausible.

Jack London's famous dog heroes embody the traditional manly virtues of courage, fighting ability, endurance, and leadership, even though he set them in an up-to-date context of the Nietzschean morality of power. He rendered his canine protagonists' thoughts and feelings quite authentically, while showing their kinship with humans; but he shaped their lives and consciousness to endorse the strength he admired. He set up situations in which the ability to survive in a harshly competitive—a "dog eat dog"—world is the ultimate value, and invited us to identify with the protagonist who could make the grade. More clearly than humans in civilized society can do, the dogs enact the struggle by which superior animals establish hierarchical order by mastering inferior ones. A dog can openly assert his power to establish mastery over others without incurring the guilt of a human subject to civilized law; he is only expressing his nature. Yet Buck and White Fang embody qualities that are admired in men.

Buck in *The Call of the Wild*, like the dilettante Humphrey Van Weyden in *The Sea Wolf*, is stripped of the comfortable certainties of his life and becomes a better male animal as a result of his hardships. He thinks more or less like a dog, but functions symbolically as a junior man. Everyone who looks at him recognizes his natural physical superiority, which, it is implied, means his spiritual superiority as well. He goes through horrible, brutalizing experiences; but they are salutary because they make a "man" of him. Buck started out as a 140-pound Saint Bernard–collie mix in his prime, living a privileged life on a rich estate, which he ruled with "the dignity that comes of good living and universal respect." But then he was stolen and sold to meet the demand for big dogs to pull sleds in the Alaskan Gold Rush, and his complacency and civilized values were stripped away. He had always been able to restrain humans with a menacing growl; now men ignored his displeasure and beat him into understanding that he must obey whatever hard orders men gave him. In a hideous early scene, a breaker clubbed him again and again, finally clubbing him directly on the nose, until he submitted to accepting a pat on the head, a drink, and meat from the breaker's hand. London denounced cruelty to dogs, but he subjected his heroes to dreadful suffering to prove their toughness, and he described it with enthusiastic vividness.

Once at the Arctic camp, Buck was taught by the whip and punishment from experienced dogs to pull a sled and to steal food.

This first theft marked Buck as fit to survive in the hostile Northland environment. It marked his adaptability, his capacity to adjust himself to changing conditions, the lack of which would have meant swift and terrible death. It marked, further, the decay . . . of his moral nature, a vain thing and a handicap in the ruthless struggle for existence. It was all well enough in the Southland, under the law of love and fellowship, to respect private property and personal feelings; but in the Northland, under the law of club and fang, whoso took such things into account was a fool.

As he became stronger and more assertive, Buck challenged the lead dog, Spitz, and finally beat him in combat. He insisted on taking over the lead position, even though his owner tried repeatedly to place a more experienced dog there; and he immediately became the perfect leader—accurate in judging, quick in acting, forceful "in giving the law and making his mates live up to it."

Sold to a group of incompetents, Buck was rescued by John Thornton, who was as virile as Buck was himself (and as oblivious to females). Thornton, a considerate master who attended to his dogs' emotional needs, aroused passionate love in Buck for the first time. Like a nobly devoted Victorian dog, "He would lie by the hour, eager, alert, at Thornton's feet, looking up into his face, dwelling upon it, studying it, following with keenest interest each fleeting expression." When Thornton thoughtlessly bet that Buck could start a thousand-pound sled and urged him on—"As you love me, Buck. As you love me"—Buck pulled, strained, and succeeded. Then the buddies triumphed—Thornton wept, Buck affectionately took his hand in his teeth, and the spectators "drew back to a respectful distance," realizing they must not interrupt this blissful communion. Later, living with Thornton in the wilderness, Buck reverted more and more toward his wolf ancestors. But he was a super wolf, able to kill a great bull moose all by himself. And he retained a dog's chivalry, or rather the chivalry that men attribute to dogs: when he killed a half-grown calf, "he wished strongly for larger and more formidable quarry." Ultimately Buck joined the local wolf pack and soon, of course, became its leader. He came, after all, out of white American civilization. At the same time, he is the classic American hero who finds freedom in the wilderness, where there is no artificial authority and natural powers can find their full expression.

London's second canine hero, White Fang, who established dominance over every other dog in an Indian village by fighting better and more ruthlessly than any, instinctively recognized the superiority of men to dogs (he accepted all men as gods), of men to women (a piece of meat tossed him by his harsh master was "worth more, in some strange way, than a dozen pieces of meat from the hand of a squaw"), and of whites to Indians (whites were superior gods). He was bought by a sadist who kept him caged and successively pitted dogs against him, and killed every opponent until he could not deal with a bulldog's grip. London recognizes the cruel victimization of the dogs, yet he cannot resist endorsing it to the extent of holding up the indomitable White Fang for admiration. Finally White Fang was rescued by a man who tamed him with love and made him his lead dog: "The wisest as well as the strongest dog was the leader, and the team obeyed him and feared him. That White Fang should quickly gain this post was inevitable."[14] In London's world, the best male animal always wins.

The heroic dogs of Albert Payson Terhune, London's slightly younger contemporary, likewise promote manly—or rather, gentlemanly—virtues, though in a softer way and without the Nietzschean philosophy. Terhune insisted on his canine heroes' courage, fighting ability, and natural superiority, although these appear less starkly in the normal civilized settings of his stories. Their superiority was based on social class rather than genetic endowment; Americans often use dog stories to express the pleasurable snobbery that they would be abashed to express in relation to humans. Terhune's highbred collies are superior in every way to the mongrels they meet. Lad, his "greatest" dog, was obviously an aristocrat even as a half-grown puppy. When he attacked a burglar, he stopped when the thief fell and broke his leg, for "the sporting instincts of a hundred generations of thoroughbreds cried out to him not to mangle the defenseless." Lad was "thoroughbred in spirit as well as in blood. He had the benign dignity that was a heritage from endless generations of high-strain ancestors. He had, too, the gay courage of a d'Artagnan, and an uncanny wisdom. Also—who could doubt it, after a look into his mournful brown eyes—he had a Soul." And with all his wonderful qualities, Lad was a true dog and worshiped Master. Both he and his mate, Lady, accepted Terhune not just as their "mere owner but the absolute Master. To them he was the unquestioned lord of life and death, the hearer and answerer, the Eternal Law; his the voice that must be obeyed, whatever the command."

Lad's thoroughbred spirit ensured his chivalric forbearance to the weaker sex. When Lady arrived as a puppy, he felt "the natural impulse of the thoroughbred—brute or human—to guard the helpless"; when she grew up, he fell in love with her and let her do anything. Alas for them, Master agreed to take care of a friend's collie, appropriately named Knave, whose bad character was revealed by his prick ears (a collie should have tulip ears—three quarters erect). Since Master forbade him to fight Knave, Lad had to watch the interloper flirt with Lady. Finally he could restrain himself no longer and attacked Knave, who howled with pain and fear like "any gutter cur" and ran away. Lad, the soul of chivalry, remained devoted to Lady despite her inconstancy and general unworthiness. She got tired of devotedly caring for their pup, but Lad's compassionate solicitude never ended. Accordingly, the pup grew to love him as he had never loved Lady and also valued his sire's discipline and firm kindliness over her sporadic affection. Lad was wise, loving, patient, and disciplined; Lady, the only bitch in the story, was fickle, selfish, and irresponsible.

It was not enough for Lad to be dauntlessly brave; he had to match the virile ideal of fighting ability as well, even though collies were not bred for fighting and are not particularly well armed in body or temperament. As in old-fashioned adventure stories where gentlemen are always braver and better fighters than common men, highly bred dogs have to be braver and better than mongrels. Terhune reiterates that thoroughbred collies are great fighters because of their wolf heritage (as if this were not shared by all dogs), while mongrels are cowardly and inept. In *Buff, a Collie*, a huge, vicious black mongrel lunged at the hero's belly, a maneuver that would destroy the average dog; but his "opponent was a collie. And, in the back of his brain, though never in his chivalrous heart, a collie is forever reverting to his own wolf ancestors." So he eluded the bite and killed the mongrel.[15]

The pit bull terrier (spiritual successor to the nineteenth-century bulldog) actually has the courage and fighting prowess to make it a perfect emblem of macho virility; in life and fiction, it is a gratifying surrogate for men who wish they were equally valiant. Its blind fearlessness and tenacity can be interpreted as superlative courage, resolution, and unshakable loyalty. Rudyard Kipling's "Garm—a Hostage" idealizes the bull terrier as the manly man's dog and contrasts him with an officer's fat, contemptible retriever, who dotes on his master but disregards his call and cares mainly for food.

The original pit bull (or bull and terrier) was developed for dogfighting, a lowlife dog for a lowlife sport. Many disdained it as a ferocious brute, lacking in all the higher qualities of dogs. But at the same time, its zeal and aptitude for fighting gave it a heroic aura that impressed men preoccupied with virility. So raffish young gentlemen took it up, as well as toughs. They demanded a smart-looking, all-white dog, and James Hinks developed one in 1860. Once it was enthusiastically adopted by fashionable men, the dog became a status symbol and was endowed with the qualities of an idealized aristocrat. According to its breed club, the bull terrier "was bred by gentlemen for gentlemen, for those who had a great sense of fair play, and who scorned the liar and the deceiver in any game. The dog was taught to defend himself and his master courageously, yet he was not to seek or provoke a fight—and so the white variety became known as 'the white cavalier.' "[16] The dog's upper-class admirers could indulge their snobbery and at the same time imagine themselves to be just as tough as any fighter in the slums.

Stories about pit bulls are contrived to provide their readers with these contradictory gratifications: the canine hero must display blind courage and fighting prowess (which are supposedly idolized by all men), but must also be amiable and highbred, since thuggish, abused street fighters are not appealing subjects. Although he is a show champion and a pet, the aristocrat, as in Terhune, must fight better than the professionals. In R. G. Kirk's "White Monarch and the Gas-House Pup," a gentleman is provoked by a lowlife's insult to pit his show champion bull terrier against the other man's champion fighter, Grip, the Gas-House Pup. So he puts his good-natured, pampered pet through the cruel training necessary for a fighting dog, including everincreasing hours of circling on a treadmill, so that he will develop "the power to endure under monotonous suffering—and endure—and endure—and endure." For five hours, "Shoulder to shoulder, breast to breast, brisket to brisket . . . fangs to fangs, those two beautiful brutes fought," until White

Monarch broke Grip's foreleg. Grip continued to fight nimbly on his broken leg, striking the male audience with awe by this display of "the noblest attribute in dogs and men—unbreakable courage." In the end it is a draw between two dogs half dead with exhaustion. The two owners almost fight also (demonstrating that the aristocratic dandy has become a Man), but they are dissuaded and shake hands with mutual respect.[17]

The average sentimental reader must further be assured that putting dogs through such an ordeal is compatible with loving them. A good trainer in the story deeply loves dogs and his "heart broke when he lost his pets in the pit," but he has convinced himself that "given their choice, they would have asked him to be allowed to come to their end in the rapture of deadly combat." In another tale, the owner of a redoubtable fighting bitch "could watch a pit dog take its punishment in a fair fight," but "was tender as a woman where animals were concerned."[18]

Hunting stories naturally provide fine opportunities for dogs to promote masculine values, especially since the rigid rules of hunting make it easy to place canine heroes in clear-cut moral situations in which they come close to disgrace and can clear themselves by one decisive action. Reck, a promising young setter in Ben Ames Williams's "Mine Enemy's Dog," is victimized and misjudged, but in the end triumphantly justifies himself by his display of gentlemanly virtue. Out of a foolish desire to conciliate Proutt, a sadistic dog trainer with a grudge against him, the game warden Westley hands his beloved Reck over to him for breaking (as training is called here). Proutt seizes his opportunity to destroy "Reck's honor and reputation and life" by deliberately training the dog to hunt deer—an awful crime in the hunting society of this story. This distresses the dog greatly, causing him to act furtive and consequently to be suspected of being the dog who is killing deer in the neighborhood. If he is indeed guilty, his master will have to shoot him, although he "would as soon have shot one of his own blood as the dog he loved." But Reck proves to be virtuously going after birds only, so his master can triumph: "Didn't you know that you could not kill the soul and the honor of a dog like mine? Reck is a thoroughbred." Not surprisingly, it turns out that Proutt's hound was the deer hunter.[19] The owner loves his dog and attaches great importance to him, and yet he feels neither doubts nor guilt about subjecting the dog to needless suffering or condemning him to death for failing to meet arbitrary human standards. The callous injustice of the owner is wiped out by the dog's inspiring display of virtue.

As conventionally masculine values are increasingly being questioned, dog fiction is no longer dominated by canine heroes who are models of courage in a tough world; now dogs are more apt to be models of the softer domestic virtues in a blandly wholesome world where everything works out as we would like it to. Even sporting dog stories may focus on heartwarming family values rather than the heroic aspects of sport. In Vereen Bell's "Brag Dog," a poor black man works really hard and trains the apparently worthless pointer he's been given so that it wins him the prize at the field trials and he can buy his crippled wife a wheelchair. In Richard Harding Davis's "The Bar Sinister," an abused fighting bull terrier mix gets some sympathetic training and becomes a top show dog; the genes of his father, a super champion, so dominate those of his street-dog mother that he has the satisfaction of defeating the father who had callously abandoned her. After his triumph, he rescues his broken-down old mother and brings her into his new luxurious home.[20]

Twentieth-century American writers have taken up the Victorian association of dogs with the wholesome home in order to celebrate the traditional values of a simpler and better time. The cocker spaniel Spot is an important character in the Dick and Jane primers, included in more stories than Mother and Father combined. These readers—which appeared in the 1930s, dominated 80 percent of the market in the 1950s, and remained on the scene until 1970—provided role models for first graders that they fondly retained into adulthood. Dick and Jane live in a prosperous home in a friendly suburban neighborhood, sheltered from the problems and complexities of the real world. Everyone happily fulfills his or her role: Father as the head of the family; Mother as the capable homemaker; six-year-old Dick as the responsible, enterprising boy; five-year-old Jane as the helpmate-in-training; and Spot as Dick's playful dog, always eager to be part of the action. Spot is Dick's dog, but he, like Father and Dick, is part of a family rather than an individual achiever. The three male characters no longer represent stereotypical virility, but togetherness.[21]

A major appeal of boy-dog memoirs is that they commemorate an earlier time when life was more innocent, secure, and simple—not only because the narrator was a carefree boy, but because he lived in an old-fashioned small town. Willie Morris and his fox terrier Skip grew up in a Mississippi town where everyone was neighborly and life was all games and harmless practical jokes and Skip was recognized by "everybody of any consequence." When Farley Mowat's setter mix Mutt was killed by a car, it marked "an end to the best years that I had lived."[22] The dog symbolizes the idyllic state of boyhood; when he dies, the boy becomes aware that this state cannot last.

Lassie in Eric Knight's *Lassie Come-Home* is more dramatically devoted to her boy than any real-life dog, crossing "a thousand miles of tor and brae, of snow and rain and fog and sun; of wire and thistle and thorn and flint and rock to tear the feet" to rejoin her beloved Joe. Like the other boys' dogs, she is associated with a traditional nonurban environment, where people are responsible, unequivocally honest, and respectful, and the only bad character is a shifty kennel man from London who mishandles Lassie. Moreover, she plays an important part in maintaining family harmony, which disintegrated after the father's inability to find work made it necessary to sell her to the Duke of Rudling. "When they had had Lassie," Joe thinks, "the home had been comfortable and warm and fine and friendly. Now that she was gone nothing went right. If Lassie were only back again, then everything once more would be as it used to be." His feeling is supported by the story. Once Lassie was back in their house, his mother bustled happily to put his father's dinner on the table the moment he came home, and his father came home cheerful, asked about Joe's day at school, and flattered his mother. Through Joe, a change that presumably resulted from his father's new job and steady income is attributed to Lassie.

In addition to her domestic virtues, Lassie has the high breeding of Terhune's dogs, together with the fighting ability that was supposed to go with it. Although she belonged to a poor mining family, Lassie was a show-quality collie. When she was attacked by two sturdy working sheepdogs in the course of her journey, she vanquished them despite her exhaustion, because "She had blood. She was a pure-bred dog, and behind her were long generations of the proudest and best of her kind. . . . where the mongrel dog will whine and slink away, the pure-bred will stand with uncomplaining fearlessness."[23] At the same time that the story appeals to democratic sentiment through its upstanding working-class human characters, it appeals to snobbery with its aristocratic dog.

As Lassie's story developed in film and television—a film of *Lassie Come-Home* in 1943, followed by eight sequels and a television series that ran from 1954 through 1973—she and her people developed increasingly into models of fifties family values. She also became a superdog, not only devoted and courageous but so intelligent that she regularly saved her family and friends from disaster. Thus she fulfills the sentimental fantasy of a dog who is capable of understanding complex situations, responding to elaborate directions from humans, and replying in woofs that are as meaningful as words—and who nevertheless thinks of nothing but service to people. In "Guide Dog," a 1964 episode in the television series, Timmy (an excruciatingly cute, polite, and obliging little boy) and Lassie rush to help their friends, a blind man and his guide dog, Duke, when a careless motorcyclist runs into them. Although the two seem to be uninjured, the dog refuses to reassume his harness. The veterinarian can find nothing physically wrong with Duke and concludes he must have been too emotionally traumatized to carry on his work. What can be done, since we cannot reason with a dog? But Timmy has an idea: "Even if we can't reason with Duke, maybe Lassie can." Timmy and Lassie work together to rebuild Duke's confidence, but when Lassie brings his harness, he again shies away, and Timmy cannot figure out what to do. Fortunately, Lassie can: she pushes her own body into the harness, and Duke, encouraged by her example, accepts it. That night, Timmy kneels by his bedside and prays that he and Lassie will succeed in rehabilitating Duke. As the two big dogs are sitting beside him, we see a row of three pious, benevolent faces, presided over by Mom.

T. Coraghessan Boyle hilariously deflated the Lassie mystique in his burlesque "Heart of a Champion." Lassie comes running to Mom and Dad, who instantly interpret her barks: "Timmy's trapped under a pine tree out by the old Indian burial ground . . . a mile and a half past the north pasture." Dad sends Lassie to stand watch over Timmy while he and Mom go for Dr. Walker, and the scene shifts to Timmy, unable to move, in a valley that is just about to be flooded by a bursting dam. A scruffy coyote slinks up and starts to gnaw on Timmy's hand. But then Lassie comes bounding up, accompanied by loud heroic music. The coyote looks up at her—and her "look of offended AKC morality" dissolves. "She skids to a halt, drops her tail and approaches him, a buttery gaze in her golden eyes." While the dam bursts and a wall of water moves into the valley toward Timmy, the two canids dash away together, "the white-tipped tail retreating side by side with the hacked and tick-blistered gray one—wagging like raggled [sic] banners as they disappear into the trees at the top of the rise."[24]

Reincarnated in a 1993 film, *Lassie,* the superdog unerringly attaches herself to the family that needs her, a tense group in conflict over their move from Baltimore to the country. She reconciles the troubled boy to his family and his new life and brings everyone into harmony. Since she has somehow acquired the ability to herd sheep like the best professional, she enables the urban family to adopt the more wholesome lifestyle of sheep ranchers. She also dispatches a wolf and twice saves her boy's life, as well as her family's flock. And through it all, she retains the appearance of a show dog, keeping her luxuriant white ruff impeccable through every stressful situation.[25]

People increasingly need affirmations of the old-fashioned virtues, as these seem to be disappearing in the modern world; and it was always more plausible to attribute them to dogs than humans. As Garber astutely points out, "The dog becomes the repository of those model human properties that we have cynically ceased to find among humans. Where today can we find the full panoply of William Bennett's *Book of Virtues*—from Courage and Responsibility to Loyalty and Family Values—but in Lassie and Beethoven and Millie and Checkers and Spot?"[26] Dogs can set an example of traditional values for humans because they happily continue to play the role they always have; their characters and attitudes do not change, they dislike innovation and accept authority, and they are untroubled by moral complexities.[27]

Dogs now represent goodness as often as they do virility. And alongside the macho stories there is a feminized type with equally stereotyped values, where canine heroes are preternaturally sweet, pious, and obliging, and live in a benign world in which virtually everyone is well-meaning and everything works out for the best. Stories in anthologies such as Beth Brown's *All Dogs Go to Heaven* overflow with piety and goodwill, both canine and human. All dogs are devoted and friendly, and all human hearts warm to them. In

Brown's title story, her deceased fox terrier, Hobo, reminisces with other dogs in the pet cemetery about his life with his mistress, when they were all in all to each other: during his last illness, he would lie beside her, "sleepless, thinking what would happen to her if I left her. Who would take care of her . . . once I was gone?" She buried Hobo with his clothes and every toy he had ever had, her own red jacket, a down pillow, and "our little black Bible in case I [that is, the dog] forgot my prayers." In Nancy Byrd Turner and Gertrude Nichols's "The Great Penborough Race," Balto not only leads his sled team to victory and responsibly prevents them from ruining the race by chasing a cat, he is a great friend of children; even though he is exhausted from his race and still in harness, he gratifies them by performing the trick they taught him of walking around in a circle on his hind legs. In Dodie Smith's *The 101 Dalmatians,* all the decent characters, human and canine, put themselves out to help the family of the "young married" Dalmatian protagonists. Although the male human who belongs to them is a high-powered financier busy negotiating an important business deal, he is happy to spend his day at home feeding their puppies.[28]

Endings are always happy, however improbable, and even death is not painful. If a woman takes in a miserable stray, he will develop into a marvelously sleek and self-confident dog that will beg and run errands so as to support her when she becomes bedridden (Elsie Noble Caldwell, "Pickpocket, Financier"). If poor children face losing their Great Dane because their family cannot afford to feed him, they will find a valuable portrait that can be sold to pay for his meals (Alice Dalgliesh, "Meals for Mickey"). If a wounded soldier lies waiting to die under the wreckage of his tank, he will be saved by the ghost of the cocker mix he had as a boy, who digs around the tank so he finds hope to climb out and be found by stretcher bearers; they, too, were guided by the dog, whose ghost was summoned by the prayers of a nurse (Gladys Taber, "Sometimes a Man Needs a Friend"). If a firefighter's Dalmatian dies while taking a lifeline to his second master, it is only to have a blissful reunion with his original master in heaven (Howard M. Brier, "The Fire Fighter").[29]

Story after story relates the vindication of an apparently unpromising dog who makes good. The runt of a prize spaniel's litter saves herself from a puppy mill when, placed temporarily with a trainer who keeps chickens, she

spontaneously flushes one and drops; the trainer develops this natural aptitude, and she covers herself with glory at her first field trial competition. Not
only does her success save her, but her prize money saves her trainer's farm
(Taber, "Little Goat"). An unpromising collie pup attaches himself to a shepherd, who finally manages to train him. The shepherd is shot while they are
out with the herd and must go off to seek help, leaving the dog in charge.
The dog not only keeps the herd together, he drives off a wolf and brings the
sheep back to his master over impossible terrain (Frank K. Robertson, "Bone-
head").[30] Such gratifying opportunities can be more plausibly offered to dogs
than to human characters.

Because realistic canine characters are intrinsically limited, authors often attempt to hold their readers' interest with factitious appeals to the feelings,
whether admiration of a hero or warm sympathy with a charmer or evocation
of the nicer world that we would like to live in. They may also draw on sentimental appeals of the opposite kind by dwelling morbidly on canine suffering. Mournful pity can be as pleasurable as complacent optimism, especially
when the suffering innocents are sufficiently removed from readers that there
is no uncomfortable identification with them. Even the virile adventure stories include gratuitous suffering, as authors like London prove the worth of
their canine heroes by subjecting them to pain, which is often related in lingering detail. Ouida's children's classic *A Dog of Flanders* was motivated by a
genuine concern for the poor and animated by a genuine value for dogs. Nevertheless, it piles on sufferings with harrowing excess. Patrasche was a draft
dog whose master, a drunken tinker, overloaded his cart and beat him when
he failed to pull. After two years of this treatment, he collapsed on the road
one hot day, and when the tinker could not revive him with kicks and cudgel
blows, he "left the dying dog there for the ants to sting and the crows to
pick."[31] The few passersby who noticed him went right on, but a crippled old
man and his grandson took pity on Patrasche, dragged him home, and nursed
him back to health. The dog repaid them by insisting on pulling the old
man's milk delivery cart, and for a few years, working within his strength, being caressed instead of beaten, he was happy. But neither he nor his human
friends could be allowed a happy ending. Despite their courageous efforts and
refusal to despair, they were defeated by misfortune after misfortune. In the

end, the boy and the dog were found on the cathedral floor on Christmas morning, dead of cold and hunger.

The first novel written to promote kindness to dogs, (Margaret) Marshall Saunders's *Beautiful Joe: An Autobiography,* is memorable only for the hero's gruesome sufferings at the beginning of his life. Joe, a medium-sized cur born in a stable to a half-starved mother, started out as the property of a sadistic milkman. His master stabbed and clubbed Joe's littermates to death in front of their mother, Joe, and his own children. When the mother died of grief and inadequate feeding and Joe was grieving for her, the man kicked Joe, and when Joe bit him, cut off his tail and both his ears as closely as possible. The kind clergyman who ultimately rescued Joe called him Beautiful in sarcasm because he was so ugly.

Donald McCaig's *Nop's Trials* shows that the taste for canine suffering still persists. McCaig successfully creates the consciousness of his border collie hero, but his subject is the dog's misfortunes: the lengthy series of trials through which he puts Nop. The valuable herding dog is stolen by a sadistic villain and narrowly escapes being used as training material for fighting dogs—that is, being pitted against them for three or four fights until they chew him up. Then he is sold to a dog jobber, who throws him into a truck with a crowd of other frantic dogs, most of them stolen. The cocker spaniels are destined for a National Institutes of Health project, some eight- to nine-year-old Labrador retrievers will go to Harvard for research on aging, young purebred bitches will be sent to puppy mills, young dogs of fashionable breeds will go to pet stores, and others will be sold to furriers, since Dobermans' skins can pass for sealskin and German shepherds' for wolf. Nop goes to Detweiler Labs to be a subject in a retest designed to clear a drug that in its first test had caused cancer in dogs, but he manages to escape by rattling a technician with his sheepdog stare and darting out an open door. McCaig's indictment of the wrongs humans inflict on blameless, loving animals that trust them is obviously justified, and he develops it with moving detail, as when the dogs keep trying to win sympathetic attention by sitting up and offering their paw; but he could have made his point without inflicting such prolonged abuse upon an amiable hero.

So could Ouida and Saunders, but at least these three writers had the moral purpose of denouncing cruelty to dogs. Some others represent dogs as actually seeking suffering, as if it were somehow appropriate to their nature. In Mary E. Wilkins Freeman's "The Lost Dog," a frantic lost dog was taken in by a young stranger who became a famous opera singer and gave him a loving and luxurious home. But when he saw his former master, a poor and mean-spirited old man whose only redeeming feature was that he loved the dog to the limited extent that he could love anything, the dog flew eagerly to him. He was "faithful not only to his old master, but to a nobler thing, the faithfulness which was in himself—and maybe by so doing gained another level in the spiritual evolution of his race." Freeman uses the dog to illustrate supererogatory abstract virtue, even though that is meaningful to humans, not to dogs. Even that factitious satisfaction is denied in R. K. Narayan's painful story "The Blind Dog." A common street dog befriended a blind beggar, sitting with him, coercing passersby to leave him a coin, protecting him from a nasty boy who teased him. Then someone gave the beggar a cord to tie the dog to him. Thus the dog "lost his freedom, completely," while the blind man could move about on his own for the first time and trebled his income. Kicked by his new master whenever he tried to approach another dog, the animal gave up thoughts of "contact with his fellow creatures." Once, when the beggar kicked him for straining to reach a bone, a neighbor felt sorry for the dog and cut his string. He ran off, delighting in his regained freedom. But twenty days later the beggar reappeared with the dog, who had voluntarily returned to him. "Once again there was the dead, despairing look in the dog's eyes," as the man drove him on with shouts and blows.[32]

This is one of the nine out of thirty-one stories in Roger Caras's *Treasury of Great Dog Stories* that is built on gratuitous canine suffering. In the others, Jack London's Buck painfully overstrains himself to save his master's idle bet, an amiable mother dog sees her puppy blinded and killed when her beloved master decides to amuse himself by experimenting on him (Mark Twain's "A Dog's Tale"), a boy's nice little dog is routinely beaten and ultimately flung out the window by the child's drunken father (Stephen Crane's "A Dark-Brown Dog"), a serf's beloved spaniel is killed by command of his selfish old mistress (Ivan Turgenev's "Mumú"), repeated vain attempts to get rid of an annoying dog are presented for our amusement (Ellis Parker Butler's "Getting Rid of Fluff"), a man botches the shooting of his old golden retriever (Dion

Henderson's "Broken Treaty"), a fox terrier made affectionate by the love of a family of children is shot by his owner for being soft (D. H. Lawrence's "Rex"), and an innocent but consistently abused dog serves as the perfect symbol for the victimization of inoffensive Jews throughout history (Sholom Aleichem's "Rabchik, a Jewish Dog").

Ten of the twenty-one stories in Michael J. Rosen's anthology, *The Company of Dogs,* deal with the death of a dog, in one case a particularly painful one, and two more with an aged dog's approaching death. Dogs die in fifteen of the thirty-four stories in Jeanne Schinto's *The Literary Dog.* In Antonya Nelson's "Dog Problems," a husband "accidentally" kills his wife's beloved aged dog by stressing it with an unnecessary bath. In Jim Shepard's "Reach for the Sky," a man rationalizes that the unwanted dog he is bringing to a shelter will find a new home, when in fact it will certainly be euthanized. In Jack Matthews's "The Immortal Dog," an old man is forced by the neighborhood women to kill his big dog, who they claim is a danger to the children; two poisonings and a shooting, described in gruesome detail, fail to do the job. In Lee K. Abbott's "Where Is Garland Steeples Now?" a disturbed Vietnam veteran tells wildly varying tales about a dog he had adopted and loved in Vietnam, but had to kill to save his life. In B. Wongar's "The Dingo," the oppression of an aboriginal family by whites culminates in their pet dingo's being caught in a leg-hold trap. The canine friendship in Doris Lessing's "The Story of Two Dogs" ends with one dog shot for stealing eggs and the other, aged by the loss of his friend, euthanized. After a boy's dog saves his life in Alistair MacLeod's "Winter Dog," the dog becomes too powerful and protective, and the boy's father arranges for a neighbor to shoot him; the dog is fatally hit but dies slowly. Granny and her hostile granddaughter are brought together by a narrow escape in Mary Hood's "How Far She Went," but Granny has to drown her beloved little dog to effect it. In Barbara Nodine's "Dog Stories," a tenderhearted American couple in India drown a series of dogs to save them from worse fates. The dog in Stephanie Vaughn's "Dog Heaven" could always turn a sour day into a joyful one for a little girl and her family and friends; but he was killed, along with all the other dogs on the block, when someone threw poisoned hamburger into every yard. These stories are more sophisticated than those in the earlier anthologies: they examine canine and human character with more honesty and insight and recognize that relationships between dogs and people can bring troubles as well as joy and love. Nevertheless, too many have as their main point the suffering of one or more dogs.[33]

Dan Rhodes's *Timoleon Vieta Come Home: A Sentimental Journey* almost explicitly makes an inoffensive dog the scapegoat for human moral weakness and misery. Timoleon Vieta, the dog and only friend of a forlorn, aging gay man, is taken far from home and abandoned by his owner, who let himself be persuaded by "the Bosnian," an unpleasant young rotter who lives off him in exchange for weekly sex. Throughout the book, the aging man regrets what he did and the dog strives valiantly to return home. In the end, the man is made happy by the return of his most satisfactory young lover. And the dog, starving and exhausted, perks up because he has almost reached home. But at this point, anyone familiar with dog stories is seized by sickening apprehension. Sure enough, the Bosnian catches Timoleon and slits his throat. The dog is the most amiable of the central characters and the only one with a steady, definite purpose—and yet all the humans' prospects improve while he is gratuitously slaughtered. Is the dog being offered up as an appropriate sacrifice to gain happiness for rather undeserving humans?

When stories center on canine characters, their writers too often rely on readers' warm feelings for their subject to carry the fiction. Instead of engaging our feelings with portrayals of individual animals in realistic situations, they draw on a stock of conventional attitudes, stereotyped characters, and contrived plots that automatically elicit comfortable good feelings or pleasurable pity. Where the main characters are dogs, readers are more ready to accept stories in which ruthless fighting ability demonstrates superiority, or limited mortal creatures embody absolute fidelity, or losers regularly get the chance to make good, or good feeling overcomes all problems, or gratuitous suffering evokes virtuous compassion. The stereotyped themes and treatment and the appeal to traditional values in these stories are conducive to an atmosphere of casual racist and sexist prejudices. Bell's "Brag Dog" presents its poor black characters with ostensible sympathy and celebrates the hero's triumph with his unpromising pointer, but in fact it is disfigured throughout by humor based on the ignorant mispronunciations and simple-minded thought processes that Bell attributes to black people. It is fortunate that males are ever-ready to help females in Smith's cloying *101 Dalmatians,* for they are helpless on their own. "Missis" Dalmatian gets hopelessly lost when she goes off by herself and must be rescued by a gallant old spaniel; the male puppies "struggled along bravely" on the long walk from Cruella de Vil's house, "but the girls stumbled and panted and had to have many rests."[34]

10

The Negative Side of Our Friendship with Dogs

NOT EVERYONE, OF course, shares the appreciation of dogs that seems so natural to dog lovers. For some people, dogs are no more than beasts that are particularly conspicuous on the human scene, and it is fatuous, if not impious, to love or value them in anything like human terms. Even people who like dogs find them a convenient source for degrading epithets and comparisons and a convenient embodiment of animal impulses that we would like to deny in ourselves. Hence we routinely abuse women as bitches and villains as dogs and degrade someone by putting him in the doghouse.

Humans are taught to control and conceal appetites such as lust, gluttony, and pugnacity. Dogs are not, and when they indulge them freely in our view, they provide us with a ready source of negative examples for humans. The animality that dogs represent is not necessarily distasteful: those that pursue their doggy concerns in Venetian religious paintings, oblivious to the human subjects' spiritual experience, are attractively portrayed and seem to have been included to bring the sacred events closer to the everyday world that ordinary viewers can understand.[1] But the dogs that participate eagerly in seventeenth-century Dutch representations of sensuality and disorder were probably placed there to reinforce the point that the people in these scenes are behaving like animals rather than rational, moral humans. A large eager dog stands in the foreground of Jacob Jordaens's painting of an Epiphany celebration, embodying the animality of the coarse and fleshy king, the blowsy women, and the vomiting man. Dogs are equally conspicuous in Jordaens's other pictures on this theme, gazing at a bit of food in a child's hand or licking at food-stained linen in a basket or jumping exuberantly at the lap of a drinking man. Jan Steen's roistering tavern scenes usually include a dog either caught up in the general merriment or gazing hopefully at someone in hopes of a handout. Typically, the atmosphere in these paintings is more joyful than censorious, but Steen's recurrent presentations of the disordered household definitely convey a moral warning and usually include misbehaving dogs to highlight human disregard for order and discipline. Amid the general disarray of *The World Upside Down* (c. 1663), a dog stands on a table eating a pie while the housewife sits asleep next to it. In *The Dissolute Household* (1668), a young couple pet each other, a child steals money from the pocket of the sleeping drunken housewife, and a dog helps itself to meat left in a platter on the floor.

When humans become morbidly anxious to deny their animal nature, they vilify beasts for being beastly, and dogs are always at hand. The Puritan clergyman Cotton Mather spelled out his distaste for sharing bodily functions with other animals in a diary entry of 1700: once, when he was "making water at the wall," a dog came by and did the same thing. "Thought I; 'What mean and vile things are the children of men . . . How much do our natural necessities abase us, and place us . . . on the same level with the very dogs!'" He solved his problem by resolving to distinguish himself from dogs by thinking holy, noble thoughts while he relieved nature. When the eighteenth-century hymn writer Isaac Watts exhorted children to be sweet and well-behaved, he told them to avoid behaving like dogs: "Let Dogs delight to bark and bite, / For God hath made them so"; but children's "little Hands" were not made for aggression.[2]

Because dogs live with us, we tend to judge them by standards of morality and hygiene to which they are oblivious; and of course we find them wanting. We condemn them as lustful because they practice promiscuity and incest. We despise them for eating their own vomit because the act is revolting to us, forgetting that it is natural for dogs to eat regurgitated food and that their regurgitations are quite inoffensive compared to what we throw up. And when we recall the familiar verse in Proverbs that makes returning to one's vomit an emblem of human unregeneracy, we identify the dog innocently following its instincts with a human stubbornly persisting in vice.

Apart from unfair projections, it must be admitted that dogs have unattractive characteristics ready for exploitation by an unsympathetic observer. Shakespeare, insofar as we can judge from the references in his works, had no personal affection for dogs. As a result, he made brilliant use of their characteristics to degrade humans. Kent, the loyal retainer who protested King Lear's misjudgment of Cordelia, contrasts virtuous servants who try to correct their masters' faults with opportunists like Oswald, who keep in favor by catering to their unworthy passions and agreeing with their every varying opinion—in other words, "Knowing nought, like dogs, but following." The dog's unquestioning loyalty, so praised by sentimentalists, is here a mark of its inferiority to the human, who can and should exercise moral judgment. When Lear at last realizes that people established in authority by society are often spiritually inferior to those subject to their power, he thinks of the watchdog who drives a beggar off its master's property—"a dog's obeyed in office." The horrifying scene in which Regan and her husband gouge out the Duke of Gloucester's eyes becomes even more appalling when Regan orders that the blinded man be thrust out to "smell his way to Dover." The man Gloucester is symbolically reduced to a dog, walking on all fours and snuffling with his nose to the ground.

Julius Caesar spurns a plea from the conspirators as "base spaniel fawning." When Mark Antony recognizes his political ruin after the battle of Actium, he describes the opportunistic followers who will now desert him as dogs:

> . . . The hearts
> That spaniel'd me at heels, to whom I gave
> Their wishes, do discandy, melt their sweets
> On blossoming Caesar.[3]

The flatterers who followed him when he was powerful were like spaniels obsequiously pressing at his heels. The image merges into melting candy, suggesting dogs' greedy love and slobbering consumption of sweets. The association of dogs, especially spaniels, with flattery is justified by their expressive displays of devotion and submission. It does seem unfair, though, to revile them for a trait that humans have bred into them.

In *Animal Farm* George Orwell, like Shakespeare, used a conspicuous quality of dogs to stigmatize debased human behavior. As the pigs represent the greedy leaders and the sheep the stupid masses, the dogs represent the elite class that supports their leader from unquestioning loyalty to the one they perceive as their superior: namely, the strongest member of the group. After the animal revolution, they transfer their allegiance from Farmer Jones to the new "top dog," the vicious pig Napoleon. They attend him constantly, bare their teeth at anyone that displeases him, and tear out anyone's throat without hesitation at his command. In their single-minded loyalty to him, they give up attachment to all the other animals; and in return the pigs give them special privileges. The unwavering loyalty of dogs to their leader becomes a sinister force when it supports a police state.

Even people who are fond of dogs may be provoked by doggy characteristics like their indiscriminate appetites for love and food. D. H. Lawrence was revolted on occasion by the effusive, all-inclusive love of his French bull mix, Bibbles. Once when he found her capering around an old Mexican woman who was cursing her, "I had a moment's pure detestation of you." Though "You don't care a rap for anybody. . . . You love to lap up affection, to wallow in it, / And then turn tail to the next comer, for a new dollop." She follows Walt Whitman's exhortation "Reject nothing"—whether it means gobbling up filth in the street or leaping lovingly on the dirtiest scallywag who comes to the door (who, with fatuous human susceptibility to dogs thinks "This dog sure has taken a fancy to me"). She knows nothing of fidelity or loyalty—only LOVE: "Such a waggle of love you can hardly distinguish one human from another."[4] So much for the fulsomely praised quality of canine affection.

Often, however, it is not the actual characteristics of dogs that irritate people, but rather the overestimation of their qualities by humans. Assertions that dogs are morally superior to people or that anyone who fails to love them is "utterly dead to all the better feelings of our nature" naturally provoke a reaction. Such critics claim that the noble qualities of dogs were simply projected onto them by fatuous humans or created by unduly indulgent interpretation of their natural behavior. Perhaps the enthusiastic devotion and responsiveness to human feelings that make us value dogs above all other animals are just stupidity or servility that we call virtues because they flatter our vanity. It is surely true that one reason we like dogs is that they make us feel good about ourselves. As the cat explains in Oliver Herford's verse:

> *At Human jokes, however stale,*
> *He jumps about and wags his tail,*
> *And Human People clap their hands*
> *And think he really understands.*

Or as Dave Barry put it, "Most dogs are earnest, which is why most people like them. You can say any fool thing to a dog, and the dog will give you this look that says, 'My God, you're *right! I never* would have thought of that!' So we come to think of dogs as understanding and loving and compassionate, and after a while we hardly even notice that they spend the bulk of their free time circling around with other dogs to see which one can sniff the other the most times in the crotch."[5]

Dorothy Canfield Fisher persuasively argues that the uncritical devotion dogs offer us has a "debauching influence on the human ego." When we take comfort in the thought that we can be sure of the admiration of our dog whatever we do, we reveal our own unhealthy need to be admired whether or not we are admirable. It is what religious leaders would like from their congregations, noblemen from peasants, officers from soldiers, and old-line husbands from wives. She is sickened by the thought "that my dog will always be sure that I'm right and he's wrong, no matter how unjustly and selfishly I treat him" and would prefer dogs to have a decent amount of self-respect, like cats: to judge human beings at their real value, bite those who mistreat them, and love them only if they are lovable. Fisher finds dogs too dependent on people: the dog's much-praised eagerness to comply with human wishes is in fact a pitiful striving "to fit himself to ideas which he does not understand, which he takes on blind faith that they must be better than his." "When my beautiful collie (as he has just this minute done) feels my eye speculatively on him, and, after a moment's uneasy pause, gets up hastily to come to lay his head on my lap and beg me to assure him that he is really all right, and that I do love him as much as I did five minutes ago, and that I do not love another dog, and that he has not inadvertently done something bad," I long to tell him not to take me so seriously and to live his *own* life.[6]

People who are uncomfortable with the dog's effusive, uncritical admiration for humans often contrast it unfavorably with the cat, in opposition to the prevailing opinion of Buffon and so many others that the cat is a less deserving animal. Perhaps the cat's self-centeredness is more sensible than the dog's unquestioning love. In an eighteenth-century French fable, a dog sold by his master broke his chain and returned home, and as a reward for his devotion was beaten back to his new dwelling. He was utterly bewildered, but the old cat remarked that only a simpleton would count on human love. François-René de Chateaubriand was attracted by the independence and self-sufficiency of the cat, who merely takes physical pleasure from your caresses, not, like the dog, "a silly satisfaction in loving and being faithful to a master who returns thanks in kicks." Alexandre Dumas saw the cat as an aristocrat because she refuses to comply and will leave a home where she is not properly treated, while the vulgar dog is slavishly eager to please and submits to anything. Nicely exploding the image of the noble sporting dog, Dumas pointed out that yes, the cat kills birds; but so would the dog if he were not "too clumsy and stupid." Moreover, the dog fatuously consents to hunt for man, whereas the cat has the sense to kill prey for the purpose of eating it herself.[7]

Still, majority opinion favors the dog above all other animals, for perverse reasons that Thorstein Veblen analyzed with hostile acuteness in his *Theory of the Leisure Class*. Typically useless and often expensive, the dog serves as an item of conspicuous consumption, as well as flattering the human's ego with his "unquestioning subservience and a slave's quickness in guessing his master's mood." These qualities, miscalled fidelity and intelligence, more than compensate for his being "the filthiest of domestic animals in his person and the nastiest in his habits." He affords "play to our propensity for mastery, and as he is also an item of expense, and commonly serves no industrial [i.e., practical] purpose, he holds a well-assured place in men's regard as a thing of good repute." His association in our imagination with the aristocratic and manly occupation of hunting adds to his value. "Even those varieties . . . which have been bred into grotesque deformity by the dog-fancier are in good faith accounted beautiful by many"; in fact, distortion actually adds to their value because it makes it harder and more expensive to keep them alive and reproducing. The cat is less valuable as a status symbol because she is cheaper to maintain, is more apt to serve a useful purpose, and "lives with man on terms of equality."[8]

The eccentric horror writer H. P. Lovecraft despised dogs precisely because they embody the wholesome social values that stupid people admire; cats are superior because they ignore them. Dogs fit into our society so well because they share the conventional American's sentimental morality and foolish ideals of manliness and sociability. Because it is affectionate and wants to please its friends, the dog is "the favorite of superficial, sentimental, and emotional people—people who feel rather than think, who attach importance to manhood and the popular conventional emotions of the simple, and who find their greatest consolation in the fawning and dependent attachments of a gregarious society." The cat lover proves his superiority by rejecting "the fallacy that pointless sociability and friendliness, or slavering devotion and obedience, constitute anything intrinsically admirable or exalted."[9]

William Plomer claimed equal fatuity for British dog lovers through Miss Haymer, a perversely iconoclastic old lady who is the cleverest character in his novel *The Case Is Altered.* She maintains that the English love dogs as incarnations of their own stupidest qualities. "Dogs are simply full of public-school spirit and cheerful stupidity and false pride—all the things the English admire so much in themselves." British people's patriotism during the war in fact consisted of the doggy qualities of "unthinking cheerfulness . . . blind faithfulness, hard fighting, tail-wagging at the end, and then two minutes' silence, with the head on the paws." If it is true that dogs are "often much more faithful and affectionate and better companions than human beings"—first, "That's not saying much"; and second, it's only "because they're often more kindly treated than human beings."[10]

Whether they were animal lovers with reservations about overpraising dogs' virtues, like Fisher, or cold observers, like Shakespeare and Veblen, these critics focused on characteristics that dogs really have. Others, however, are so provoked by the very idea of humans loving dogs that they pour intemperate abuse on the animals without regard to their actual nature. These diatribes are sometimes motivated by a desire to shock as much as genuine outrage at what is seen as dotage on lower animals, but in any case they exist because love and indulgence of dogs is so widespread. In *The Devil's Dictionary*, Ambrose Bierce defined the dog as a "subsidiary Deity" that lies "upon a doormat all day long, sun-soaked and fly-fed and fat, while his master . . . [works] for the means wherewith to purchase an idle wag of the Solomonic tail, seasoned with a look of tolerant recognition." The dog is not only idle, but "a detestable quadruped that knows more ways to be unmentionable than can be named in seven languages." Bierce celebrated a world rid of dogs in his poem "The Oakland Dog" and suggested that hungry Klondike prospectors build up their manly strength with dog meat.[11]

In O. Henry's story "Ulysses and the Dogman," hostility to overindulged dogs is united with hostility to overindulged wives. Every evening in New York City, the narrator witnesses "one of the most melancholy sights of urban life": namely, "beings that were once men," who now follow dogs because each "has been either cajoled, bribed, or commanded by his own particular Circe to take the dear Household pet out for an airing." These dogs "are one in fatness, in pampered, diseased vileness of temper, in insolent, snarling capriciousness of behavior. . . . These unfortunate dry nurses of dogdom, the cur cuddlers, mongrel managers, Spitz stalkers, poodle pullers, Skye scrapers, dachshund dandlers, terrier trailers, and Pomeranian pushers" meekly follow charges who "neither fear nor respect them." In the end, one particularly depressed man leashed to a particularly vile white dog meets an old comrade from the West, where both were real men, and is persuaded to go off with him to Denver, after sending the dog howling away with a vigorous kick.[12] This story both recalls the eighteenth-century satires on silly women who neglect men to dote on their lapdogs and reflects the perennial convention that, while men's love for dogs may be idealized, women's is unwholesome and self-indulgent.

Raymond Hull in *Man's Best Fiend,* a title he must have chosen to be misread at first glance, scrapes together shoddy evidence to attack dogs and the "canophiles" who fatuously dote on them. He holds the dog responsible for injurious idioms like biting the hand that feeds it, rather than recognizing them as examples of human projection. He irrelevantly reproaches Browning for writing a poem about a dog that saved a child from drowning (the antivivisectionist "Tray") and not writing one "about a dog that gave a child rabies, which leads to a death much more unpleasant." Because Pope and Byron were satirists and loved their dogs, he concludes with blatant falsehood that they hated people and had no friends. The book culminates with a long glee-ful discussion of eating dogs, offering a collection of realistic-sounding recipes for Dalmatian with Dumplings, Barbecued Bloodhound, and so forth. Rich people could enjoy eating expensive dogs at $250 a serving, while "There would . . . be plenty of cheaper dogs for humbler tables. So . . . every hungry child may come to know that happiness is a grilled puppy."[13]

Ralph Steadman's *No Good Dogs* and Peter Desberg's *No Good Dogs: Sure-fire Dog-Training Techniques* are sadistic picture books based on the idea that harsh methods must be devised to curb dogs' native obnoxiousness. Stead-man's methods include applying hobnailed boots and dragging a dog by its collar behind a speeding motorcycle. Desberg's humorous suggestions include holding a dog up by its tongue to keep it from licking people. Productions such as these, while obviously based on the assumption that many book buy-ers dislike dogs enough to enjoy japes at their expense, do not necessarily ex-press sincere detestation.

Some people, however, are genuinely disgusted by the number of dogs among us and our attachment to them, and convinced that they bring trouble rather than benefit to humankind. Such people can always find some reason why dogs are harmful and dangerous. Back in 1791, when George Clark urged Parliament to impose a tax on dogs, he admitted that "Such a tax would no doubt cause a devastation" among them, but claimed that result would be desirable. Dogs consume food that could go to poor people and they destroy sheep and lambs. And, above all, they spread rabies, a cruel malady by which "husbands, wives, children are snatched from each other . . . in the midst of horrors which human nature in no other case feels," which sinks "human na-ture . . . to its lowest state of degradation," so "we see nothing but the wretched form of humanity left; and that abject form convulsed by a mind, dreadfully changed from the image of God, to the condition of a brute ani-mal!" Even if the tax might not bring in as much as he calculates, it will surely produce one "blessing of great value . . . a destruction of dogs; and that will be an additional security to our lives, our health, and our happiness."[14]

Rabies aroused disproportionate horror in the eighteenth and nineteenth centuries, like leprosy in the Middle Ages. In both cases, the likelihood of catching the disease was greatly exaggerated. Even Théophile Gautier, a lover of animals, felt an understratum of fear to his affection for dogs, because "These excellent creatures, so good, so faithful, so devoted, so loving, may go mad at any moment, and . . . become more dangerous than a lance-head snake." Actually, although rabies is a hideous and fatal disease, it is and was rare. It was never so prevalent among dogs nor so frequently communicated to humans as to justify a general suspicion of dogs. The early veterinarian Delabere Blaine deplored the "inconceivably" intense dread of rabies that caused people to fear and hate "the whole race of dogs . . . solely on this account."[15] The legitimate threat was exaggerated to justify hostility to and destruction of animals that were unwanted, disliked, or vulnerable.

There were periodic panics during which any agitated dog might be presumed to be rabid, the most trivial dog bite convinced the terrified victim he had been infected, and a single case could be magnified by rumor into a terrifying epidemic. In England in the summer of 1760, many deaths were attributed to the bites of mad dogs, and the Common Council of London ordered the constables and watchmen to kill every dog they found in the streets. The animal-loving Horace Walpole was convinced this action had no legitimate basis but was simply a pretext for killing. "In London . . . the streets are a very picture of the murder of the innocents—one drives over nothing but poor dead dogs!" slaughtered because the English "desire nothing better than to be halloo'd in blood." Satirizing the same campaign, Oliver Goldsmith reported that "A dread of mad dogs is the *epidemic terror* which now prevails. . . . Their manner of knowing whether a dog be mad or no, somewhat resembles the ancient European custom of trying witches . . . a crowd gather round a dog suspected of madness, and they begin by teasing the devoted animal on every side; if he attempts to stand upon the defensive and bite, then is he unanimously found guilty, for *a mad dog always snaps at every thing*; if, on the contrary, he strives to escape by running away, then he can expect no compassion, *for mad dogs always run straight forward before them*." Alarming stories grow and spread, as a little dog that runs frantically through a village becomes a mastiff that bit a lady and drove her into "running mad upon all four, barking like a dog, biting her servants."[16]

Taplin drew attention to the sadistic element in these attacks on dogs who could be supposed dangerous. If a dog is distraught because he has lost track of his master and runs "eager in pursuit, and panting with hope and anxious in fear, wanton boys throw stones, sticks, and halloo other dogs to overtake and worry him . . . butchers, labourers, blackguards, and their whole fraternity join the inhuman hunt. 'Mad dog!' is exclaimed from every mouth, both brutes and beasts being determined upon destruction."[17] Louisa May Alcott's beguiling poodle in *Under the Lilacs* is almost killed when, lost, bedraggled, and terrified, he is surrounded by a group of sadistic urchins who clamor that he is mad. That year a great fear of rabies had arisen in Boston for no apparent reason, and a committee was set up that proposed calling for stray dogs to be shot on sight.[18]

In 1978, Iris Nowell modernized the traditional charges against dogs in a two-hundred-page diatribe called *The Dog Crisis*. She had to find a replacement for rabies, which is no longer a major threat because of improvements in vaccination, and came up with various obscure diseases that could be contracted from dogs and imperil our lives; but even her most substantial example, canine roundworm, is not persuasive. True, it *can* be picked up by ingesting dog feces, and it *can* cause partial blindness, even death. However, even setting aside the unlikelihood that people will eat dog feces, she had to admit that roundworm infection rarely produces "serious illness or debility" in humans. Nowell produced secular versions of the sermons of medieval and Puritan preachers against people who preferred dogs to Christians. Not only is much good, protein-rich food wasted on pets while humans starve, but humane societies' campaigns for abused and homeless animals distract attention from children in the same situation. (She was unaware of the well-documented connection between abuse of animals and abuse of children.) We should be buying kidney dialysis units instead of building animal shelters. The "few" cases where dogs guide blind people, find lost children, patrol streets with the police, and keep children and old people company by no means "justify half the population owning pets and indulging in a useless extravagance at the expense of all of society." By arbitrarily setting the interests of humans and dogs in opposition, she reduced the pros and cons of pet ownership to the question of "whose rights are deemed more important, those of dogs or people."

Dogs detract far more from society, Nowell concluded, than they contribute to it; and any sentimental attachment to them must therefore be stamped out. Since adult pet owners are a hopeless cause, she recommended rigorous censorship in portraying animals for children. "It is essential that anthropomorphizing and idealizing of animals be eradicated from animal education. The Lassie syndrome—in which such traits as loyalty and dependability are exaggerated to an unrealistic extent—must be obliterated. . . . Lassie on film never dumped on a neighbor's property" or "kept anyone awake with her barking."[19]

Nowell did raise one genuine problem: dog bites, especially of children. An alarming number of bites are reported, some causing serious injury, disfigurement, and even death; and some have been perpetrated by the family dog. In 2002, a couple's dachshund chewed through a playpen, dragged out their six-week-old baby, and severely mauled him. An eleven-year-old in suburban Prince Georges County, Maryland, was attacked in his own backyard by his neighbor's two pit bulls, who leaped over a chain-link fence, hunted him down, mauled his leg, and left him with nightmares that lasted for years. Between 1979 and 1998, pit bulls were responsible for sixty-six human deaths. A San Francisco couple with Nazi connections kept two Presa Canario mastiffs known to be dangerous, and one day one of them mangled and killed a young woman neighbor.

Obviously, such events are appalling. And it is disgusting when people extenuate them. After the owners of the dachshund resolved to euthanize the dog that had permanently injured their child, Dachshund Rescue went to work and found several families willing to adopt it. The owners of the Presa Canarios, who had ignored numerous orders to muzzle and control their dogs, expressed no remorse for their neighbor's horrible death and denied responsibility when they were arraigned for murder.

On the other hand, the fact that a few dogs are vicious, and should be appropriately dealt with, does not condemn the entire species. (Suppose the same standard were applied to humans.) The legislators of Prince Georges County tried to solve the vicious pit bull problem by banning the entire breed. As a result of the ban, a neighbor complained about a family's mixed breed dog and they were forced to bring her in to the chief of animal control. Simply because she looked like a pit bull, he ordered them to get her out of the county within two weeks, despite the tears of the mother and child. When they failed to comply in time, an officer seized the dog when the family was at church and euthanized her. This was a family pet that had never bitten anybody.[20] Actually, there are no vicious breeds, although some are more easily provoked to aggression than others. It is hostile, irresponsible owners who pervert dogs into machines of destruction. Bullies breed pit bulls for ferocity and debase them with abusive training so that they will attack anything—an inoffensive person or dog, even a bitch in heat. But properly trained and socialized pit bulls are amiable and friendly to people, including children, and can be taught to get along with other dogs and even cats. Attempts to eliminate vicious dogs by banning certain breeds are futile, since the same thugs who now train pit bulls to be killers could easily transfer their attentions to rottweilers, German shepherds, or some other assertive breed.[21]

One does not have to be a lover of dogs to see that the blanket charges leveled by cynophobes are flimsy. However, those humans who are impervious to the value and appeal of dogs or any other animals will never be able to imagine why we, as the dominant species, should love dogs or enjoy their company or spend resources on them or put ourselves out for them. Such people can see nothing but distasteful characteristics and unnecessary problems: dogs are greedy, dirty in their tastes, indiscriminate in their affections, and often annoyingly boisterous; they foul the streets, frighten and sometimes bite people, and fill the air with barks and yaps. The more dogs are loved and idealized as friends of humanity, the more indignation will be produced in those humans who cannot see anything about them to like.

11

Dogs as Equals

READERS ARE BECOMING increasingly uncomfortable with stories that nominally focus on dogs but in fact push aside their identities to indulge human feelings—whether the animals are made to incarnate human values, or exist to give their all to Master, or are victimized to give readers an opportunity to dwell on others' suffering without discomfort. Even when such stories glorify their canine subjects, they emphasize the dogs' subjection to man, which is presented as proper because they are by nature ancillary and subordinate. Many people today are not comfortable with Victorian notions of hierarchy, even with regard to our animals. We cannot enjoy reading about the suffering and exploitation of dogs because we see them as animals very like ourselves, who therefore deserve to be treated with similar consideration. We feel awkward calling ourselves the master or mistress of our dog (although we have not yet figured out an adequate replacement term). E. B. White happily accepted his dachshund Fred's refusal to worship him and obliviousness to his commands: "in the miniature democracy that was, and is, our household he lived undisturbed and at peace with his conscience."[1]

Nowadays many people think of dogs as more human than bestial—speaking to and treating them as junior family members, assuming them "to have virtually the same thoughts, feelings, and desires as people." These desires include a healthy self-interest. We no longer assume that dogs live to serve their master; rather, like other animals including ourselves, they live to fulfill their emotional needs, which include love for their pack leader but are not limited to it. This attitude can lead humans to mawkish overconsideration for dogs, which can amount even to deference. But it also clears away the stereotyped images of single-minded, uncritical devotion and eager submission to human aims. We no longer expect dogs to be morally perfect, but accept their faults as we do our own. Discarding the traditional mystique, we can see dogs more realistically, assume their point of view more accurately, and be more alert to the comic aspects of dogs and human attitudes toward them.[2] This change has made possible new and delightfully imaginative types of dog stories.

Of course it did not set in universally or at any particular time. As the older attitude persists (for example in the gratuitous sacrifice of Timoleon Vieta), the new one occasionally appeared in past centuries. At the turn of the twentieth century, Edith Somerville and Martin Ross praised Maurice Maeterlinck's discerning appreciation of dogs, but deplored his assumption of human superiority. "No dogs, save perhaps hounds [presumably of a hunting pack], should speak of 'Master,' or 'Mistress.' The relationship should be as that of a parent; at farthest, that of a fond governess." Virginia Woolf, writing an epitaph on her Skye terrier mix Shag, questioned the very basis of our relationship with our domestic animals:

> There is some impertinence as well as foolhardiness in the way in which we buy animals for so much gold and silver and call them ours. . . . There is something, too, profane in the familiarity, half contemptuous, with which we treat our animals. We deliberately transplant a little bit of simple wild life, and make it grow up beside ours, which is neither simple nor wild. You may often see in a dog's eyes a sudden look of the primitive animal, as though he were once more a wild dog hunting in the solitary places of his youth. How have we the impertinence to make these wild creatures forgo their nature for ours, which at best they can but imitate?

On the other hand, Shag's "best friend could not claim for him any romantic or mysterious animal nature, but that made him all the better company for mere human beings." He was sociable but crusty and insisted on being "treated with due respect." The title of master or mistress "was absurd where

Shag was concerned, so we called ourselves his uncles and aunts." All was well until an engaging sheepdog puppy entered the household and won attention by its social graces. "In a kind of blundering and shamefaced way," Shag "lifted one stiff old paw and gave it to me to shake, which was one of the young dog's most successful tricks. It almost brought the tears to my eyes. I could not help thinking, though I smiled, of old King Lear."[3]

John Galsworthy noted the conflict between his spaniel Chris's urge for roving and his devotion to his people; and like Woolf, he "wondered how far this civilization of ours was justifiably imposed on him; how far the love for us that we had so carefully implanted could ever replace in him the satisfaction of primitive wild yearnings. He was like a man, naturally polygamous, married to one loved woman." Galsworthy would not have dreamed of subjecting Chris to the indignity of the dog show, because that would be using him. For true companionship with his dog, a man must "soon pass beyond the thought: 'By what shall this dog profit me?' into the large state of simple gladness to be with dog." He recognized that he and Chris had legitimately different priorities. Although Chris "never tried to hinder or distract, or asked for attention" "when one was too absorbed in work to be so close to him as he thought proper," he looked sad, and, if he could have spoken, would have said: "I have been a long time alone, and I cannot always be asleep; but you know best, and I must not criticize."[4] At the same time that Galsworthy appreciated Chris's doggy abstention from criticism, he acknowledged that he had a counterinterest to his human companion.

People now explicitly recognize that dogs have rights. The trainer Barbara Woodhouse maintains that "A dog should be a complete member of the family, its rights and privileges should have the same consideration as any other member . . . within reason." In the case of a well-behaved, loving, and intelligent dog, "the words 'family pet' can be dropped, for the dog has indeed become one of the family." Since the development of the animal liberation movement in the 1970s, the case against cruelty to animals may be made on the grounds of rights and justice rather than compassion. Peter Singer explicitly denies that animals' interests can be lightly set aside in favor of humans': "There is no ethical basis for elevating membership of one particular species into a morally crucial characteristic," although different species have different requirements for welfare and happiness. But "where animals and humans have similar interests," such as avoiding pain, "those interests are to be counted equally, with no automatic discount just because one of the beings is not human."[5]

Konrad Lorenz declared that "The fidelity of a dog is a precious gift demanding no less binding moral responsibilities than the friendship of a human being." Although he insisted that dogs be well-disciplined, he was gratified when his dogs taught themselves to fulfill the spirit rather than the letter of his orders. His beloved Alsatian-chow mix, Stasi, would lie down on command to guard his bicycle; but she felt free to move around within a radius of a few yards. It pleased him to think that lessons, "once learned, can be carried out by a dog not only with slavish exactitude but also in the form of a most sensible, one is almost tempted to say creative, variation."[6]

Many poems in *Dog Music,* an anthology of contemporary American poetry, celebrate not what dogs do for people, but how the two species relate to each other. Howard Nemerov's "Walking the Dog" precisely describes the communion between two distinct, differing animals:

> *Two universes mosey down the street*
> *Connected by love and a leash and nothing else.*

While the man contemplates light effects through the leaves, the dog

> *. . . mooches along with tail up and snout down,*
> *Getting a secret knowledge through the nose*
> *Almost entirely hidden from my sight.*

The man watches his dog investigating a bush as long as he can stand it, then hauls him off. But regardless of the tugging and dragging involved on both sides, they remain "contented not to think each other's thoughts."[7]

The model of master with blindly loyal, subservient dog has been explicitly challenged by women, who simultaneously deny that there is an exclusive sacred bond between dogs and men or boys, to which female humans are irrelevant and often hostile. *Dogs and Their Women,* a feminist book of photographs with autobiographical accounts, is an organized attack on this

stereotype. The editors see an equally strong and emotionally deeper bond between dogs and women, where the dog's unconditional love is complemented
by the woman's nurturing. "Women's unique bond with their dogs," they
claim, "honors them as equals." Even if woman's "nurturing" may be as
much a stereotype as man's "leadership," the relationships described in this
book are clearly as close and rewarding as any between virile men and the
dogs that worship them. Paula Bennett was saved by her spaniel, Topper,
when she was a hostile, troubled thirteen-year-old: "he was the only thing I
loved. And . . . he was the only thing I let love me." Alix Smith appreciates
the welcome home she can count on from her bull terrier, Buzzsaw: "Nobody
else has ever been that happy to see me." Eve S. Minson doesn't consider her
three dogs "as my pets; it's more that we're all fortunate to be sharing the
same rocky road." Jo Giese happily reports that she "replaced a six-foot
Swedish husband with a five-pound" Yorkshire terrier.[8] Jennifer Crusie's
novel *Crazy for You* dramatizes a similar situation: the protagonist's bond with
a dog liberates her to do what she wants and get out of her relationship with
an apparently perfect but actually uncongenial man. In the beginning, Quinn
thinks she has a good life with Bill. But when she insists on adopting Katie, a
scrawny, neurotic mutt, Bill's patronizing ultimata that of course she will not
and does not even want to keep "it" jar her into realizing that she doesn't
want to keep him. Finally Bill sneaks the dog off to the pound, and Quinn's
new man proves his worth by breaking the law to save Katie from execution.

While it is self-evidently more moral and enlightened to regard dogs as
friends than as slaves to be exploited at will, modern egalitarian feelings can
be exaggerated to the point of denying any differences between the sensibilities, priorities, and rightful claims of dogs and humans. In *My Dog Tulip*
(1956), a thinly fictionalized biography of his German shepherd, Queenie,
the distinguished gay literary man J. R. Ackerley made clear that the dog was
his dearest friend and met his fastidious standards better than his human acquaintance. The book, which has been praised as the finest dog book ever
written, gracefully conveys Tulip's beauty and Ackerley's delight in her; but it
is tainted by distorted judgment. Every detail about Tulip is worth recording,
including her urination and defecation habits, the subject of an entire chap-

ter. Ackerley plumes himself on his dotage on Tulip and his inability to discipline her. Although his text reveals her as an unusually nervous and badly behaved dog, he presents her as totally lovable.

At the same time that he adores the dog, he does not hesitate to sneer at humans he considers inferior. Tulip's preferences must always be respected, but women's are annoying. When Tulip produced a litter of crossbreeds and Ackerley had to place the puppies, he complained that "Many of my applicants were working-class people; my ambitions rose to a higher aim." Such people hadn't sufficient money, time, physical energy, or mental capacity to care properly for *Tulip's* puppies. One of the bitch puppies did go to a young man, his sister, and their crippled father, all of whom "doted upon her"; but because she had to live in "a dark basement flat with a small backyard" (as they did), the arrangement could not work. The joy the dog might give two overworked young people and their crippled father is not, evidently, worth consideration.

Ackerley expected everyone else to share his doting indulgence of a dog who cared for no one but himself. When Tulip deposited a loose load in the entrance to a greengrocer shop, the owners' resentment proved they were "a surly, disobliging couple." Ackerley was mildly aggrieved when friends in the country failed to welcome Tulip a second time as a houseguest. "Her unconquerable belief that every building we enter, even a railway carriage, belongs from that moment exclusively to us, may have something to do with it; people seem to resent being challenged whenever they approach their own sitting or dining rooms." Yes, indeed. Tulip was even more than a best friend; she was very close to a lover. Ackerley constantly extols her beauty, including that of her swollen pink vulva when she was in heat; she rejected male Alsatians, hated to let him out of her sight, and constantly mounted his leg. Her prototype, Queenie, offered him a "waiting love and unstaling welcome" that he had never received from human lovers.[9] Bitch and man loved each other as absolute equals.

If anyone in past centuries had felt Ackerley's effusive love, he certainly would never have expressed it openly. But Ackerley's contemporary T. H. White poured out much the same feelings for his setter, Brownie. "She was wife, mother, mistress & child." Her death moved him to thoughts of suicide, and he repeatedly visited her grave on the chance that her consciousness persisted.[10]

Elizabeth Marshall Thomas's *The Hidden Life of Dogs* purports to be a scientific investigation of canine psychology, but in fact is permeated with as much sentimental anthropomorphizing as Ackerley's story of Tulip. Thomas treats her dogs exactly like humans, giving utmost respect to their preferences and abstaining from exerting any authority over them. The key part of her research was following her Siberian husky Misha as he roamed freely over a range of 130 square miles—approaching that of a wolf—in suburban Cambridge, Massachusetts. (She did not consider the consequences of unlimited mating and the dangers to Misha and car drivers when he crossed busy thoroughfares.) She discovered, not surprisingly, that maintaining a territory and asserting dominance over other dogs are important canine motives. She developed a pack of huskies, oriented toward each other rather than to humans, and left the older dogs to train the younger generation, without attempting to mold their behavior to her own needs. She does not explain what was gained by reversing fourteen thousand years of domestication or why an almost feral dog is more genuine or better than one trained to live in human society. Her dogs, happily free to do what they like in and out of her house without paying much attention to the human inmates, are boarders rather than pets or members of a human family.

Her excessive consideration for dogs is even more evident in her second book, *The Social Lives of Dogs: The Grace of Canine Company*. Sundog, for example, had grown accustomed to eating popcorn from her husband's hand, rather than from his bowl; but one day Steve was preoccupied and just put some on the floor for Sundog. The dog stared in dismay and dejectedly left the room, ignoring the popcorn. "Horrified that we had seriously hurt his feelings," the Thomases followed and offered him popcorn, "but he turned his face away from the bowl. We saw that we had humiliated him . . . had shown him, bitterly, that he really wasn't one of us after all, that we were people, that we controlled everything, that he was just a dog, that he had presumed beyond his station in trying to be like one of us . . . *and for the rest of his life he never ate popcorn again*." She rightly perceives that the dog valued the fellowship of sharing rather than the food, but surely she feels exaggerated guilt for offending his sensibility.

Pearl, a hefty Australian shepherd-chow mix, "was my sister." But Thomas would hardly have tolerated the greeting behavior from a human sister that she did from Pearl. "No matter how much I yelled at her to stop, when she jumped up on me in greeting, as she would after even the shortest absence, her claws dug bleeding furrows down my skin." On two occasions Pearl's rush tripped Thomas up, once breaking her ankle and once knocking her downstairs. "Still, I continued to adore her. I liked her strength and her self-reliance. And . . . her good intentions."[11] Thomas allowed Pearl to train her, by increasingly loud barks, to get up at four-thirty, when the dog required her breakfast.

Jeffrey Moussaieff Masson, in *Dogs Never Lie About Love: Reflections on the Emotional World of Dogs*, gives his old-fashioned eulogy of canine virtue a contemporary twist by dissociating it from any allegiance to humans. He attributes dogs' unconditional love and general friendliness entirely to superior goodness, discounting the probable influence of their simpler minds and social instincts as pack animals. He shares Thomas's abhorrence of imposing human restrictions on the free canine spirit, reproaching himself for getting angry when his dog begged food from strangers at a picnic and refused to come when he called her away: "Why do I think that she is thwarting my will . . . when she wants to do what she wants to do?"[12]

The detective story writer Susan Conant rightly derides Thomas's portentous scientific conclusion, pointing out that anyone who has ever walked a male dog knows that he wants "to leave his mark as ostentatiously as possible on absolutely every object in the vicinity of which he could possibly cock a leg." Conant goes on to ridicule Thomas's argument that domestication victimizes dogs by making her detective sarcastically describe a walk with her beloved malamute: "with my product of pitiless domestication oppressively reduced to an unnatural and abnormal condition, which is to say, with Rowdy safely hitched to his flex lead and thus . . . linked to his devoted oppressor, I started out along the bank of the lake." Conant dismisses Thomas's book as "the pitiful story of a woman so terrified of a normal, protective human relationship with dogs that she fled the responsibility and mutuality that love entails."[13] Actually, however, Conant herself projects an overindulgent view of dogs.

Dogs have become increasingly prominent in detective stories from the time the Charleses' schnauzer, Asta, added a bit of wholesome, normal domesticity to the hard-boiled, ultrasophisticated world of Dashiell Hammett's Thin Man novels of the 1930s. In Lindsey Davis's novels set in ancient

Rome, the scruffy sleuth, Marcus Didius Falco, has an appropriately ratty, overindulged dog named Nux.[14] The mystery novel featuring dogs (or cats) has become a genre, in which the detective's companion animals may provide the main interest. Conant's detective, Holly Winter, is a columnist for *Dog's Life* who dotes on her two malamutes. Rowdy and Kimi are always conspicuously present to provide humor and local color. Conant follows the convention of praising her breed as more wonderful than any other, despite endearing idiosyncrasies that ordinary people might find objectionable, such as uncontrollable willfulness. Even though their owner has trained them for competition in obedience trials, they are not even normally well behaved. They greet her with enthusiasm that produces "a scratched chin, a sore nose, and a bruised jaw. Since winning the unconditional love of these two dogs . . . I have been dragged down the back stairs three times . . . most malamutes will steal food, raid the trash, chase cats, kill livestock, and kiss the burglar . . . But as soul mates? As kindred spirits? As an intelligent companion in a partnership of equals, the Alaskan malamute is without peer."[15]

Holly's large, wild sled dogs have become such cosseted pets that *she* feels the need to protect *them* from a murderer, even though he is puny and unarmed. In the climax of *Animal Appetite*, this man keeps her immobilized by threatening to give poisoned hamburger to the dogs, who will eagerly devour it instead of attending to a situation that, as should be obvious to any canine nose and ears, imperils the life of their mistress as well as their own.

Michael Bond's Monsieur Pamplemousse and his bloodhound Pommes Frites make a far more satisfactory detective pair. Pommes Frites accompanies Pamplemousse everywhere (more plausible in France, where dogs are welcome in first-class restaurants) and shares his avid interest in fine food. He is Pamplemousse's friend and confidant, but he is also a dog: his master values his companionship and considers his wishes, but there is no question that the man gives the directions and sets the agenda. Bond keeps his readers aware of what Pommes Frites senses and feels, but the dog is a well-trained junior partner. *Monsieur Pamplemousse Aloft* opens with Pommes Frites being the only one to notice a model airship flying overhead, because he happened to look up "for want of something better to do while bestowing his favours on a convenient tree . . . wondering idly whether, if he kept very still, a pigeon perched on top of . . . [a nearby statue's] hat might be lulled into a false sense of security and land on his own head by mistake."[16] The dog plausibly contributes to the resolution of the plot by his scenting ability, together with his canine distrust of things that are out of the ordinary. Pamplemousse was embarrassed when his dog seized and refused to let go of a bag of ballast that was being loaded onto an airship that was to carry both the French and British heads of state. It turns out that Pommes Frites had scented a bomb in the bag that would have blown them up and caused an international disaster.

Actually, people who like and respect their dogs as animal companions, rather than idealizing or indulging them as privileged equals, are more apt to observe them precisely. It is possible to adopt a dog's point of view and examine its mental processes independently of human interests and convenience without placing it on the same level as a person. Any owner has noticed how upset a dog becomes when its people are going away, but Galsworthy clarified the dog's feelings by imagining its thought processes. When his spaniel Chris "smelled packing," he

> *curled his head round over his left paw and pressed his chin very hard against the ground. . . . What necessity,—he seemed continually to be saying,—what real necessity is there for change of any kind whatever? Here we were all together, and one day was like another, so that I knew where I was—and now you only know what will happen next. . . . Some careless word, some unmuted compassion in voice, the stealthy wrapping of a pair of boots, the unaccustomed shutting of a door that ought to be open . . . one tiny thing, and he knows for certain that he is not going too. He fights against the knowledge just as we do against what we cannot bear; he gives up hope, but not effort, protesting in the only way he knows of, and now and then heaving a great sigh*

—more affecting than a human's because it is not intended for effect. "The words: 'Yes—going too!' spoken in a certain tone, would call up in his eyes a still-questioning half-happiness, and from his tail a quiet flutter, but did not quite serve to put to rest either his doubt or his feeling that it was all unnecessary—until the cab arrived," when he would leap into the vehicle.[17]

When sixty-year-old John Steinbeck took a long trip across America, he brought along a pal to keep him from feeling lonely and helpless—his poodle, Charley. He accepted Charley's doggy preferences as one would the foibles of a human friend:

> *Charley likes to get up early, and he likes me to get up early too. And why shouldn't he? Right after his breakfast he goes back to sleep. Over the years he has developed a number of innocent-appearing ways to get me up. He can shake himself and his collar loud enough to wake the dead. If that doesn't work he gets a sneezing fit. But perhaps his most irritating method is to sit quietly beside the bed and stare into my face with a sweet and forgiving look on his face; I come out of deep sleep with the feeling of being looked at. But I have learned to keep my eyes tight shut. If I even blink he sneezes and stretches, and that night's sleep is over for me. Often the war of wills goes on for quite a time, I squinching my eyes shut and he forgiving me, but he nearly always wins.*[18]

We not only recognize that dogs have their own agendas and get many benefits out of their human friends—we do not mind. Stephen Budiansky argues semi-facetiously in *The Truth About Dogs: An Inquiry into the Ancestry, Social Conventions, Mental Habits, and Moral Fiber of Canis familiaris* that dogs are superb con artists who delude us into thinking they "are loyal, trustworthy, selfless, loving, courageous, noble, and obedient," while all the while exploiting us to give them pleasant lives. We cheerfully support them in comfort, inconvenience ourselves for them without getting any tangible return, and put up with behavior from them that we would never tolerate in humans. Nevertheless, Budiansky, like so many of us, is happy to have them. We can enjoy their company even though the doggy behavior that pleases us is derived from expediency rather than overflowing worshipful love, even though their affectionate greetings, wish to be near us, and so forth are no more than ways to get along as subordinates in the wolf pack. "Dogs unquestionably enjoy our company," he admits, "find reassurance . . . [in] a stable place in the social hierarchy of human society," may help us through their sensory prowess and natural skills; "but we are guilty of . . . self-centeredness, when we see every useful thing they do for us as proof that they are doing it all for us."[19]

Carl Hiaasen's novel *Sick Puppy* dramatizes the situation Budiansky describes, and with the same indulgent humor. His plot is based on contemporary Americans' devotion to dogs and brings out the absurdity of idealizing a sensual animal. His hero, the Labrador retriever Boodle, is a comic take on a dog much like Greene's Buller. In Boodle's world, a not-too-wild exaggeration of modern America, ingenuous universal friendliness makes one loved, at least if one is a dog; and even a sleazy, unscrupulous lobbyist can be controlled by threats to his dog. A fanatical environmentalist kidnaps Boodle in order to force his owner to abort a destructive deal and then sends him first an ear and then a paw from a Labrador retriever. Since the kidnapper would not dream of hurting a dog, he must go to great trouble to find a freshly killed Labrador from which to cut the parts. Meanwhile Boodle is having a grand time, as Labradors always do, since their minds are uncluttered by contemplation or worry. "Every day was a romp. . . . Eating was a thrill. Pissing was a treat. Shitting was a joy. And licking your own balls? Bliss. And everywhere you went were gullible humans who patted and hugged and fussed over you."[20] He finds his kidnapper a nice man, and who can tell whether he misses his owner? When he finds him tied to a chair, he sniffs casually at the knots at his wrists, pokes his nose into his groin, and ambles off to make friends on the beach.

Once we see the similarity between canine motives and our own, we can imagine plausible fictions of role reversal, which increase our insights into dogs and people at the same time that they amuse with their ingenuity. Corey Ford confides in "Every Dog Should Own a Man" that he happens "to belong to an English setter who acquired me when he was about six months old and has been training me quite successfully ever since. . . . I've learned not to tug at the leash when he takes me for a walk." Soon Ford may be cured of the habit of running away by getting long reproachful looks whenever a suitcase appears. The setter recognizes that "Training a man takes time. Some men are a little slow to respond, but a dog who makes allowances and tries to put himself in the man's place will be rewarded with a loyal pal. Men are apt to be high-strung and sensitive, and a dog who loses his temper will only break the man's spirit."[21] By cleverly reversing the conventional precepts for training dogs, Ford brings out truths about our actual relationships with them.

A. R. Gurney's play *Sylvia* brilliantly conveys our present feeling of quasi-equality with dogs by using a human actor to represent a dog. Sylvia is not a human doing antics in a dog suit, as she would have been in the past. Rather, she seems to be expressing the authentic feelings of a dog, except with an articulateness that makes her wishes and claims seem more justified. Sylvia, a stray that Greg picks up in the park and adopts over his wife's objections, has all the demonstrative love, gratitude, enthusiasm, and superficial eagerness to please that endear dogs to us, together with the healthy self-interest, emotional demands, and readiness to encroach on human prerogatives that we now recognize in canine behavior. When Greg brings her into his apartment, she wanders around, taking an occasional sniff, until he orders her to sit and stay, enforcing obedience by hitting her. She reproaches him for the blow but immediately tells him, "I love you . . . I really do . . . I think you're God, if you want to know." He keeps trying to read his paper, while she keeps distracting him by gazing at him adoringly. His wife wants to get rid of Sylvia, with whom she obviously cannot compete in demonstrative, unqualified affection. Besides, she complains, she and Greg spent their wedding anniversary night "with Sylvia wandering restlessly around the room, peering over the bed, and panting." Sylvia also drinks noisily from the toilet when they are eating dinner and says hello by poking at strangers' crotches. Greg's disclosure that he is unhappy in his increasingly abstract job and longs to become "more connected" with "living" prepares us for the cliché that dogs give us a mystical connection with Nature, but instead Sylvia just wishes she "could contribute something here, but I just plain can't." All she can do is try unsuccessfully to conceal her boredom.[22]

Sylvia is a convincing dog, despite her human voice; but Peter Mayle's Briard mix, Boy, whose memoirs written in emulation of Proust were published as *A Dog's Life,* is a worldly wise human, despite his canine motives and opinions. Imagining the dog's independent point of view provides Mayle with a fresh approach for mocking human foibles, particularly the vanity that requires a dog's adoration. Boy's ability to criticize is sufficiently plausible because he is a typical contemporary companion dog—engaging and fond of his people, but by no means adoringly dependent on a human master. He has an entirely human interest in making himself a comfortable life, pursues his ends with shrewd common sense, and is not burdened by reverence for people. Left alone while the management—Mr. and Mrs. Mayle—selfishly went out for a long lunch, Boy looked for something to amuse himself with. So he entered the forbidden guest bedroom, leapt on the antique white bedspread, rearranged the pillows in a circular nest, and settled down for a nap. He would have liked to stay there all afternoon, but he realized he had better bound downstairs to greet the management. For

> *people who live with dogs like a full turnout when they come home after an absence. It makes them feel loved and appreciated. It can also make them feel slightly guilty at having left their faithful companions all alone. This, in turn, can lead to what they call "treats" and what I regard as conscience payments to make up for willful neglect. However you look at it, the fact is that it is usually worth presenting yourself at the door with bright eye and jaunty tail and generally behaving as if life had been an arid desert without them.*

Then he must deal with their anger over the mess in the guest bedroom. He has learned that any crime can be redeemed with a sound "conciliation technique." However, "Punishment in our house, as in the legal system generally, depends" more "on the mood and general disposition of the presiding judge and the jury" than "on the gravity of the offense." In this case, the judge is in a bad mood from having overeaten at lunch, so Boy must go through the "seven gestures of appeasement." Boy uses his human articulateness to explain and justify the canine nose-to-crotch routine that so revolts humans. He observes that shaking hands or pecking at cheeks is not "what I would call informative body contact. . . . How can you hope to discover anything of interest from an arm's-length handshake or a brief contact just west of the earrings? My greeting methods, on the other hand, are genuinely cordial, or so I like to think, and extremely revealing." His approach with vigorously wagging tail "prepares the way for a more intimate salute—a probing sniff to the guest's central areas."[23]

Michael Z. Lewin's *Rover's Tales: A Canine Crusader and His Travels in the Dog World* are narrated by Rover, a stray or, as he calls himself, an "independent dog." Even more than Boy, he is a canine picaro, set up to satirize humans and made a dog to simulate a detached view of human foibles. He joins in conversation with a pack of dogs who argue whether humans have intelligence. "Just being good with their paws isn't enough to prove they're . . . truly intelligent. . . . They can't talk . . . and has any of you ever seen a human being do a genuinely intelligent thing? Something that couldn't be explained as natural cunning?" He meets a dog named Pal, who made the mistake of eating some free meat humans were giving out. It was drugged, and he woke to find a collar fixed around his neck that itched and hummed. "And half the time when I stop somewhere one of those fiends in white jackets turns up." Rover guesses that they are doing research on independent dogs. "But why?" Pal asks. "What's it to them?"

Going to investigate cries that are neither canine nor feline, Rover finds a man raping a woman and cannot understand why: "What is the point of trying to do it with a female when she doesn't want to? With us no means no. No hard feelings. Maybe some other time." Even though it was not his problem, he "felt the impulse to get involved" and rescued the woman by biting the man and running away with his pants.[24] The incongruities resulting from reversing human and canine points of view are thought-provoking as well as comic. The dogs' debate on human intelligence parodies arrogant human analyses of dogs' mental inadequacies and makes the valid point that human superiority does in fact owe much to our hands as well as our brains. It is hard to understand why men so commonly impose sex upon women who are "not in the mood." Obviously, Lewin was not making a serious effort to represent a dog's consciousness realistically: Rover is too smart and thoughtful for a dog and too happy and carefree for a solitary, homeless stray. But Lewin created Rover's canine tastes and interests with sufficient plausibility to make his hero engaging and create a fresh point of view for his satire. This makes *Rover's Tales* much more effective than Coventry's *Pompey the Little*, written before a genuine interest in dogs would be assumed necessary for a work with a canine hero.

Aside from these playful inventions, some twentieth-century authors have seriously tried to create a dog's consciousness. Although Kipling retained the old hierarchical attitude in "Thy Servant a Dog," narrated by the Scottish terrier Boots, he made a genuine effort at authenticity. He confined the narrative to a dog's interests and (more or less) to a dog's understanding; his attempt to render all this in canine Basic English is less successful, suggesting failed attempts at human dialect. Boots describes his first meeting with the dog who belongs to the young woman his master will marry: "There is walk-in-Park-on-lead. There is off-lead-when-we-come-to-the-grass. There is 'nother dog, like me, off-lead. I say: 'Name?' He says: 'Slippers.' He says: 'Name?' I say: 'Boots.' He says: 'I am fine dog. I have Own God called Miss.' I say: 'I am very fine dog. I have Own God called Master.' There is walk-round-on-toes. There is Scrap. There is Proper Whacking." Boots reports, without understanding, that his friend Ravager, a foxhound, is going to be killed for being "snipey-about-the-nose"—"I were not comfy." A hunt terrier tells him that "if he had me for two seasons, he would make me earn-my-keep. But I would not like. I am afraid I would be put-in-ponds and sunk, because I am snipey-about-the-nose."[25]

Virginia Woolf's *Flush*, written from the point of view of Elizabeth Barrett Browning's cocker spaniel, Flush, is more successful because she uses him as a central consciousness but makes no attempt to give him a near-human voice. Inspired by Woolf's relationship with her own cocker spaniel, Pinka, the book is filled with smells and emotions never formulated in words, and brings out the intimate interdependence between woman and dog. After one intense mutual gaze, Flush cast off his whole past life of chasing freely in the country to center his life on an invalid in her room. Woolf playfully points to their similarity in appearance—large expressive eyes, wide mouths, long ringlets on Elizabeth and long hairy ears on Flush—and goes on to speculate that each completed what was dormant in the other. Flush shared his youthful animal vitality with the pale invalid, while she brought out such depths in his nature that the intensity of his emotional life compensated for its physical limitations. Although Woolf articulates his thoughts better than he could, her rendition of his thought processes sounds authentic. On his first trip to Regent's Park, where "he saw once more, after years of absence it seemed, grass, flowers and trees, the old hunting cry of the fields hallooed in his ears and he dashed forward to run as he had run in the fields at home. But now a heavy weight jerked at his throat; he was thrown back on his haunches. Were there not trees and grass? he asked. Were these not the signals of freedom?" But then he noticed the flowers massed in beds, the hard black paths, and the men patrolling them in shiny black hats. After a number of these walks, "he had arrived at a conclusion. Where there are flowerbeds and asphalt paths and men in shiny top-hats, dogs must be led on chains. Without being able to decipher a word of the placard at the Gate he had learned his lesson—in Regent's Park dogs must be led on chains."

As the relationship became closer and closer, Flush became ever more sensitive to Miss Barrett's feelings. When Robert Browning first began to call, Flush had the horribly novel experience of being left out of their conversation, and "Though he could make no sense of the little words that hurtled over his head from 2:30 to 4:30 sometimes three times a week, he could detect with terrible accuracy that the tone of the words was changing. Miss Barrett's voice had been forced and unnaturally lively at first. Now it had gained a warmth and an ease that he had never heard in it before."[26] It is a convincing presentation of what a dog would perceive in a human situation.

In *Thor*, Wayne Smith set up a fictional situation through which he could portray a canine mind with deep sympathy and insight, showing the limitations and abilities that distinguish it from a human mind. The story is told through the central consciousness of Thor, a conscientious German shepherd, who is placed in an intolerable dilemma where his natural instincts and perceptions conflict with the law laid down by his pack leader, Dad. He must resolve a problem he cannot understand and the humans he believes wiser than himself cannot even recognize. Smith convincingly represents the dog's perceptions, comprehension, values, and struggles to reconcile his conflicting imperatives. Thor recognizes Dad as the alpha male; distinguishes between the Mating Pair and the pups, who are to be protected but not obeyed; understands human tones and body language and a few words; dreads Dad's disapproval and separation from the Pack. His difficulties arise when he becomes suspicious of Uncle Ted, whom he has always liked: he catches a strange Wild Animal scent from Uncle Ted and sees in him the body language of a Bad Dog. He senses what the humans cannot smell or see: that Uncle Ted has become a werewolf. Somehow he must fulfill his duty to protect his Pack, even though the oblivious humans keep frustrating his attempts. When he finally attacks Uncle Ted to save the rest of the family, Dad is convinced that he has turned vicious and throws him in the cellar. In doing what he had to do, Thor has violated both Dad's law of behaving himself and the Natural Law against attacking a member of the Pack with intent to kill; he feels he is irretrievably a Bad Dog, forever excluded from the Pack, and he wants to die. Smith's novel is superior by far to earlier treatments of the conventional misjudged dog theme, for it presents a significant moral issue—as opposed to whether or not a bird dog has been killing deer—and is founded on real differences between canine and human perception.

Stephen King's *Cujo* is deeper and more touching than a mere horror story about a demon dog because King takes us into Cujo's mind. Cujo is more horrible than Doyle's Hound of the Baskervilles because he torments human beings for excruciating hours, and even more because he was originally a family pet of a notably benevolent breed. We are not disposed to credit dogs with supernatural powers, and King skillfully makes Cujo terrifying without making him supernatural.[27] A normal good dog could be transformed into a mindless killer by rabies, a two-hundred-pound Saint Bernard could easily kill people if it wanted to, unfortunate circumstances could cause people to be trapped in their overheating car with such a dog outside. A rabid dog provides the perfect trigger for King's pattern of horror writing, in which something that is normally friendly and ordinary turns into a hideously alien, deadly force.

After drawing us into sympathy with Cujo by convincingly rendering his perceptions and understanding, King carries us along with the dog as the disease produces its awful changes: from Cujo's growling at a friend for the first time in his life and realizing with confusion that he had wanted to bite him; to his hideous mad disorientation, when nothing makes sense anymore, all the certainties of his life are shaken, and his confidence in human friendship turns into a conviction that everyone he meets is responsible for his agony; until nothing is left in him but destructive rage. Thus in the final sequence we are harrowed both by suspense about whether the two suffering humans in the car will escape and by horror at what has happened to Cujo. He is a monster, but not simply a monster; for by articulating his delusions, King keeps us aware of the good dog, the friend of man, that he could and should have been.

By seeing dogs as autonomous creatures with their own point of view, wishes, and priorities, people can understand their motivation more accurately. Writers can use these insights to create a fresh, amusing view of humans. Or they can create dog-centered stories that are interesting and convincing because their protagonists have their own minds and feelings rather than standing in for simplified humans. *Thor* is more moving than other stories on the same theme because the hero's dilemma comes from genuine canine rather than imputed human imperatives.

12

Myth and Reality

For the past two or three centuries at least, we have considered our First Friend to be amiable and special. We warm to pictures of or anecdotes about dogs, we like our politicians better when we see them with their dogs, we keep dogs for company rather than for any utilitarian purpose, and we value them as members of the family. In 2003, there were 61,278,000 owned dogs in the United States, 94 percent of whom were kept as companions.[1] Even the vociferous hostility to dogs is in part a reaction against the high estimation in which most people hold them.

Indeed, our love of dogs sometimes causes us to forget that they are mammals of the order Carnivora that do not have the same tastes and sensitivities as civilized humans. Already in the nineteenth century, there were mourning outfits and fur-trimmed driving coats for dogs, as well as elaborate canine funerals and burials; and increasingly widespread prosperity has engendered an ever-increasing variety of luxuries for dogs. Three Dog Bakery, a rapidly expanding chain, sells bone-shaped birthday cakes for $18.00 and petits fours dipped in carob sauce at two for $1.50. Although dogs undoubtedly enjoy them, some *Washington Post* reporters set up a reality check to find out whether they prefer them to traditional canine treats such as garbage. The testers offered five dogs a buffet of Three Dog Bakery's birthday cake and petits fours, old McDonald's hamburgers, hunks of Spam, Milk-Bone dog biscuits, strawberry cream cake, cat feces dusted with kitty litter, and a freshly soiled Pamper. The dogs preferred the Spam (ten points) and the old hamburger (eight), with the birthday cake coming in a distant third with four points and the petit four with three.[2]

Some owners feel they should treat their dogs with exactly the same kind and degree of consideration they should give to human beings. Ackerley apologized profusely to Tulip for failing to understand her wishes in time when she needed to go out, and even then mourned that he could never atone for his insensitivity. Of course, people who make humans of their dogs cannot subject them to the indignity of training and discipline, even though these pack animals are more comfortable with clear rules and a definite social order. Moreover, the resulting obnoxious behavior increases the hostility of those who do not care for dogs even under the best circumstances.

Sheri S. Tepper perceptively uses fantasy to explore the kinship and distinctions between humans and dogs in her science fiction novel *The Companions*. It is set in a technologically advanced dystopian future in which a powerful party on Earth is preaching that all nonhuman animals should be wiped out on the grounds that they use up air and water required by the overgrown human population; its slogan is, "In God's Image—Humans First and Only." Enlightened humans collaborate with independent dogs to fight for the rights of all animals. The small pack of dogs, who have been bred to be brighter, longer-lived, and more self-sufficient than those of today, are and consider themselves to be equal to humans. The woman hero and the alpha bitch think of themselves as sisters, and the alpha dog leads his pack where he thinks best, regardless of human wishes. The hero sets out with the dogs to find a planet where they can be settled safely on their own. In the course of their travels they tangle with an unprincipled shape-shifting super-race who have adopted the forms of dogs, as well as the canine morality of pack loyalty and pack hierarchy. While these values are acceptable in dogs, they become evil when practiced by rational beings (whether invented super-race or humans), who have a greater capacity for doing harm. The dogs are briefly seduced by the dog-shaped villains, but realize just in time that their interests lie with their human friends.[3]

Jon Katz reports in his sociological study *The New Work of Dogs* that people are increasingly relying on dogs to provide the emotional support they cannot get from other people in our disconnected society. His case studies include recently divorced women whose dogs gave them invaluable reassurance and sympathy after their husbands left them and a lonely old man whose dog fulfilled his needs for love and companionship. However, Katz points out, people who rely on their dogs to the point of making them into permanent surrogates for the spouses or children who have failed them are demanding more of the animals than they can possibly give. Dogs are not equipped to provide the complex emotional responses that humans require. Too intense, exclusive intimacy between dog and human (which the dog is helpless to resist) can produce neurotically demanding or badly behaved dogs and disappointed owners.

Owners are inclined to avoid disappointment by deluding themselves. Katz himself confesses to telling a dog trainer that his dog was so devoted to him that it would pine away if he died. The trainer "laughed and said that given two pounds of beef liver and a couple of days, my dog would forget that I ever walked the earth."[4] One of the owners Katz studied, Donna, got through terminal cancer with the support of her corgi, Harry. Donna's husband left her because he could not stand watching her deterioration, but the dog didn't mind how she looked; he was constantly on hand to cheer her, love her, keep her company, and, she could be sure, would never abandon her. Nevertheless, when she became too ill to take care of him and passed him on to a friend, he fretted and whimpered for only a few days and then began to eat again and soon became perfectly happy in his new home. Dogs live more in the present than people do and so do not retain grief so long. Harry contributed enormously to Donna's emotional well-being while she lived, but he did not give her undying devotion. Katz also points out that most dogs left five hundred miles from home would not trek back like Lassie: they would find some kind people with food and stay with them.

We cannot realistically expect our dogs to pine away after we die or even to dedicate their every thought to us while we live. Reading in Buffon or Taplin that dogs live to please their master, assiduously following every order and anticipating every wish, makes one wonder whether they ever actually looked at their dogs' behavior. Anyone who observes the dog they live with knows that it has its own priorities and can be deaf to commands that interfere with something it really wants to do. The exalted absolutes of Buffon and the others must have reflected the ideal child or servant they wanted more than the actual sentient animal they had.

Moreover, as Agnes Repplier (a cat enthusiast) astutely pointed out, extravagant exaltation of canine love reflects the author's egotism more than the dog's feeling. She remarked on Maurice Maeterlinck's impassioned tributes: "Never for a moment does he consider his dog save as a worshiper . . . think of himself save as a being worshiped . . . feel that this relationship can be otherwise than just, reasonable, and satisfying to both parties." He claims that the dog is fortunate in being "the only living being that has found, and recognizes, an indubitable, unexceptionable and definite god." And this god, Repplier deflates, is "M. Maeterlinck, you, I, anybody who has bought and reared a puppy."[5]

Absolute love is only one of the superhuman virtues with which some admirers credit dogs. Terhune rhapsodized that they immeasurably excel humans "in swerveless loyalty, in forgiveness, in foursquare honesty, in humor, in stamina, in adaptability, in conscience, in pluck, in sacrifice." But dogs' unquestioning fidelity, their eagerness to please superiors and to overlook injuries from them, owe more to the instinctive hierarchical order of the wolf pack than to moral principles; probably they cannot imagine alternative behavior. It may be true that a certain red setter "never entertained a mean or an unworthy thought," but it does not follow that its mind was filled with generous and noble ones.[6] If dogs are not capable of hypocrisy on the human scale, it is because they are unacquainted with human motives for falsification. On their own simpler level, they are quite capable of displaying instant affection to anyone holding a tasty treat.

Dogs are praised for loving without criticism, even though they do so because they are oblivious to human moral distinctions; and yet there is also a persistent myth that there must be some goodness in anyone that a dog loves. Robert Service was inspired by the sight of a filthy tramp who was always accompanied by a starved yellow cur, even when he lay dead drunk on the street, to write a poem about a criminal who was hanged and appeared, still unrepentant, before the Judgment Seat. Just as he was about to be damned for his many crimes, his cur crept to his feet, and God decreed that anyone who had won the love of a dog would ultimately be saved.[7]

In the same way, a person's love for dogs is supposed to be evidence of basic goodness. Although nice people are nice to their dogs and cruelty to dogs surely reveals a nasty nature, it is far from true that kindly feelings toward dogs necessarily reveal anything about the rest of one's character. Adolf Hitler, for example, was very fond of his German shepherds. He tenderly recalled his friendship with Foxl, an English war dog whom he adopted in the trenches and who accompanied him through most of World War I. Napoleon, too, had a soft spot for dogs. As he was touring the corpse-strewn battlefield after one of his victories in Italy, a dog leaped out from under the clothes of a dead man and ran back and forth between Napoleon's party and his dead master, howling piteously. The great soldier was moved to compassion by the sight of this man "forsaken by all except his dog!" Napoleon did go on to remark on the incongruity of his being deeply upset "by the mournful howling of a dog" when he could plan the slaughter of humans with dry eyes.[8] But this insight prompted neither regrets for the deaths he had caused nor a thought of ceasing to make war.

Surely it is possible to love and appreciate dogs without confusing them with people, or endowing them with superlative virtue or the capacity to perceive or elicit hidden goodness. Through the hero of his science fiction novel *Sirius,* a superdog with a human mind and a German shepherd's body, Olaf Stapledon judiciously classified human attitudes toward dogs. Apart from "those who were simply indifferent," there were " 'dog lovers,' whom [Sirius] detested . . . who sentimentalized dogs, and really had no accurate awareness of them," who made them into "pathetically human" dolls by "exaggerating their intelligence and loveableness, mollycoddling them and over-feeding them; and starving their natural impulses of sex, pugnacity and hunting"; "dog-detesters, who were either too highbrow to descend to companionship with a dumb animal or too frightened of their own animal nature"; and finally, "the 'dog-interested,' who combined a fairly accurate sense of the difference between dog and man with a disposition to respect a dog *as a dog,* as a rather remote but essentially like-minded relative."[9]

Like the "dog-interested," we should appreciate dogs for the loving and lovable, sensitive and responsive animals they are. We can recognize that they share many of our needs, perceptions, and feelings without supposing their requirements to be identical with our own. Attributing to them qualities they do not have reveals a lack of respect for what they are. Ted Patrick points out that those who ascribe mystical, extrasensory powers to dogs are refusing to recognize the reasoning powers that they have. A dog does not "sense" that its owner is going away; rather, it sees him taking out suitcases and has learned by experience what that means.[10] Considering that dogs have no natural familiarity with vacations and suitcases, that ability to learn is remarkable enough.

Brooks Atkinson explains that comparisons of the moral worth of dogs and humans are meaningless because "the circumstances are not equal." If Cleo, his German shepherd, "never did a mean thing in her life, there was no reason why she should. Her requirements in life were simple and continuously fulfilled. . . . It was easy to maintain a sunny disposition in [Cleo's] circumstances. . . . But it would be unfair to deny to Cleo her personal sweetness and patience. Whether her life was simple or not, she did represent a standard of good conduct. . . . She was loyal and forgiving. She loved everyone in the home. Beyond that, she was joyous and beautiful and a constant symbol of happiness."[11]

John Updike's poem about a dying dog's last pathetic effort to be a "good dog" is more touching than any contrived tale about a bird dog's proving his honor by resisting pressure to hunt deer. Updike's young dog was just learning to relieve herself on newspapers spread on the kitchen floor when she was fatally injured by a car. She died on the way to the veterinary's the next morning, and when the Updikes got home they saw that, needing to defecate during the night, she had dragged herself to a newspaper accidentally left on the floor. Within her doggy comprehension, she had risen above her pain to do the right thing. Her effort was all the more pathetic because it was useless: the newspaper was not put down for her, and no one would have blamed her for breaking training in her extremity.[12]

James Thurber demonstrates the admirable character of his black standard poodle Medve by her expert handling of a potentially disastrous situation involving her newborn puppies and a two-year-old child. When her litter arrived ahead of schedule and was discovered in the barn by the toddler, Medve averted trouble more sensibly and kindly than many humans would. "The child gaily displayed on her right forearm the almost invisible and entirely painless marks of teeth which had gently induced her to put down the live black toys she had found and wanted to play with."[13] Recognizing both that her puppies had to be protected and that the person who threatened them was innocent of bad intentions, the dog figured out a way to stop the child without hurting her. The real anecdote better persuades us of canine worth than some melodramatic fiction in which a dog saves a child's life.

Robert Westall's *The Kingdom by the Sea*, an honestly presented novel free of factitious sentimental appeals, convinces us how much a child and a dog can do for each other. After twelve-year-old Harry's home and (he believes) his family have been destroyed in a bombing raid, he is befriended by Don, an Alsatian type dog in the same situation. The dog's sympathy allays his desolation, and the dog's need stimulates Harry to buy food, which of course they share. Accepting responsibility for Don causes Harry to grow up: he realizes he must control the dog, for both their sakes, and he teaches himself to do so. Don's confidence in him spurs him to figure out how to support the two of them. During their first air raid together, Don drags Harry to shelter under the pier and Harry alleviates Don's suffering by muffling his ears with a sweater. Then Harry thinks how wonderful Don was: "He'd heard the bombers coming, long before the siren went; he'd found the best shelter. Above all, he'd been close to the dog, to its furry warm bulk. The dog had been closer to him than Mom had been, let alone Dad. He thought he and the dog made a pretty good team."[14] And indeed they do, but their comradeship is precarious. As they move from place to place, they must avoid the authorities, who would euthanize the ownerless dog. As in *Lassie Come-Home*, children and dogs are powerless in a world run by adult humans. There is no easy solution here, however. Harry learns that his family has survived, and he has to go back to them. His sister takes an unreasoning fear of Don and his father ill-temperedly refuses to pay for feeding him, so Harry has to send Don off to a friend they made on their journey. It is clear to Harry and the reader that he was better off on his own with the dog than with his second-rate family. Don is not a superdog nor an emblem of anything except himself; he offers nothing but warm, steady, sympathetic friendship, but that is quite enough to sustain the boy. Their relationship is mutual; neither dog nor boy would have come through intact without it.

Our relationships with dogs can be eminently satisfying without being ideal beyond human limits. We can enjoy their love even if we know it is based partly on dependency and is not free of self-interest. Even if we recognize that our dogs love us uncritically because they do not know any better, we all need someone who will greet us enthusiastically whenever we come home, who will never weigh our shortcomings or care about our success in society. Our First Friend may not be our Best Friend (unless we are unfortunate in our human connections), but it is a good friend whom we can count on to cheer and sustain our spirits.

Notes

Dedication adapted from P. L. Travers, *Mary Poppins* (New York: Harcourt, Brace & World, 1934), 53–54.

1. What Dogs Mean to Us

1. Marion Schwartz, *A History of Dogs in the Early Americas* (New Haven: Yale University Press, 1997), 21–22; Maria Leach, *God Had a Dog: Folklore of the Dog* (New Brunswick: Rutgers University Press), 32–33.
2. Marjorie Garber, *Dog Love* (New York: Touchstone, 1997), 77.
3. Mark Derr, *Dog's Best Friend: Annals of the Dog-Human Relationship* (New York: Henry Holt, 1997), 5.
4. Bruce Fogle, *Interrelations Between People and Pets* (Springfield, Ill.: Charles C. Thomas, 1981), 47.
5. Caroline Knapp, *Pack of Two: The Intricate Bond Between People and Dogs* (New York: Dial, 1998), 213.
6. "At the Vicar's," in Christopher Hawtree, *The Literary Companion to Dogs: From Homer to Hockney* (London: Sinclair-Stevenson, 1993), 422–24.
7. Knapp, 212.
8. "Dog," in Benjamin Spencer, *Memorable Dogs: An Anthology* (New York: Harper & Row, 1985), 125–26.
9. "Talking to Dogs [In memoriam Rolfi Strobl, run over, June 9th, 1970]," in Hawtree, 827.
10. In Lucy Menzies, *The First Friend: An Anthology of the Friendship of Man and Dog* (London: George Allen and Unwin, 1922), 177–78.
11. *Washington Post*, March 5, March 16, 2001.
12. Coolidge quotation in Roy Rowan and Brooke Janis, *First Dogs: American Presidents and*

Their Best Friends (Chapel Hill: Algonquin Books, 1997), 3; Roosevelt in Hawtree, 753–54.

13. William E. Maloney and Jean-Claude Suarès, eds., *The Literary Dog* (New York: Push Pin Press, 1978), 117.

14. The current President Bush has two Scotties.

15. Peter and Ingrid Salmon, in A. H. Katcher and A. M. Beck, *New Perspectives on Our Lives with Companion Animals* (Philadelphia: University of Pennsylvania Press, 1983), 253, 264.

16. In John Richard Stephens, *The Dog Lovers' Companion* (Rocklin, Calif.: Prima Publishing, 1992), 293. Compare William Cowper's "The Dog and the Water-Lily," where the poet wishes that humans were as prompt to oblige God as his dog was to oblige him by leaping into the water to fetch a water-lily that he noticed his master wanted. In his essay "Of Atheisme," Francis Bacon argued that the dog's relationship to man proves the existence of a parallel relationship between man and a being superior to him: as the dog's god, his master, inspires him to a nobility above his nature, the love of God inspires man.

17. Eileen Power, *Medieval People* (London: Methuen, 1963), 96–97, 103.

18. William Youatt, *The Dog* (London: Longman et al., 1852), 9–10.

19. Edmund Burke, *A Philosophical Inquiry into the Origin of Our Ideas of the Sublime and the Beautiful* (1756) (London: George Bell, 1889), 48. Jean-Jacques Rousseau, who was very fond of his pets, admitted to James Boswell that he did not much respect his dog (*Boswell on the Grand Tour, Germany, and Switzerland, 1764* [New York: McGraw-Hill, 1953], 433–34).

20. In the past, *dog* was "a particle added to any thing to mark meanness, or degeneracy, or worthlessness; as a *dog* rose" (Johnson, *Dictionary,* under "Dog"). Johnson adds *dog-trick, dog-hearted,* and *doghole.*

    Dogged persistence, however, is not necessarily negative. In the Middle Ages, the Dominicans, who were noted for their dogged pursuit of heretics, punned on the name of their order to proudly call themselves *Domini canes,* dogs of the Lord. From this perhaps arose the story that St. Dominic's mother dreamed before his birth that she was carrying a white, constantly barking whelp in her womb. A priest interpreted this to mean that she would bear a son who would be "a very good dog," who would guard the house of God, "pursue its enemies with loud barking," and "cure many with the healing of his tongue" (Leach, 259–60). Our positive word *sleuth* comes from sleuthhound, an old word for bloodhound.

21. This legend is very widespread, although the hero is not always a wolfhound; there is an almost identical French version.

22. For Carroll's Dogland, see Margaret Blount; *Animal Land: The Creatures of Children's Fiction* (New York: William Morrow, 1975), 83. Pluto was fully developed in 1934; later, of course, Disney developed anthropomorphic dogs—first Goofy (a humanized dog in the Mickey Mouse crowd), then the characters in *Lady and the Tramp* (1955) and *101 Dalmatians.* Actually, in *Tik-Tok of Oz* (1914) Toto is induced to speak a few words, but normally he communicates perfectly well by barking.

23. Lewis, *The Last Battle* (New York: Macmillan, 1956), 108–109, 151.

24. Roger Caras, *Roger Caras' Treasury of Great Dog Stories* (New York: E. P. Dutton, 1987), 420. Clarke's story is also in Caras.

25. Bram Stoker, *Dracula* (1897), chapter 7. The immense dog that sprang up on deck from below as the doomed ship landed and then disappeared was presumably Dracula himself. If so, the local SPCA's concern for him was amusingly ironic. Blackwood's story appeared in 1920.

26. The Wish Hounds, Yell-hounds, or Yeth-hounds were headless hounds driven by the devil. They understandably terrified people but did not generally attack them, although their presence portended death. The *Anglo-Saxon Chronicle* reported as fact that in 1127 a pack of black hounds with eyes like saucers streamed baying through Peterborough and the adjacent woods (Leach, 64–66).

27. Briggs, *Encyclopedia,* 301. When Jane Eyre first saw Mr. Rochester's Newfoundland by himself on a lonely road in Yorkshire, she thought fearfully of the Gytrash.

    The Black Dog of Bungay who raced through a church during services on August 4, 1557, and left two people dead and one crippled was more actively malevolent, though its motives were never described. Cotton Mather related the awful experience of John Kembal, who was pursued in the woods by a black puppy that forced him off the road so that he kept stumbling and falling and risked cutting himself with the ax he was carrying. He tried to cut the puppy as it ran between his legs, but he couldn't hit it. Then it vanished, but another, larger black puppy appeared and kept flying at his throat. He was saved by calling on God and Christ, which made it vanish (*Wonders of the Invisible World,* in Michael Parry, *The Hounds of Hell: Weird Tales About Dogs* [London: Victor Gollancz, 1974], 8).

28. Katharine Briggs, *An Encyclopedia of Fairies* (New York: Pantheon Books, 1976), 208. The headless dog story is a folktale related in Karen Zweifel, *Dog-gone Ghost Stories* (Birmingham, Ala.: Crane Hill Publishers, 1996).

29. Conan Doyle, "The Hound of the Baskervilles" (1902), in *The Annotated Sherlock Holmes* (New York: Clarkson N. Potter, 1967), 2:100.

30. Parry, 151. The other two horror stories involving real dogs are Ramsey Campbell's "The Whining," where the protagonist is persecuted by an obnoxious stray dog that thrusts itself into his life and home and continues to haunt him after he kills it, and Dion Fortune's "The Death Hound," where a cardiac patient is harassed by a ferocious-looking black dog that constantly appears in the shadows when he is trying to go to sleep; he lives in fear that some day he will be unable to resist running away from it and will be killed by the exertion. Arthur Bradford's story is in his *Dogwalker* (New York: Knopf, 2001).

31. The one exception is too far-fetched to be effective or convincing. In Anne Perry's "Daisy and the Archeologists," the neighborhood dogs and cats get rid of archaeologists who are digging up their favorite meadow by planting obviously modern dishes in the ground. Manson's *Canine Crimes II* includes three stories on the old Dog of Montargis theme.

2. How the Partnership Started

1. Rudyard Kipling, *Just So Stories* (New York: Books of Wonder, 1996), 116–17.

2. Juliet Clutton-Brock, in Ian L. Mason, ed., *Evolution of Domestic Animals* (London: Longman, 1984), 199.

3. Raymond P. and Laura Coppinger, *Dogs: A Startling New Understanding of Canine Origin, Behavior and Evolution* (New York: Scribner, 2001), 57–61. The Coppingers perhaps overestimate the differences between wolves and dogs, as when they insist that dogs have lost the lupine pack structure with its clear hierarchy.

4. Juliet Clutton-Brook, in Susan Janet Crockford, ed., *Dogs Through Time: An Archaeological Perspective* (Oxford: Archaeopress, 2000), 4.

5. John Paul Scott, "Evolution and Domestication of the Dog," in Theodosius Dobzhansky et al., eds., *Evolutionary Biology 2* (New York: Appleton-Century-Crofts, 1968), 258–59.

6. Crockford, *Dogs Through Time,* 12, 14, 17.

7. Stephen Budiansky, *The Covenant of the Wild: Why Animals Chose Domestication* (New York: Morrow, 1992), 77–78.

8. R. and L. Coppinger, *Dogs,* 63–64; Raymond Coppinger and Mark Feinstein, " 'Hark! Hark! The Dogs Do Bark . . . ' and Bark and Bark and Bark," *Smithsonian,* 21 (January 1991), 127–28; Stephen Budiansky, *The Truth About Dogs: An Inquiry into the Ancestry, Social Conventions, Mental Habits, and Moral Fiber of* Canis familiaris (New York: Viking, 2000), 46–47; Lyudmila N. Trut, "Early Canid Domestication: The Farm-Fox Experiment," *American Scientist* 87 (March/April 1999), 168. Belyaev started his project in 1959 and continued it for twenty-six years. Trut, who has continued his work, reports that these foxes can now be satisfactory house pets, as affectionate and devoted as dogs although more independent, having descended from solitary animals.

9. Dingoes and basenjis, however, both primitive breeds, retain the annual cycle.

10. Peter Steinhart, *In the Company of Wolves* (New York: Knopf, 1995), 128–29.

11. R. and L. Coppinger, *Dogs,* 49.

12. Steinhart, *Company of Wolves,* 130–31.

13. Konrad Lorenz, *Man Meets Dog,* trans. Marjorie Kerr Wilson (Baltimore: Penguin, 1964), 129, 137.

14. Stanley Coren, *The Intelligence of Dogs: A Guide to the Thoughts, Emotions, and Inner Lives of Our Canine Companions* (New York: Bantam Books, 1995), 63–64, 93–97.

15. Peter Messent, *Understanding Your Dog* (New York: Stein & Day, 1979), 30.

16. John Paul Scott and John L. Fuller, *Genetics and the Social Behavior of the Dog* (Chicago: University of Chicago Press, 1965), 76–77, 403; Scott, "Evolution and Domestication," 266.

17. John C. McLoughlin, *The Canine Clan: A New Look at Man's Best Friend* (New York: Viking, 1983), 106–108, 124–25.

18. Clutton-Brock, in Mason, 204.

19. James Serpell, ed., *The Domestic Dog: Its Evolution, Behaviour, and Interactions with People* (Cambridge: Cambridge University Press, 1995), 15, 247.

20. Richard B. Lee and Irven De Vore, eds., *Man the Hunter* (Chicago: Aldine, 1968), 295.

21. F. E. Zeuner, *A History of Domesticated Animals* (New York: Harper & Row, 1963), 61–62.

22. Clutton-Brock, in Serpell, 10; Stanley J. Olsen, *Origins of the Domestic Dog: The Fossil Record* (Tucson: University of Arizona Press, 1985), 31; Zeuner, 93–94; Crockford, 302. Teeth tend to be crowded in the jaws of early dogs because jaw size was reduced before teeth were.

23. In Mason, 199. A study of canine DNA by P. Savolainen et al. suggests that the original domestication of dogs occurred in the Far East about fifteen thousand years ago. See their "Genetic Evidence for an East Asian Origin of Domestic Dogs" in *Science* 298 (November 22, 2002), 1610–13.

24. "Evolution and Domestication," 249, 261.

25. Sandra Olsen, in Crockford, 71–72, 82–85; Coppinger in Serpell, *Domestic Dog*, 22.

26. Crockford, in Crockford, 303–305.

27. Olsen, in Crockford, 71–72.

28. Leach, 137–38. Dogs in the other world fulfilled another important canine role by guiding dead souls through the underworld, as they guard and guide their masters in life. The Aztecs sacrificed a dog when someone died to guide the soul to the underworld kingdom of the dead. Yama, the Hindu god of the dead, had two "four-eyed" dogs who ran to earth to seek out those chosen to die and conduct them to his city; they also guarded the road to heaven (Leach, 137, 140).

29. Schwartz, 89.

3. Dogs in the Ancient World

1. John McLoughlin, an amateur runner, reports that the only dogs that have ever bitten him are sight hounds (100, 103). On the earliest sight hounds, see Lois E. Bueler, *Wild Dogs of the World* (New York: Stein & Day, 1973), 109.

2. Beatrice Fox Griffith, *Historic Dogs: An Outline in Pictures of the Story of the Dog* (Haverford, Pa.: Clinton L. Mellor, 1953), picture following p. 11.

3. Brian Vesey-Fitzgerald, *The Domestic Dog: An Introduction to Its History* (London: Routledge and Kegan Paul, 1957), Supplementary Notes, 54.

4. Herodotus, *The Histories,* trans. Robin Waterfield (Oxford: Oxford University Press, 1998), 121.

5. Nina M. Davies, *Ancient Egyptian Paintings, Selected, Copied, and Described* (Chicago: University of Chicago, 1936), vol. 1, Plate 15.

6. Letter from Zeuner, 108–109; story (second millennium BCE) from Anthony S. Mercatante, *Who's Who in Egyptian Mythology* (New York: Clarkson N. Potter, 1978), 36–38.

7. *The Odyssey,* trans. E. V. Rieu (Baltimore: Penguin Books, 1946), 266–67.

8. Herodotus, 17.

9. *Cynegetica* (fourth century BCE), in *Scripta Minora*, trans. E. C. Marchant (Cambridge: Harvard University Press, 1925), 367, 377–85, 387. Although classical writers listed

many varieties of hounds, they usually identified them by their place of origin rather than by characteristics we could recognize today. Molossians from Epirus were huge, heavy mastiff types; Laconians were more lightly built.

10. Second century CE, in Denison Bingham Hull, *Hounds and Hunting in Ancient Greece* (Chicago: University of Chicago Press, 1964), 166–70.

11. *The Republic* (fourth century BCE), trans. Francis MacDonald Cornford (London: Oxford University Press, 1945), 64–65; Homer, *Odyssey,* 304.

12. "Cynics," in *Encyclopaedia of Religion and Ethics,* ed. James Hastings (Edinburgh: T. and T. Clark, 1911), 4:378–83, and *Concise Routledge Encyclopedia of Philosophy* (London: Routledge, 2000), 186.

13. Herodotus, 304, 470.

14. Homer, *Odyssey,* 245.

15. Marcus Terentius Varro, *Varro on Farming,* trans. Lloyd Storr-Best (London: G. Bell, 1912), 218–19, 224.

16. Lucius Junius Moderatus Columella, *On Agriculture* (c. 60 CE), trans. E. S. Forster and Edward H. Heffner (Cambridge: Harvard University Press, 1954), 2:305–307, 309–11, 315. Columella may have been inspired by Cicero's famous eulogy in *De Natura Deorum*: "Such fidelity of dogs in protecting what is committed to their charge, such affectionate attachment to their masters, such jealousy of strangers, such incredible acuteness of nose in following a track, such keenness in hunting—what else do they evince but that these animals were created for the use of man" (Vesey-Fitzgerald, *Domestic Dog,* Supplement, 45). Quotation from Lawrence in Jack Goodman, ed., *The Fireside Book of Dog Stories* (New York: Simon & Schuster, 1943), 216.

17. Lucretius, *On the Nature of the Universe,* trans. Ronald Latham (Baltimore: Penguin Books, 1951), 203–204.

18. Vesey-Fitzgerald, *Domestic Dog,* 164.

19. *Aristotle's History of Animals,* trans. Richard Cresswell (London: George Bell, 1891), 239. In general, Aristotle had little to say about dogs, merely listing a few facts or superstitions, such as that they eat grass to purge themselves and that the ferocious Indian dogs were sired by tigers (204, 227, 230).

20. In Jocelyn M. C. Toynbee, *Animals in Roman Life and Art* (Ithaca, N.Y.: Cornell University Press, 1973), 120.

21. Ibid., 106, 110–111, 121.

22. Marcus Valerius Martialis, *Epigrams,* trans. D. R. Shackleton Bailey (Cambridge: Harvard University Press, 1993), 1:125. Toynbee cites Petronius, 109. Lucian quotation comes from Ethel E. Bicknell, ed., *Praise of the Dog: An Anthology* (London: Grant Richards, 1902), 5–6.

Fabulists typically focused on the everyday failings of dogs to bring out the same failings in humans. Besides "The Dog in the Manger," who will not let the hungry ox eat hay even though the dog has no use for it, there is a dog who loses the piece of meat he has when he tries to seize the meat of "another" dog, who is actually his own reflection in the river ("The Dog Carrying a Piece of Meat") and the dogs who send a delegation to Jupiter to plead for "a better lot in life," but lose their opportunity by dawdling on the way, busily sniffing about in dung heaps ("An Embassy"). Aesop's Fables (sixth century BCE) are known from Phaedrus' Latin version (first century CE); "The Dog in the Manger," in Joseph Jacobs's collection, may have been added to Aesop in postclassical times. The Dog in the Manger behaves realistically, but took on exaggerated significance in later times, when it passed into proverb. As a result, by medieval times the dog became unfairly associated with the deadly sin of Envy. In poetry and pictures, Envy was personified riding on or accompanied by a dog. The dog appears in a good light only in "The Faithful Dog," where a watchdog refuses a bribe of bread from a thief.

23. Plutarch, *Moralia* (first–second centuries CE), trans. Harold Cherniss and William C. Helmbold (Cambridge: Harvard University Press, 1957), 12:325, 379, 381, 405.

24. Claudius Aelianus, *On the Characteristics of Animals,* trans. A. F. Scholfield (Cambridge: Harvard University Press, 1958), 2:137, 155, 175–79, 359–61.

25. Ovid, *Metamorphoses,* trans. Rolfe Humphries (Bloomington: Indiana University Press, 1968), 63–64.

26. Pliny the Elder, *Natural History,* trans. H. Rackham (Cambridge: Harvard University Press, 1947), 8:107. Pliny also highly praised the dog's intelligence and character. Homer refers to "Orion's Dog, . . . brightest among the stars, and yet . . . a sign of evil / and brings on the great fever for unfortunate mortals," in *The Iliad,* trans. Richmond Lattimore (Chicago: University of Chicago Press, 1951), 436. The Dog Star had a positive connotation only in Egypt, because the Nile rises when the Dog Star rises, "and so the Egyptians pay honor to the Dog for bringing and summoning this fertilizing water" (Aelian 2:341). Sirius, faithful as a dog, appeared every year to warn them to move their cattle to higher land.

27. *Iliad,* 437.

28. *Theogony* (c. 700 BCE), in Stephens, 271; Virgil, *The Aeneid* (first century BCE), trans. W. F. Jackson Knight (Baltimore: Penguin, 1956), 159–60; Dante Alighieri, *The Inferno* (early fourteenth century), trans. John Ciardi (New York: New American Library, 1954), 66.

In the same way, Milton elaborated on classical myth to create a horrid canine picture in *Paradise Lost* (1667). When the nymph Scylla rejected a suitor, she was punished by having heads of barking dogs sprout all around below her waist: "feeling for her thighs, / Her legs, her feet, she finds in all these parts, / The heads of dogs, jaws gaping wide and hellish. / She stands on dogs gone mad, and loins and belly / Are circled by these monstrous forms" (Ovid, 340). When Milton reworked this figure as Sin in *Paradise Lost,* he emphasized the awful noise of their incessant barking, which continued even when they crawled back into her womb that had borne them and gnawed her insides (*Complete Poetry and Selected Prose* [Glasgow: Nonesuch Press, 1948], 115, 118).

29. Jezebel's story is told in II Kings 9:10, 33–35. For an illustration of her end, see, for example, the early-fifteenth-century Bible of King Wenceslas. For other references to dogs eating dead bodies, see I Kings 14:11, 16:4, 21:19, 21:24, 22:38. For degrading canine comparisons, see I Samuel 24:14, II Samuel 9:8, 16:9, II Kings 8:13, Psalms 22:16, 59:6,

14–15, Proverbs 26:11, II Peter 2:22. Favorable references are found in Proverbs 30:31, Isaiah 56:10–11, Job 30:1. The only hunters mentioned in the Bible are Esau, Isaac's less favored son, and Nimrod, leader of an enemy people.

30. Luke 16:21. For Tobias's dog, see *The Book of Tobit* (200–175 BCE), in *The Apocrypha: An American Translation,* trans. Edgar J. Goodspeed (Chicago: University of Chicago Press, 1938), 117, 124.

31. Plato, 158.

4. Hunting Dogs

1. A. C. Fox-Davies, *A Complete Guide to Heraldry*, revised J. P. Brooke-Little (London: Nelson, 1969), 154–55. Three other sporting dogs appear on at least one crest (a foxhound, a water spaniel, and a fox terrier) and a mastiff on at least one.

2. These medieval methods of hunting persisted into modern times when circumstances were appropriate. In the American West in 1909, a wolf would be found and started by scent hounds and pursued by a mixed pack—two greyhounds to run the wolf down and hold it until the heavier dogs (bloodhounds, foxhounds, wolfhounds, or crosses among them) arrived to do the actual fighting. The hunters followed the hounds on horseback (A. R. Harding, in Clifford Hubbard, *A Kennel of Dogs* [London: Elek, 1977], 87–88).

3. Edward, Second Duke of York, *The Master of Game*, ed. William A. and F. Baillie-Grohman, with foreword by Theodore Roosevelt (London: Ballantyne, Hanson, 1904), xlvii, 60, 95–99, Appendix 127, 173. Although Edward left out a few of Gaston's chapters and added five of his own, everything I have quoted is directly translated from Gaston. On sleuth hounds, see Hector Boece's *History and Chronicles of Scotland,* 1536, in George R. Jesse, *Researches into the History of the British Dog, from Ancient Laws, Charters and Historical Records* (London: Robert Hardwicke, 1866), 2:170–71.

4. One is represented in an exquisitely detailed bronze statue from a third century CE shrine in Gloucestershire, lying down and turning its head backward and upward, perhaps looking soulfully at its master. The Irish chieftains used their great wolfhounds to guard their herds and property and regularly turned them out at night, after making sure that no legitimate visitor was still outside. This is why the great hero Setanta, whom no one knew was in the vicinity, had to kill the ferocious hound of the smith Culand in self-defense. Moved by Culand's lament over the loss, Setanta volunteered to take over watching the house until a replacement dog grew up; and thus Setanta acquired the name Cu-Culand (Cuchullain), Culand's hound. See Alfred W. DeQuoy, *The Irish Wolfhound in Irish Literature and Law* (Alfred W. DeQuoy, 1971), 21–22.

5. Edward, Duke of York, 42–44, 46, 63. Dame Juliana Berners's constantly quoted *The Book of Saint Albans* (fifteenth century) puts bits of Gaston's manual into doggerel verse and elaborates his description of the greyhound in a fanciful and not very informative way. She says a good greyhound should be "heeded lyke a snake / and neckyd lyke a drake / fotyd lyke a catte and tayllyd lyke a ratte / syded lyke a teme / and chyned lyke a beme." This evidently means that it should have a long narrow head, a long flexible neck so it can stoop

and grab a hare without breaking its stride, round compact feet, a long thin tail, a capacious chest providing plenty of room for lungs, and a spine like a long, straight, strong beam. She ruthlessly elaborates on Edward's time line: a hound will do nothing but grow for the first year, will learn for the next two, will be at his peak for the fourth year, will gradually decline during the fifth and sixth, can be a stud the seventh, will only hang around the eighth, and in the ninth year he will be good for nothing and should be sent to the tanner (in Edward Cecil Ash, *Dogs: Their History and Development* [New York: Benjamin Blom, 1972], 1:175).

6. Sir Walter Scott, *The Talisman* (New York: Dodd, Mead, 1941), 105, 292. Maida was also the model for the deerhound Bevis, who plays a prominent role in Scott's *Woodstock*. His noble, unthinking loyalty parallels that of his royalist human family.

7. Arthur Frederick Jones and John Rendel, eds., *The Treasury of Dogs* (New York: Golden Press, 1964), 43.

8. Brian Vesey-Fitzgerald, *The Book of the Dog* (London: Nicholson & Watson, 1948), 799, 800, 805.

9. Edward, Duke of York, 64, 65, 68; Geoffrey Chaucer, *The Canterbury Tales,* trans. Nevill Coghill (Harmandsworth, Middlesex: Penguin Books, 1951), 77.

10. Edward, Duke of York, 66–67.

11. Ibid., Appendix, 197.

12. Richard Surflet in 1600, in John Henry Walsh, *The Dogs of the British Islands* (London: Horace Cox, 1872), 2–3.

13. Nicholas Cox, *The Gentleman's Recreation* (Yorkshire: E. P. Publishing, 1973), Section III, 44, 47–48.

14. Moxon in Vesey-Fitzgerald, *Book of the Dog,* 229–30; Ford in Beth Brown, ed., *All Dogs Go to Heaven* (New York: Grosset & Dunlap, 1961), 438–40.

15. Anne Brontë, *Agnes Grey* (Oxford: Oxford University Press, 1988), 155; Vesey-Fitzgerald, *Book of the Dog,* 933. Terriers were not mentioned by name until the Middle Ages, but a Roman metal figurine of the first to fourth century CE, found in Northumberland, has the characteristic square head, rough coat, and medium-short legs, together with prick ears and a tail curved over its back.

16. Bonnie Wilcox and Chris Walkowicz, *Atlas of Dog Breeds of the World,* 4th ed. (Neptune City; N.J.: T.F.H. Publications, 1993), 763–64.

17. Edward, Duke of York, 69–71, Appendix 188 (the hounds' pilgrimage, from accounts kept by the master huntsman of Charles VI of France, 1388).

18. Cox, Section I,1–13; *Institucion of a Gentleman* (1568), in Roger B. Manning, *Hunters and Poachers: A Social and Cultural History of Unlawful Hunting in England, 1485–1640* (Oxford: Clarendon, 1993), 4; William Taplin, *The Sportsman's Cabinet, or a Correct Delineation of the Canine Race* (London, 1803), 2:185–86.

19. William Somervile, *The Chace* (Garden City, N.Y.: Doubleday, Doran, 1929), 16, 18, 34, 37–38, 96–99.

Voice has always been given great importance in evaluating hounds. Gervase

Markham, in *Country Contentments* (1615), gravely explained how to arrange "your kennel for sweetness of cry": "compound it of some large dogs, that have deep solemn mouths . . . which must bear the bass in the consort, then a double number of roaring, and loud ringing mouths, which must bear the counter-tenor, then some hollow plain sweet mouths, which must bear the mean or middle part: and so with these three parts of music you shall make your cry perfect: and herein you shall observe that these hounds thus mixed, do run just and even together, and not hang off loose from one another." You should add "a couple or two of small singing beagles, which as small trebles may warble amongst them." In Joseph Wood Krutch, ed., *The World of Animals: A Treasury of Love, Legend and Literature by Great Writers and Naturalists from the Fifth Century B.C. to the Present* (New York: Simon & Schuster, 1961), 84–85.

20. William Cowper, *The Selected Letters* (New York: Farrar, Straus and Young, 1951), 243. In a couple of engaging poems, Cowper reproaches his spaniel, Beau, for killing a baby bird without even the excuse of hunger, for he left the corpse untouched; and Beau replies that he could not resist a voice even louder than his master's, namely that of nature; he also reminds his master that he spared his pet linnet when it had fallen helpless to the floor ("On a Spaniel Called Beau Killing a Young Bird," "Beau's Reply").

Doubts about the value of hunting were rare in the early modern period, but Michel de Montaigne, Thomas More in *Utopia,* James Thomson (who attacked stag hunting in *The Seasons*), and Grimm (who in 1756 wrote to Diderot: "there is no pleasure less worthy of a thinking being than that of hunting") rejected the conventional assumptions of their times. See Heather Hastings, *Man and Beast in French Thought of the 18th Century* (Baltimore: Johns Hopkins University Press, 1936), 265–67.

21. William Secord, *A Breed Apart: The Art Collection of the American Kennel Club and the American Kennel Club Museum of the Dog* (Woodbridge, Suffolk: Antique Collectors Club, 2001), 120; Griffith, 54.

22. Angus Phillips, "Wolf to Woof: The Evolution of Dogs," *National Geographic,* January 2002, 20–21.

23. Manning, 58.

24. Scott, *Talisman,* 109.

25. P. B. Munsche, *Gentlemen and Poachers: The English Game Laws 1671–1831* (Cambridge: Cambridge University Press, 1981), 12, 180–82.

26. Munsche, 82; Henry Fielding, *Joseph Andrews* (Boston: Houghton Mifflin, 1961), 192–93.

27. Munsche 82; Thomas Bell, *A History of British Quadrupeds* (London: John Van Voorst, 1837), 236–37; Ralph Beilby, *A General History of Quadrupeds* (Newcastle upon Tyne: T. Bewick and S. Hodgson, 1790), 343.

Another working-class group who hunted for a living were the commercial fowl shooters on the barren Scots coast, where the land was too poor to farm. They had water dogs who would retrieve fowl from water at a considerable distance from land or from clefts in the rock cliffs and then figure out a route along which they could carry a heavy bird, such as a gannet or a Soland goose. The meat and down from these birds was the principal support of these families, and it could not have been obtained without the dogs (Taplin, *Sportsman's Cabinet*, 1:223–25).

28. Milton, 30; William Shakespeare, *The Tragedies* (London: Oxford University Press, 1912), 512, 705; *The Comedies* (London: Oxford University Press, 1911), 336, 568, 751–52; *The Histories and Poems* (London: Oxford University Press, 1912), 974.

29. Fielding, 203–205.

30. Rawdon B. Lee, *A History and Description of the Modern Dogs of Great Britain and Ireland* (London: Horace Cox, 1906), 1:57–58; Gordon Stables, *Our Friend the Dog* (London: Dean and Son, 190?), 12–13; Glenn Frankel, "A Regal Pursuit Is Run Down," *Washington Post*, November 19, 2004, A15.

31. Edward, Duke of York, xii.

32. William Faulkner, "The Bear," in *Bear, Man, and God: Seven Approaches to William Faulkner's "The Bear,"* ed. Francis Lee Utley, Lyn Z. Bloom, and Arthur F. Kinney (New York: Random House, 1964), 10–11, 22–23, 24–27, 30, 41, 49, 135 (from the original version of the story).

33. Kantor's story (1935) appears in Caras and others, Foote's (1917) in Zistel, Dion Henderson, *Algonquin* (1953), in *Top Dogs* (Madison, Wis.: Northwood, 1985), 96–97.

34. Rick Bass, *Colter: The True Story of the Best Dog I Ever Had* (Boston: Houghton Mifflin, 2000), 1, 5–6, 86–87, 96–97.

35. McLoughlin, 112. For the foxhound as the model dog, see John Henry Walsh, *The Dogs of the British Islands* (London: Horace Cox, 1872), 194.

36. Barker's essay is in Jim Kjlegaard, ed., *Hound Dogs and Others: A Collection of Stories by Members of Western Writers of America* (New York: Dodd, Mead, 1958); Hamilton's poem (1706) and Scott's comment, in Jesse, *Researches* 1:83–89; the *Essay on Shooting* (1789), quoted in Vesey-Fitzgerald, *Book of the Dog*, 197.

    My subject is dogs, so I abstain from comment on the fate of the bobcat family, as well as statements like this from Vesey-Fitzgerald: "There is no greater achievement for both hounds and huntsman than to kill a beaten fox after a three-hour hunt" (*Book of the Dog*, 774).

37. A bloodhound, the champion of them all, can distinguish between the scent of identical twins and follow one of them. Humans have long marveled at its ability: one tested in the seventeenth century traced the footsteps of a man it had never seen to a country town four miles off and then a market town three miles beyond, ignoring all other footsteps (Robert Boyle, "Essays of Effluvia," in Sydenham Teak Edwards, "Blood-hound," *Cynographia Britannica* ([Leeds: Peregrine Books, 1992)].

38. Phillips, 25, 27. Stanley Coren tells how a dog saved her mistress's life when her nose alerted her to a situation that went unnoticed by human vision. A Shetland sheepdog kept sniffing and nuzzling a dark mole on her mistress's lower back. Since it produced no symptoms, the woman ignored it. Finally the dog actually bit her back, trying to remove the mole. So the woman showed it to her doctor at her next examination; he immediately recognized a melanoma, which was removed just in time. Apparently, dogs can detect

melanomas and certain other types of cancer, presumably by odor, before other symptoms appear (*How to Speak Dog: Mastering the Art of Dog-Human Communication* [New York: Simon & Schuster, 2001], 184–85).

39. Robin Meadows, "Scat-Sniffing Dogs," *Zoogoer*, September/October 2002, 22–27.

5. Working Dogs

1. Sir Walter Scott, *Ivanhoe* (New York: Dodd, Mead, 1941), 35–37, 199–201, 345.

2. *Ancient Laws and Institutes of Wales; Comprising Laws Supposed to Be Enacted by Howel the Good, Modified by Subsequent Regulations Under the Native Princes Prior to the Conquest by Edward I* (printed by command of his late majesty King William IV under the direction of the Commissioners of the Public Records, 1841), 242, 244.

3. Raymond and Lorna Coppinger, *Dogs,* 208–209, "Dogs in Sheep's Clothing Guard Flocks," *Smithsonian,* 21 (January 1991): 69; Coppinger in Serpell, *Domestic Dog,* 27. The Coppingers report that flock guards are so inhibited that they will not consume a carcass until someone else has opened it; they will remain by a dead lamb for days, longing to eat it, but unable to because they lack the dissect motor patterns.

4. In Hawtree, 214–15.

5. Raymond and Lorna Coppinger, "Dogs in Sheep's Clothing," 65–69.

6. Wilcox and Walkowicz, 58. For centuries northern dogs had been making their way into Europe, although they are not clearly documented; Shakespeare's Pistol in *Henry V* abuses an associate as a "prick-eared cur of Iceland" (II, 1:43–44).

7. Johannes Caius, *Of Englishe Dogges, the diversities, the names, the natures, and the properties,* trans. Abraham Fleming (Amsterdam: Theatrum Orbis Terrarum, 1969), 23–24; plate and description in Edwards.

8. Rawdon Lee in *Modern Dogs,* Hugh Dalziel on the collie, in Harriet Ritvo, *The Animal Estate: The English and Other Creatures in the Victorian Age* (Cambridge: Harvard University Press, 1987), 115; Watson's poem, "A Study in Contrasts," in Claire Necker, *Cats and Dogs* (New York: A. S. Barnes, 1969), 236–37.

9. James Hogg, *The Shepherd's Calendar* (Edinburgh: University Press, 1995), 57.

10. Desmond Morris, *The Animal Contract: An Impassioned and Rational Guide to Sharing the Planet and Saving Our Common World* (New York: Warner Books, 1990), 137.

11. Edwards, "Shepherd's Dog"; Hogg, 65–66.

12. Ruth L. Tongue, ed., *Forgotten Folk-Tales of the English Counties* (London: Routledge & Kegan Paul, 1970), 81–84.

13. Ash, 1: 281–83; Hogg, 58–59, 60, 62; Donald McCaig, *Nop's Trials* (New York: Crown, 1984), 103–104, 108–109; "Address to His Auld Dog Hector," in Bicknell, 111.

   The harsh necessities of the relationship between poor men and their working dogs are brought out in Thomas Hardy's *Far from the Madding Crowd,* where Gabriel Oak's young dog, in a burst of misguided enthusiasm, initiates a herding operation on his own and drives Oak's entire flock of sheep over a cliff. The consequence is clear even to the intensely humane Oak: the dog is shot that very day.

The nineteenth-century physician and dog lover John Brown provides further evidence of the sheepdog's devotion to its work. Wylie, "an exquisite shepherd's dog" he inherited when her master retired, adapted perfectly to her new life as a pet, but unaccountably disappeared every Tuesday evening and appeared the next morning weary and covered with mud. Eventually Brown found out that she went to the market at dawn and worked incessantly to help the shepherds get their sheep and lambs into the pens. The shepherds wondered who "the wonderful wee bitch" was—"She's a perfect meeracle; flees aboot like a speerit, and never gaes wrang; wears but never grups, and beats a' oor dowgs"—but she would never let them catch her. "She continued this amateur work until she died" (Menzies, 123–25).

14. *The Uncommercial Traveller,* in Hawtree, 295–96.

15. Charles Dickens, *Bleak House* (New York: W. W. Norton, 1977), 199.

16. G. Vines, "Wolves in Dogs' Clothing," *New Scientist* 91:1270 (September 10, 1981), 649–52.

   Nop, the border collie hero of Donald McCaig's *Nop's Trials* (1984), gives his Virginia farmer master essential help with his herds of eight hundred sheep and seventy cows, as well as winning championship sheepdog trials. Nop loves the farmer, but he loves his work even more. In an amusingly imagined encounter with a young hound bitch, Nop gathers sheep to impress her, but she cannot see the point; in her opinion, a dog's work is pursuing scents and giving tongue. He could smell a deer trail like her, but "attached no significance to the scent" (32–33).

17. Ash, 1:285.

   From the time that Australia was settled, herding dogs were in great demand to manage the stock on the vast ranches. But British collies could not endure the high temperatures and lengthy treks to saleyards in the city. A dog with more stamina that would work quietly but more forcefully (to control relatively wild cattle without stampeding them) was needed. In the mid-nineteenth century, a drover crossed smooth collies with dingoes, adding traces of other breeds. The result was a compact active dog, a thicker set version of the dingo, that controlled cattle silently by nipping their heels and combined the stamina of the dingo with the faithfulness and willingness to work of the traditional herding dogs. It was called the Australian heeler and then the Australian cattle dog. The most common sheepherder in Australia today is the kelpie, also produced by crossing collies with native dogs; and it is still of great economic importance. See the American Kennel Club's *Complete Dog Book,* 19th ed. (New York: Howell Book House, 1997), 576–77; *The International Encyclopedia of Dogs,* ed. Stanley Dangerfield and Elsworth Howell (New York: McGraw-Hill, 1971), 263.

18. In a parallel development in the late 1800s, Belgian fanciers examined the various shepherd dogs of their country and determined that there was a particularly Belgian type. Now there are three American Kennel Club recognized breeds of Belgian shepherds, each of which must be kept separate and pure. One of them, the Malinois, could pass for a German shepherd, although it is happily free of the failings engendered by overproduction of that breed.

19. Taplin, *Sportsman's Cabinet,* 1: 117–18; *Man's Best Friend: The National Geographic Book*

of Dogs, rev. ed. (Washington, D.C.: National Geographical Society, 1974), 185–88. Because large watchdogs were so general, the half-starved mastiff at the gate was a conventional feature in characterizations of misers. See, e.g., Fang in George Crabbe's "The Dealer and Clerk," in Bicknell, 99–100.

20. Caius, 25–33; Harrison's "Description" (included in Holinshed's *Chronicles,* 1577), in Jesse, 2:223–25; Edwards, "Mastiff"; McLoughlin, 110.

21. The modern breed, however, has become too large, heavily furred, and lumbering for mountain rescue duties.

22. Stanley Coren, *The Pawprints of History: Dogs and the Course of Human Events* (New York: Free Press, 2002), 152; Ouida, *A Dog of Flanders,* in *English Stories,* ed. Edward Everett Hale (Freeport, N.Y.: Books for Libraries, 1969), 133–34.

23. Aaron, the flamboyant villain of Shakespeare's *Titus Andronicus,* boasts of being "as true a dog as ever fought at head" (V.1.102). Enemies of Henry VIII's efficient, ruthless minister Cardinal Thomas Wolsey called him a butcher's cur, referring to his low origins and bulky, brutal appearance (*Henry VIII,* I.1.120).

24. John Evelyn, *The Diary* (Oxford: Clarendon, 1955), 3:549 (June 16, 1670); preacher quoted in William Taplin, *The Sporting Dictionary, and Rural Repository* (London: Vernor and Hood et al., 1803), 1:96–100; Joseph Strutt, *The Sports and Pastimes of the People of England* (New York: Augustus M. Kelley, 1970), 204–205.

25. Ash, 1:91, 2:521; Vero Shaw, *The Classic Encyclopedia of the Dog* (New York: Bonanza Books, 1984), 83. Bull-dog Drummond was created by "Sapper," Herman Cyril McNeile. Bulldogs were often used for dogfighting as well as bullbaiting. Belcher fought in 104 dogfights and was never defeated.

26. Bruce Watson, "The Dogs of War," 104.

    War mastiffs were still being used in the sixteenth century, when Henry VIII sent four hundred dogs with spiked collars along with four hundred soldiers to fight with the French army against Charles V of Spain. The war dog was trained to "be an enemy to everybody except his master; so much so that he will not allow himself to be stroked even by those he knows best, but threatens everybody alike with the fulminations of his teeth . . . and glares around in every direction with a hostile glance"; he was trained from earliest youth to pursue and bite men (protected in leather suits) (Ulisse Aldrovandi, in Stephens, 130). The Spanish invaders used such dogs to terrorize American Indians, who had seen only small dogs. Shakespeare used mastiffs to signify brainless fighters like Ajax and Achilles in *Troilus and Cressida* (I.3.391).

27. Colette, *Creatures Great and Small,* trans. Enid McLeod (New York: Farrar, Straus, & Giroux, 1951), 289–90. In "The One Who Came Back," Colette sympathetically presents a Briard's traumatic experience of combat (126–27).

28. Michael G. Lemish, *War Dogs: Canines in Combat* (Washington, D.C.: Brassey's, 1996), 18–20, 32, 73–75, 124–25, 148, 186, 231–32. Messenger dogs, important as long as communication depended on mechanical gear, have not been needed since the development of reliable radio communication.

The army had originally intended to destroy the war dogs as unreclaimable killers after World War II, but fortunately, Captain William Putney, who was the commanding officer of the 110 human Marines and 72 dogs who freed Guam in 1944, led a successful campaign to get the Marine Corps dogs de-trained. Of 559 surviving Marine Corps dogs, 540 were successfully de-trained and returned to civilian life, 15 were euthanized for physical health problems, and only 4 had to be euthanized for incorrigible behavior. See William W. Putney, *Always Faithful: A Memoir of the Marine Dogs of World War II* (New York: Free Press, 2001), 216.

29. Barbara Cohen and Louise Taylor, *Dogs and Their Women* (Boston: Little, Brown, 1989), 12.

30. Michel de Montaigne, *Essays,* trans. John Florio (London: J. M. Dent, 1910), 2:156–57. Actually, dogs were probably helping blind people from even earlier times. A wall painting at Herculaneum shows a woman offering food to a ragged man with a dog on a leash—probably a blind beggar with his guide dog. See Michael Tucker, *The Eyes That Lead: The Story of Guide Dogs for the Blind* (London: Robert Hale, 1984), 15.

31. Tucker, 72–76, 132–33, 179; Vesey-Fitzgerald, *Book of the Dog,* 951–52; Clinton R. Sanders, *Understanding Dogs: Living and Working with Canine Companions* (Philadelphia: Temple University Press, 1999), 56.

32. Vesey-Fitzgerald, *Book of the Dog,* 945; Katcher and Beck, 478.

33. Pamela Gerhardt, "Heal, Doggie, Heal," *Washington Post Health,* July 25, 2000, 10, 12–13.

34. American Humane Society, *Advocate* 17:1 (1999): 8–9, 23.

35. Alan Beck and Aaron Katcher, *Between Pets and People: The Importance of Animal Companionship* (New York: Putnam, 1983), 159–62.

Back in 1860, Florence Nightingale had noticed the therapeutic benefits of dogs, especially in long chronic cases, and remarked that "an invalid in giving an account of his nursing by a nurse and a dog, infinitely preferred that of the dog. 'Above all,' he said, 'it did not talk' " (*Notes on Nursing,* in Hawtree, 230).

36. Mary Flanagan, *The Blue Woman and Other Stories* (New York: W. W. Norton, 1994), 276.

6. Pets in Early Modern Times

1. G. R. Owst, *Literature and Pulpit in Medieval England: A Neglected Chapter in the History of English Letters and of the English People* (Oxford: Basil Blackwell, 1966), 11; George Jesse, 377–78; Keith Thomas, *Man and the Natural World: A History of the Modern Sensibility* (New York: Pantheon, 1983), 40.

2. E. and M. W. Radford, *Encyclopedia of Superstitions,* ed. and rev. Christina Hole (Chester Springs, Pa.: Dufour Editions, 1969), 136; Ash, vol. 1, Plate 44.

3. *Observations upon Prince Ruppert's White Dogge Called Boy* (1643); when Boye was killed at Marston Moor, a Puritan celebrated the disaster to the Cavaliers in *A Dogs Elegy, or Rupert's Tears* (July 27, 1644); letter of 1717. See Katharine MacDonogh, *Reigning Cats and Dogs* (New York: St. Martin's, 1999), 209, 211; Maurice Ashley, *Rupert of the Rhine* (London: Hart Davis, MacGibbon, 1976), 40–41, 80.

4. Chaucer, 23; "Janvier," in *Très Riches Heurs de Jean de Berry*.

5. Evelyn, 3:331, 4:410.

6. Hawtree, 80–81; Jesse, 2:255–57, 260.

7. Wilcox and Walkowicz, 690. Jean-Jacques Bachelier's *Dog of the Havannah Breed* (1768) portrays the quintessential poodle as toy and entertainer. The dog has been bred down to tiny size, as measured by the coins and slippers placed in front of it. Its hair has been elaborately clipped, luxuriantly fluffy in some places and shaved to the skin in others; and it wears a hair ribbon. It concentrates painfully upon its trick of sitting up, anxiously eying human observers.

8. Horace Walpole, *Correspondence* (New Haven: Yale University Press, 1937–74), 1:178, 2:271, 29:145, 32:137, 35:387.

9. Samuel Pepys, *The Diary* (Berkeley: University of California Press, 1970), 1:46, 54, 4:99, 5:239, 8:421, 9:296, 308–309.

10. Frances Burney d'Arblay, *The Journals and Letters of Fanny Burney (Mme. d'Arblay)* (Oxford: Clarendon, 1982), 10:691–702.

11. "The White Cat" (1698) in Andrew Lang, ed., *The Blue Fairy Book* (New York: Viking Press, 1975), 169.

The present bichon breeds are the bichon frise, the bichon Bolognese, and the Maltese (also called bichon Maltais). The present-day Maltese looks different from the others because American Kennel Club standards require that the long flowing coat, presumably lengthened by selective breeding, be left unclipped.

A picture of eighteenth-century cocking spaniels at work, probably by Morland, shows five quite small dogs, which would be perceived as large toy dogs in another context. Toy spaniels were originally used as ratters, and even today the papillon will attack a rat; too small to kill it outright, it will worry the rat to exhaustion and then dispatch it (American Kennel Club, *Dog Book,* 467). Horace Walpole humorously told a friend that, despite his age and the season, he went out for birds with his toy spaniel: "Rosette put up one robin-redbreast; but we did not kill. The first rat or mouse, or such small deer that she runs down, I will take the liberty of sending your Ladyship some venison" (32:66–67).

12. Caius, 20–22. Caius's diatribe got wider circulation when it was repeated almost word for word in William Harrison's "Description of England" in Holinshed's *Chronicles*, 1577.

13. John Gay, "The Spaniel and the Chameleon" (1727), *Poetry and Prose* (Oxford: Clarendon, 1974), 2:304; Oliver Goldsmith, *A History of the Earth and Animated Nature* (Edinburgh: A. Fullarton, 1879), 1:383–84; Beilby, 364.

14. Taplin, *Sportsman's Cabinet*, 2:122, 278.

15. Youatt, 104; Hudson in Hawtree, 424; Judith Lytton, *Toy Dogs and Their Ancestors* (London: Duckworth, 1911), 108; Terhune in Harold Berman, ed., *The Pocket Book of Dog Stories* (New York: Pocket Books, 1942), 115.

16. *Tatler* Number 121, in Jodi L. Wyett, "The Lap of Luxury: Lapdogs, Literature, and Social Meaning in the 'Long' Eighteenth Century," *Lit* 10:4 (2000), 288; *Astrophel and Stella* (c. 1582), in Celia Haddon, *Faithful to the End: An Illustrated Anthology About Dogs*

and Their Owners (New York: St. Martin's, 1991), 55; Alexander Pope, *Collected Poems* (London: J. M. Dent and Sons, 1983), 80; Wyett, 281, 285–86.

17. Ward's "Panegyrick upon My Lady *Fizzleton's* Lap-Dog" (1709) and Gould's *Love Given O're* (1682) in Garber, 143; Collins's "Fatal Dream" (1762) in *The New Oxford Book of Eighteenth-Century Verse,* ed. Roger Lonsdale (Oxford: Oxford University Press, 1984), 500–501.

In contrast to these men's sexualized and disparaging images of ladies' dogs, two folk-tales, which I am tempted to ascribe to female authors, present little dogs as heroes. "Grim's Dyke" relates a heroic adventure of a lady in which her lapdog plays a key role. A mother went to rescue her daughter from the monster in Grim's Wood, supported by her horse and her great boarhound. The lady's lapdog jumped into her lap when she was mounted "and crept up her sleeve and she smiled and let him stay. 'You'll all need me,' he said, but nobody heard him." The lapdog gave her the advice that defeated the monster Grim and helped the big dog bite him until he yielded up the lady's daughter. The hero of the folktale "The Little Wee Tyke [dog]" is a small, apparently worthless dog of low social station, who is rescued from drowning by a little ragged girl. Her family, destitute because of a witch's spell, wants to throw him out; but the tiny dog saves them all by sending the witch away with a good bite in her left leg. See Tongue, 42–44, 117.

18. Tobias Smollett, *The Expedition of Humphry Clinker* (London: Oxford University Press, 1925), 72, 93, 100–101, 120. Smollett's callousness toward dogs is further displayed when Tabitha's nephew, a supposedly sympathetic character, flippantly laughs off the drowning of his dog by a practical jokester (15). Wyett suggests that relinquishing Chowder enables Tabitha to marry Lismahago, that Chowder "serves as a shield from compulsory heterosexuality and marriage, allowing women a measure of emotional and perhaps physical pleasure completely outside of the bounds of patriarchally prescribed behavior. The dog . . . must go" (290). This tidily fits the pattern of dogs competing with lovers/husbands that she outlines in her essay, but it does not seem to me consistent with Tabitha's blatant husband-hunting throughout the novel.

19. Frances Burney d'Arblay, *The Wanderer, or Female Difficulties* (London: Pandora, 1988), 455, 472, 497, 657, 835.

D'Arblay used a dog more conventionally in her earlier novel *Cecilia.* The hero's spaniel, Fidel, serves as a rather contrived plot device: he helps to bring the two separated lovers together by attaching himself to the heroine and receiving the endearments she cannot give the hero, and thus moves a long-drawn out relationship along when the man, overhearing her outright declaration of affection, is at last convinced of her love.

20. Georges-Louis Leclerc de Buffon, *Histoire Naturelle, Generale et Particulière* (Paris: F. Dufart, 1799), 23:164–67.

21. In Elizabeth Richardson, ed., *Poets' Dogs* (New York: G. P. Putnam's, 1895), 101.

22. Sarah Kirby Trimmer, *Fabulous Histories, Designed for the Instruction of Children, Respecting Their Treatment of Animals* (London: T. Longman and G. G. J. and J. Robinson, 1793), 70, 160.

23. Francis Coventry, *The History of Pompey the Little: or, The Life and Adventures of a Lap-Dog* (London: Oxford University Press, 1974), 26, 30–31, 49–54. The novel does open with "A Panegyric upon Dogs" that is half serious. Unlike all other animals, "Dogs alone enter into voluntary Friendship with us . . . Nor do they trouble us only with officious Fidelity, and useless Good-will, but take care to earn their Livelihood by many meritorious Services: they guard our Houses, supply our Tables with Provision, amuse our leisure Hours" and perform onstage (2).

24. Edward Augustus Kendall, *Keeper's Travels in Search of His Master* (Boston: Lilly, Wait, 1833), 48, 120.

25. Thomas Aquinas, *The Summa Theologica*, trans. Lawrence Shapcote (Chicago: Encyclopedia Britannica, 1990), 2:297 502–503; Stephen H. Webb, *On God and Dogs: A Christian Theology of Compassion for Animals* (New York: Oxford University Press, 1998), 33. Montaigne did recognize that the lower animals are of God's household as well as ourselves and declared that it is only human pride that separates us absolutely from them and inspires us to glibly define the limits of their abilities—but his voice is unique in the sixteenth century (2:117, 122, 142).

26. Montaigne, 2:150; Tom Regan and Peter Singer, eds., *Animal Rights and Human Obligations* (Englewood Cliffs, N.J.: Prentice-Hall, 1976), 64; René Descartes, *Oeuvres* (Paris, 1899), 3:121; 4:573, 576; Leonora Cohen Rosenfield, *From Beast-Machine to Man-Machine: Animal Soul in French Letters from Descartes to La Mettrie* (New York: Oxford University Press, 1941), 42, 70.

   Like many theorists, Descartes fortunately did not live up to his rigid principles: he treated his own dog nicely and recognized that it had thoughts and feelings. Unfortunately, colder-hearted disciples followed his theories to the letter. And, alas, there are still professional philosophers who deny that animals feel pain and that there is any moral objection to abusing them. In 1989, one P. Carruthers asserted in the prestigious *Journal of Philosophy* that animals lack consciousness and hence concluded: "since their experiences, including their pains, are nonconscious ones, their pains are of no immediate moral concern. Indeed, since all of the mental states of brutes are nonconscious, their injuries are lacking even in indirect moral concern" (Coren, *Intelligence*, 65).

27. Adrian Tinniswood, *His Invention So Fertile: A Life of Christopher Wren* (Oxford: Oxford University Press, 2001), 34, 36–37, Pepys 7:370–71, 9:203.

28. Evelyn 3:497–98; Spence's *Anecdotes*, in George Jesse 1:12.

29. *Idler* Number 17 (1758), in Samuel Johnson, *Selected Writings* (New York: New American Library, 1981), 109–10. Joseph Addison's criticism of vivisection in *The Spectator* fifty years earlier lacks Johnson's righteous indignation. His description of "a very barbarous Experiment"—an often repeated example in which a suffering bitch was cut open and ignored her own sufferings to caress her puppy—is weakened by being embedded in a bland essay on animal behavior (*The Spectator* [London: J. M. Dent, 1945], 1:365).

   Pompey the Little's narrow escape from a vivisectionist prompted the sardonic comment: "A dog might have been the emblematic animal of *Esculapius* or *Apollo,* for no creatures I believe have been of more service to the healing tribe than dogs. Incredible is the number of these animals, who have been sacrificed . . . at the shrines of physic and surgery" (Coventry, 185).

30. Voltaire, "Bêtes: Animals," *Philosophical Dictionary,* trans. Theodore Besterman (New York: Penguin Books, 1971), 64–65.

31. Jeremy Bentham, *The Principles of Morals and Legislation* (Buffalo: Prometheus Books, 1988), 311n.

32. Jenny Uglow, *Hogarth: A Life and a World* (New York: Farrar, Straus & Giroux, 1997), 500.

7. Dogs in the Nineteenth Century

1. Both Southey poems in Bicknell, 138–39, 145–49.

2. John Montgomery, *Royal Dogs: The Pets of the British Sovereigns from Victoria to Elizabeth II* (London: Max Parrish, 1962), 14–18, 21, 75.

3. Taplin, *Sportsman's Cabinet,* 72–74.

4. Stephens, 318; Hawtree, 180. During Byron's last days, his dog Lyon "was perhaps his dearest and most affectionate friend." The dog accompanied him everywhere, and Byron would commune with him constantly; the dog was particularly delighted when Byron complimented him (William Parry, *The Last Days of Lord Byron,* in Hawtrey, 185).

5. Walsh, 160; Bicknell, 98; Ash, 2:579, 581.

6. Taplin, *Cabinet,* 1:2.

7. Hawtree, 447–48.

8. Branch, "To a Dog," in Spencer, 114; Delabere Blaine, *Canine Pathology, or a Full Description of the Diseases of Dogs* (London: T. Boosey, 1817), xviii–xxx; Ouida in Helen and George Papashvily, *Dogs and People* (Philadelphia: J. B. Lippincott, 1954), 143; Philip G. Hamerton, *Chapters on Animals* (Boston: Roberts Brothers, 1882), 235.

9. Taplin, *Cabinet,* 132–36; Youatt, 9–10.

10. H. D. Richardson, *Dogs, Their Origin and Varieties* (New York: Orange Judd, 1874), 13, 15–16; Jesse, 1:341. William T. Hornaday, longtime director of the New York Zoological Park (who ought to have had more knowledge and a better attitude), wrote in 1904: "Of all the wild creatures of North America, none are more despicable than wolves. There is no depth of meanness, treachery or cruelty to which they do not cheerfully descend" (Steinhart, 52).

A story by Edison Marshall called "Shag of the Packs" (1922) epitomizes denigration of the wolf used to glorify the dog. A mountain man whose beloved shepherd bitch had been mortally wounded by wolves hoped to save the strongest of her pups by placing it in a wolf's litter. The mother wolf, too stupid to notice the substitution at first, did develop doubts when the interloper's ears drooped and his tail was carried uplifted; but "she couldn't question his superiority. He was the strongest of her litter . . . and . . . always quickest to learn." Yet even when he happily ran with the pack, he yearned for "some one very brave and very strong, whose will must never be opposed," so he hung around human settlements, and when he saw his owner's sixteen-year-old daughter, "he felt strangely and deeply humbled" and immediately forgot his mate. When he "felt the touch of her hand upon his head, . . . it was a glory and magic that stirred and enraptured him to the roots of his being." The dog's superiority to other animals and its glad subjection to humans are gratifyingly asserted. See Charles Wright Gray, ed., *"Dawgs!" An Anthology of Stories About Them* (Garden City, N.Y.: Sun Dial Press, 1937), 199, 207, 209, 224.

11. Katcher in Fogle, *Interrelations,* 45.

12. Joseph Taylor, *The General Character of the Dog: Illustrated by a Variety of Original and Interesting Anecdotes of That Beautiful and Useful Animal* (Philadelphia: Benjamin Johnson, 1807), iii, 35–36, 86. For Aelian's story, see Aelian, 2:143.

13. Joyce and Maurice Lindsay, eds., *The Scottish Dog* (Aberdeen: Aberdeen University Press, 1989), 102–105.

   Not all Victorians swallowed such tales. Thomas Hardy wrote a sardonic poem in which a newly buried woman asks who is digging on her grave. It is not her fiancé planting rue, nor her dearest kin, but her little dog. Why had she not known? the woman asks: "What feeling do we ever find / To equal among human kind / A dog's fidelity!" Alas, no: the dog was only burying a bone and had quite forgotten it was her resting place. See Louis Untermeyer, ed., *Modern British Poetry* (New York: Harcourt, Brace, 1942), 29. Hardy himself had an overindulged wirehaired terrier, Wessex; and he wrote a poem in the dog's voice that reveals a self-assured, self-centered character who would not think of sacrificing himself for his master.

14. John St. Loe Strachey, ed., *Dog Stories from the "Spectator": Being Anecdotes of the Intelligence, Reasoning Power, Affection and Sympathy of Dogs, Selected from the Correspondence Columns of "The Spectator,"* 2nd ed. (London: T. Fisher Unwin, 1896), 23, 55, 172–73.

15. Charles Darwin, *The Descent of Man, and Selection in Relation to Sex* (New York: Appleton, 1871), 1:46, 75; *The Expression of the Emotions in Man and Animals* (New York: New York University Press, 1989), 8.

16. Charles Dickens, *The Old Curiosity Shop* (London: Oxford University Press, 1957), 139–42.

17. *The Uncommercial Traveller* (1860), in Hawtree, 292–93.

18. Hamerton, 236–46; trainer quoted in Timothy Clarke, ed., *The Dog Lover's Reader* (New York: Hart Publishing Co., 1974), 367.

19. Hawtree, 606–607. Dogs were taxed in England from 1796, with considerable variations in rates and conditions. The process was regularized in 1867, when all dogs except puppies under six months old were to be licensed at five shillings per year, with a register of licenses kept and a fine of five pounds for keeping a dog without a license. Hardy's poem may have been occasioned by this or by an increase of the tax to seven shillings sixpence per year in 1878 (Vesey-Fitzgerald, *Book of the Dog,* 724).

   The essayist Dr. John Brown told how his brother William saved a poor cur from being drowned by buying him for twopence. They persuaded their father to let them keep him, but their grandmother hated dogs and dirt, and one day, when Toby stole a cold leg of mutton (perhaps because the servant had neglected to feed him), she summarily pronounced sentence on him. William came home from school to find him "dangling by his own chain from his own lamp post, one of his hind feet just touching the pavement," dead but still warm. The milk-delivery boy, Toby's friend with whom he played every morning, had done the execution for twopence. See Lindsay, 107–108. The callousness of those who so lightly killed a child's pet is shocking, and yet Brown, despite being fond of dogs, narrates it with a touch of levity.

20. Hamerton, 37; Coren, *How to Speak Dog,* 104; Josephine Z. Rine, *The World of Dogs* (Garden City, N.Y.: Doubleday, 1965), 59.

21. Inspired by the British example, Henry Bergh in New York City got tens of thousands of people to sign his petition to the New York state legislature for laws against animal abuse, got laws passed, and in 1866 got a charter to establish the ASPCA, with rights to enforce the new anticruelty laws. He was particularly moved by the plight of fighting dogs, draft dogs, and turnspit dogs, the latter often used for show in saloon windows.

22. Coral Lansbury, *The Old Brown Dog: Women, Workers, and Vivisection in Edwardian England* (Madison: University of Wisconsin Press, 1985), 8–9, 11, 155, 163, 171; Jesse, 279.

   Ultimately a wealthy woman erected a fountain adorned with the dog's statue and inscribed "In Memory of the Brown Terrier Done to Death in the Laboratories of University College in February, 1903, after having endured Vivisection extending over more than Two Months and having been handed over from one Vivisector to Another Till Death came to his Release. Also in Memory of the 232 dogs Vivisected in the same place during the year 1902. Men and Women of England, how long shall these Things be?" The statue became a symbol of the conflict between scientific authorities, on the one hand, who saw antivivisectionists as superstitious, sentimental opponents of progress, and on the other, feminists and trade unionists, who saw themselves as underdogs and, in the case of the working class, apprehended that ruthless experimentation on animals might be extended to unprivileged humans (Lansbury, 3, 8–14, 21–22).

23. Wilkie Collins, *Heart and Science: A Story of the Present Time* (Peterborough, Ontario, Canada: Broadview Press, 1996), 190, 323.

24. "Tray" (1879) in Menzies, 133–34; "Rags" in Edwin S. Burtis, ed., *All the Best Dog Poems: An Anthology of Poetry About Dogs* (New York: Thomas Y. Crowell, 1946).

   Mark Twain, who constantly excoriated humans who abuse "lower" animals that actually have the advantage over them in being innocent, contributed a thin but heartfelt story, "A Dog's Tale," to the antivivisection cause. The narrator is an altruistic dog too innocent to perceive human evil; she saves her scientist master's baby from a fire, and in return he performs an experiment on her puppy that blinds and ultimately kills it. Perhaps the lowest thing about the lowlifes in *Huckleberry Finn* (chapter 21) and *The Mysterious Stranger* (chapter 6) is their abuse of dogs.

25. Richard Adams, *The Plague Dogs* (New York: Knopf, 1978), 3–6. Adams explained in his Preface that his laboratory, Animal Research (Scientific and Experimental), was a composite, but affirmed that every experiment he described "is one which has actually been carried out on animals somewhere" (xvi).

It must be pointed out that animal experimentation is much better regulated today than in past decades, with at least lip service given to the goal of reducing the number of animals used. Not long ago, dogs were routinely sacrificed as teaching tools in medical schools; now, 100 of the 126 medical schools in the United States have replaced animal laboratories with methods such as computer simulations. It is also true that research on dogs has produced great benefits for humans, as well as for other animals. Frederick Banting used thousands of dogs in the research that made it possible to isolate insulin and administer it to diabetics. As a result of his work, millions of people have led productive lives instead of inexorably starving to death. Today scientists are working out a way to transplant insulin-producing islet cells into the patient's liver, so as to avoid the need for daily injections. Again, they are using dogs as research subjects, and again diabetic dogs, as well as humans, will profit when the process is perfected. Dogs are essential in research on cardiovascular disease, because of their sturdiness, their relatively large size, and the similarity of their cardiovascular system to that of humans. Only through research on dogs could doctors have developed surgical procedures such as heart valve and artery replacement, angioplasty, and the insertion of pacemakers. With coronary bypass and heart valve surgery developed on dogs, people can be restored to full healthy functioning who in the past would have endured the disabling pain of angina or struggled for breath with congestive heart disease until their hearts ultimately failed altogether.

However, many researchers do not seem to understand that inflicting suffering on animals is an evil, even if the evil may be justified by the benefits it produces. Most states exempt scientific research from anticruelty laws as long as the pain inflicted is necessary for the increase of knowledge—leaving the researchers themselves to determine what is necessary. Consequently, experiments are still being done that have no likelihood of producing results that are useful, new, unavailable to common sense, or beneficial to humans or other animals—that at best satisfy curiosity and at worst simply augment someone's publications list. In his *Animal Liberation: A New Ethic for Our Treatment of Animals* (New York: Avon Books, 1975), Peter Singer describes experiments in which beagles were irradiated with X-rays to confirm that X-rays produced the same horrid symptoms and death that had occurred in previous experiments on dogs, experiments in which beagles and pigs were fed massive doses of the pesticide methoxychlor to find out whether it produced different symptoms in dogs and pigs, experiments in which dogs were reduced to apathetic despair by being subjected over and over to electric shocks regardless of how they responded (27–30, 35–38).

26. Lockhart quoted in Jon Winocur, ed., *Mondo Canine* (New York: Dutton, 1991), 33; Irving in Hawtree, 169; Maida's reluctance to be painted in Edgar Johnson, *Sir Walter Scott: The Great Unknown* (New York: Macmillan, 1970), 708; Scott's Journal 18 Dec. 1825, in Johnson, 954.
27. Elizabeth Gaskell, *The Life of Charlotte Brontë* (London: Oxford University Press, 1951), 219–21.

Anne, the most sweet and conventional of the sisters, had a pretty toy spaniel, Flossy.

An endearing terrier figures prominently in *Agnes Grey*; maltreated by the odious children of Agnes's employer, he is championed by the tenderhearted heroine.

28. Gaskell, 220.

Sensitivity to the feelings of dogs (and cats) is a regular hallmark of Charlotte's admirable men. Mr. Rochester of *Jane Eyre* has an awesome Newfoundland, Pilot, who at first suggests a gytrash to Jane but soon becomes her firm friend. In *Villette* (New York: Harper & Row, 1972), the devotion of an adorable toy spaniel reinforces the worth of the unprepossessing hero. Lucy Snowe describes their relationship with tenderness, but cannot resist a final waspish remark: the dog "was very tiny, and had the prettiest little innocent face, the silkiest long ears, the finest dark eyes in the world. I never saw her, but I thought of Paulina de Bassompierre [the exquisite ingénue of the story]: forgive the association, reader, it *would* occur" (403).

29. Charles Dickens, *Oliver Twist* (Boston: Jefferson Press, 1908), 105, 111; *Barnaby Rudge: A Tale of the Riots of '80* (New York: Heritage Press, 1941), 600.

30. Charles Dickens, *The Personal History of David Copperfield* (Baltimore: Penguin Books, 1966), 709.

Diogenes, the exuberant, bumbling mongrel in *Dombey and Son,* is redeemed by his warm devotion to the otherwise unloved heroine, Florence. Dickens perhaps tries to get an excessive amount of heartwarming humor from the dog's awkwardness. In *Hard Times* (New York: W. W. Norton, 1966), Mr. Gradgrind is predictably offended when Sissy Jupe speaks of Merrylegs, her father's performing dog, as a person. Merrylegs provides the occasion for a conversation in which Gradgrind reduces dogs' love and reasoning ability to instinct (37, 221–22).

31. "To Flush, My Dog" (1843), in *The Complete Poetical Works* (Boston: Houghton Mifflin, 1900), 164; letters in Spencer, 52–54.

32. Letters in Eric Parker, ed., *Best of Dogs: Stories of Many Famous Friends* (London: Hutchinson, 1949), 109–10, 112; Lindsay, 219–22; Menzies, 127.

33. "Our Dogs," in Fairfax Davies Downey, ed., *Great Dog Stories of All Time* (Garden City, N.Y.: Doubleday, 1962), 162–64.

34. Harriet Beecher Stowe, *Uncle Tom's Cabin or Life among the Lowly* (New York: Penguin Books, 1981), 62, 113–14.

35. In Haddon, 18.

36. George Eliot, *The Mill on the Floss* (New York: New American Library, 1965), 52–54. Also in *The Mill on the Floss,* Bob Jakin's bull terrier, Mumps, helps him greatly in his trade of traveling peddler. Bob, convinced dogs are "better friends nor any Christian" (298), passes the lonely hours on the road talking to Mumps and relies on him to guard his pack.

In the scene in *Middlemarch* (New York: W. W. Norton, 1977) where Mr. Brooke and Monk go to see Brooke's impoverished and mutinous tenant Dagley, the prosperous, affable landlord and his Saint Bernard make an amusing contrast to the disreputable Dagley and his sullen sheepdog, Fag (272–74). Despite her affection for dogs, Eliot, like Mary Wollstonecraft, Charlotte Brontë, and Jane Carlyle, derided the idea that "canine affection" is an appropriate feeling for women (2). For Wollstonecraft, see *A Vindication of the Rights of Woman* (New York: Norton, 1988), 34.

37. George Eliot, *Adam Bede* (New York: Washington Square Press, 1956), 38–39; *Middlemarch,* 269.

38. Rhoda Broughton, *Red as a Rose Is She* (New York: D. Appleton, 1870), 11; *Mrs. Bligh: A Novel* (New York: D. Appleton, 1892), 7; *Belinda: A Novel* (Scholarly Press, 1970), 80.

39. Graham Greene, *The Human Factor* (New York: Simon & Schuster, 1978), 14–15, 93.

40. William Maxwell, *So Long, See You Tomorrow* (New York: Knopf, 1980), 122. The editor's comment cited in Daniel Menaker's review of *So Long* in *The New York Times Book Review*, October 15, 2000, 39.

41. Alison Lurie, *Foreign Affairs* (New York: Avon Books, 1990), 3, 9, 291.

8. How Dogs Are Classified

1. Caius 2, 10–12, 20, 34–35, 40.

   Two catalogues of dogs by Shakespearean characters presumably represent the types that came first to the early-seventeenth-century mind. Macbeth lists (scent) hounds, greyhounds, mongrels, spaniels, curs, shoughs, water-rugs (water spaniels), and demi-wolves (wolf hybrids or wolflike northern dogs?) (III.1.93–94). Mad Edgar's list in *King Lear* is more diverse: mastiff, greyhound, three types of scent hound, spaniel, and three types of low-class dog: mongrel, bobtail tike, and trundle[curly]-tail (III.6.69–71). As was usual at the time, hunting dogs are overrepresented, working dogs underrepresented or classed with mongrels, and toys do not appear at all.

2. Buffon, 23:197, 251–56.

   Carolus Linnaeus had simply listed thirty-four types of dog in his *General System of Nature,* giving a few distinguishing physical characteristics for each, such as the long, pendulous ears of the spaniel.

3. American Kennel Club, 595, 598–99; Vesey-Fitzgerald, *Domestic Dog,* 148.

   In contrast to most breeds, foxhounds, the first breed to be developed by modern "scientific" standards, were bred primarily for qualities relevant to their function—nose, voice, endurance, and speed—although also for "that perfection of form and colour which is so enchanting." The ideal was to create a matched pack, and "To breed a pack of hounds exactly level and of true colour is the work of a lifetime" (Vesey-Fitzgerald, *Book of the Dog,* 441, 752–53). The Masters of Foxhounds (who manage the packs) have maintained careful stud books since before 1800.

4. Henry Herbert, *Frank Forester's Field Sports of the United States and the British Provinces of North America* (New York: W. A. Townsend, 1858), 1:322, 338.

5. Gordon Stables, *Our Friend the Dog* (London: Dean and Son, 190?), 44–45.

6. William Secord, *Dog Painting 1840–1940: A Social History of Dogs in Art* (Woodbridge, Suffolk: Antique Collectors Club, 1992), 16; Stables, 48; George B. Taylor, *Man's Friend, the Dog* (New York: Frederick A. Stokes, 1891), 5, 7–8; Ash, 1:5–6; Secord, *Breed Apart,* 248, 250.

7. Roger Caras, *Going for the Blue: Inside the World of Show Dogs and Dog Shows* (New York: Warner Books, 2001), 8–9, 34; *A Celebration of Dogs* (New York: Times Books, 1982), 159.

In the same spirit, the famous dog trainer Barbara Woodhouse concedes that "Mongrels can be perfectly charming devoted pets," but goes on to claim that "a thoroughbred always has that extra something which makes the family proud to own it." "A mongrel is always a gamble," she darkly warns, "especially one adopted from a lost dogs' home," because "Most such dogs are wanderers by nature or they wouldn't be in lost dogs' homes" (in *The Treasury of Dogs* [London: Octopus Books, 1972], 19). (In fact, of course, most such dogs are unwanted or abandoned, through no fault of their own.)

8. Cartoon in Ritvo, 114; Nathaniel Southgate Shaler, *Domesticated Animals: Their Relation to Man and to His Advancement in Civilization* (New York: Charles Scribner's, 1895), 31; Lytton, in Secord, *Dog Painting,* 13.

9. American Kennel Club, 55–58, 241–42, 601.

10. Vesey-Fitzgerald, *Domestic Dog,* 160.

11. American Kennel Club, 95.

The original King Charles spaniel was a small version of a working spaniel, with a slightly shorter muzzle. Over the centuries, it was bred to be smaller with an exaggeratedly domed skull, flat nose, and protruding jaw. Finally, in the 1920s, breeders went to great trouble to restore the original breed; and now there are two.

12. American Kennel Club, 489; Keith Stewart Thomson, "The Rise and Fall of the English Bulldog," *American Scientist* 84 (May–June 1996):220; Max Beerbohm, *Zuleika Dobson: or an Oxford Love Story* (New York: Dodd, Mead, 1946), 64.

13. Scott and Fuller, 390, 405. In the 1950s, Scott and Fuller started an extensive research project on inheritance in dogs, in which they studied the inherent characteristics of five diverse pure breeds and the results of crossbreeding their offspring. In their experimental dog population, they found a 14.4 percent average neonatal death rate among their purebreds and a 3.4 percent rate in crossbreeds. Even in their healthy breeding stock, mating between close relatives soon brought out serious defects, such as hydrocephaly in cocker spaniels, because breeders had selected for a specialized skull shape with a broad forehead, prominent eyes, and a pronounced stop between nose and forehead (406).

14. Derr, 203.

15. American Kennel Club, 602–605; Michael W. Fox, *Canine Behavior: A History of Domestication, Behavioral Development and Adult Behavior Patterns* (Springfield, Ill.: Charles C. Thomas, 1965), 61; Lemish, 248.

16. Caras, *Celebration,* 226.

In contrast, the Dutch Kennel Club has recently decided to issue pedigrees only to puppies produced under certain health stipulations. For example, a stud dog is not to be overused for mating; puppies sired after he has mated the stipulated number of times will not get pedigrees, only "certificates of descent." See "It's a Dog's Life," *The Economist,* December 21, 2002, 63.

17. Susan Conant, *Bloodlines* (New York: Doubleday, 1992), 12, 227–32.

18. Leslie O'Mara, ed., *Best Dog Stories* (New York: Wings Books, 1990), 156.

19. Jane and Michael Stern, *Dog Eat Dog: A Very Human Book About Dogs and Dog Shows* (New York: Scribner, 1997), 35, 73–75, 107, 125. Although Einstein "charges between $1,000 and $3,000 for a . . . puppy with show potential" and $1,000 stud fees, "big profits are virtually unheard-of among top breeders." Only mass-producing puppy mills are lucrative. At most, top breeders can defray the considerable costs of showing their dogs (36). It can cost $200,000 a year to show a dog in top competition—including highly paid professional handlers to train and condition the dogs and present them in the show ring, travel for dog and handler to perhaps 150 events around the country, and expensive, full-page advertisements in dog fancy magazines to predispose the judges in a dog's favor. See Ann Gerhart, "Wagging the Dog," *Washington Post*, February 13, 2002, C1, 3.

20. Vesey-Fitzgerald, *Domestic Dog*, 176–77.

21. Statistics from American Kennel Club, www.akc.org.

9. Dogs Used as Surrogates for Humans

1. Taplin, *Sportsman's Cabinet*, 1:186–87; Jesse 1:329.

2. Mary Elizabeth Thurston, *The Lost History of the Canine Race: Our 15,000-Year Love Affair with Dogs* (Kansas City: Andrews and McMeel, 1996), 160–61; Shaler, 17.

3. Downey, 213–14.

4. Taplin, *Sportsman's Cabinet*, 1:3; Ritvo, 90–91.

5. Dwight Everett Watkins and Charles H. Raymond, eds., *Best Dog Stories* (Chicago: Rand McNally, 1925), 147, 160–62.

6. Robert Michael Ballantyne, *The Dog Crusoe* (London: J. M. Dent, 1966), 57, 129–30, 163, 217, 221.

7. Hamerton, 46–48, 52; Beerbohm, 63.

8. *Cat and Dog* (1854), in Necker, 139.

9. Burtis, 69.

   Booth Tarkington's *Penrod* (1914), a quintessentially stereotypical story of a twelve-year-old American boy, as a matter of course gives Penrod a dog, Duke, who accompanies him everywhere. Today, however, we would not be amused by the extent to which the boy unthinkingly exploits, dominates, and abuses the dog, the only character in the book who absolutely cannot resist his obnoxious mischievous schemes. In spite of his unfeeling treatment of Duke, Tarkington himself had a series of three beloved dogs whom he treated very well.

10. James Thurber, *Thurber's Dogs: A Collection of the Master's Dogs, Written and Drawn, Real and Imaginary, Living and Long Ago* (New York: Simon & Schuster, 1955), 8–9; Patrick, 31.

11. Arthur H. Trapman, *Man's Best Friend: The Story of the Dog* (New York: Macmillan, 1928), 121–25. Among Trapman's many other tales of the dog's fine moral discrimination is that of the Airedale Lola, who was oppressed with melancholy and shame after committing the "carnal sin" of meeting a lover and becoming pregnant. Lola could also

detect if humans "smelt of lies or of jealousy" and communicate this information to her mistress. So, Trapman concludes, we could train dogs "to be our protectors against impostors." He gravely explains that a dog's committing suicide on his master's death is not a sin, because his "mission on earth closes when his master dies, . . . the dog commits suicide blithely because first of all he knows that his task is done and . . . secondly . . . in order the sooner to be near his master's side," for of course Trapman believes in another world where master and dog will be reunited (125–26, 143–44, 214).

12. "The Whistle" (1933), in Goodman, 573.

13. "The Character of Dogs" (1883), in Goodman, 582–83.

14. Jack London, *The Call of the Wild* (1903) and *White Fang* (1906), *Novels and Stories* (Library of America. New York: Viking, 1982), 6, 21, 38–39, 60–61, 66–70, 79–80, 172, 245.

15. "The Heart of a Dog," in Caras, *Treasury,* 158; Albert Payson Terhune, *Lad, a Dog* (1919) (New York: Puffin, 1987), 11–13, 29; "Buff" in Caras, *Treasury,* 200.

16. American Kennel Club, 330.

17. "White Monarch" (1923), in Gray, *"Dawgs!,"* 309, 326–27.

18. Gray, *"Dawgs!,"* 318; John Taintor Foote, "Allegheny," in Charles Wright Gray, *Real Dogs: An Anthology* (Garden City, N.Y.: Garden City Publishing Co., 1926), 15.

    Several women writers have broken with this macho tradition. Sheila Burnford's old bull terrier in *The Incredible Journey* (Boston: Little, Brown, 1960) is a real sweetie, who has gone through life in total comfort by charming humans and feels himself a friend to all of them, although he retains his ancestors' ability to fight dogs and kill rodents. Vicki Hearne defends the breed as good-natured and friendly when properly treated (*Adam's Task: Calling Animals by Name* [New York: Knopf, 1986], 217).

19. C. 1920, in Marguerite Bloch, ed., *Favorite Dog Stories* (Cleveland: World Publishing Co., 1950), 196, 201.

    Samuel A. Derieux's "The Comet" (1923), another often reprinted story, has a similar structure and values. A man entrusts his wonderfully gifted young pointer to a vindictive trainer who ruins the dog by making him gun-shy. His owner is totally disgusted with the "yellow" dog, and everyone agrees that he had "better be dead than called yellow." However, an old dog man believes the Comet is redeemable and with great pain (to the dog) reverses the evil training. Comet triumphs in a field trial, despite some dirty tricks by the villain, who ends up spooking his own dog (Era Zistel, ed., *Golden Book of Dog Stories* [Chicago: Ziff-Davis, 1947], 48).

20. Both stories in Goodman. Macho values are explicitly challenged in S. J. Rozan's "Cooking the Hounds," where a woman takes exquisitely appropriate revenge on owners of fighting dogs who set them on dogs incapable of defending themselves (in Marks).

21. See Carole Kismaric and Martin Heiferman, *Growing Up with Dick and Jane: Learning and Living the American Dream* (San Francisco: Collins Publishers, 1996).

22. Willie Morris, *My Dog Skip* (New York: Random House, 1995), 8; Farley Mowat, *The Dog Who Wouldn't Be* (Boston: Little, Brown, 1957), 238. When Farley Mowat's Mutt grew old and was hit by a car, "The pact of timelessness between the two of us was ended,

and I went from him into the darkening tunnel of the years" (238). In *My Dog Skip* (1995), the "mutual boyhood" of Willie Morris and Skip ended when he went off to Oxford, never to see the dog again (99). This idea had been spelled out by the Victorian Hamerton: a beloved dog "was the friend of my boyhood . . . the companion of a thousand rambles, and when she died my boyhood was dead also and became part of the irrecoverable past" (18). A cartoon by Charles Barsotti gives this wistful theme a refreshing comic turn: a dog with wagging tail rushes over the clouds to greet an elderly man at heaven's gate, and St. Peter says, "So you're little Bobbie; well, Rex here has been going on and on about you for the past fifty years."

23. Eric Knight, *Lassie Come-Home* (Thorndike, ME: G. K. Hall, 1996), 70, 143, 232.

    Knight's theme of the love between a poor boy and a rich man's aristocratic dog is a popular one, anticipated for example in Elsie Singmaster's "A Pair of Lovers" (1915). A very popular imitation is Jim Kjelgaard's *Big Red* (1945), in which Danny, a poor trapper's son, immediately recognizes the quality of Red, a show Irish setter worth $7,000, who is also a superb natural bird dog and a successful bear hunter. Red, for his part, immediately recognizes Danny as his master, although he belongs to the local rich man. Of course the man hires Danny to raise Red. The whole is a collection of the clichés of sentimental dog-boy fiction and manly hunting fiction, with tributes to the dog fancy added to the mix.

24. Schinto, 68–69.

25. Lassie's miraculous understanding and communication skills were simulated by appropriate plotting, offscreen step-by-step commands from Lassie's trainer, and clever editing. "When Lassie seemed to be looking around carefully to study a situation, Pal [the male actor who played her] was actually watching his trainer wave a rag from a catwalk. Those looks of devotion and intense concentration were usually elicited by his trainer patting the pocket in which he always kept a few dog biscuits" (Coren, *Intelligence*, 10).

26. Garber, 15.

27. For animal symbols of independent or subversive values, one must look to cats.

28. Brown, *All Dogs,* 14, 17; "The Great Penborough Race" appears in Frances Cavanah and Ruth Cromer Weir, eds., *A Treasury of Dog Stories* (Chicago: Rand McNally, 1947).

    Smith praised the unique qualities of Dalmatians as fatuously as Terhune did those of collies; together with the Disney film it inspired, *The 101 Dalmatians* misled many parents into buying this difficult breed for their children.

29. Caldwell's story appears in Brown, *All Dogs,* Dalgliesh's in Pauline Rush Evans, ed., *Best Book of Dog Stories* (Garden City, N.Y.: Doubleday, 1964), Taber's in Gladys Taber's *When Dogs Meet People* (Philadelphia: Macrae Smith, 1952), Brier's in Cavanah and Weir.

30. Taber's story appears in Gladys Taber, *Long Tails and Short* (Philadelphia: Macrae Smith, 1938), Robertson's in Kjelgaard, *Hound Dogs.*

31. Ouida, 136.

32. "Lost Dog" (1900), in Watkins and Raymond, 270–71; Narayan's story in Caras, 472–75.

Olive Schreiner's "The Adventures of Master Towser," another intolerably sad story, narrates the life of a nice terrier who seeks someone to love, is repeatedly failed by humans, and finally yields to despair. It seems to have no other point than to relate the afflictions heaped on an innocent, well-meaning dog. The author ostensibly invites our sympathy, but perhaps it is our sadism that is exercised instead. In any case, our reaction is passive rather than indignant, as if this dog's sad lot were somehow appropriate (in Brandt Aymar and Edward Sagarin, eds., *The Personality of the Dog* [New York: Crown Publishers, 1964]).

33. And too many overemphasize the unhappy aspects of our relationships with dogs. The only satisfying relationships in the book are either terminated by premature death, in "Dog Heaven," or involve an imaginary dog, in Peter Cameron's "The Secret Dog."

34. Dodie Smith, *The One Hundred and One Dalmatians* (New York: Penguin-Puffin, 1989), 121, 128.

Even the well-intentioned *Beautiful Joe* is marred by racism. In his first paragraph, the canine narrator, who had been named Beautiful Joe because he was ugly and mutilated, tells his readers why the idealized benevolent minister who adopted him found this amusingly appropriate: the minister's grandfather had named a slave boy and his mother Cupid and Venus because they were so ugly. There is no suggestion of criticism for this equation of dog and black human, nor recognition that, although the dog does not understand the belittling irony, the humans undoubtedly would be wounded by it.

Many of the stories in this chapter take their significance not from any intrinsic quality or importance, but from being typical and popular. Each valiant bull terrier, misjudged dog makes good, dog admitted to heaven, etc., story that I mention represents many more on the same theme. Most of those I have discussed were selected for at least two anthologies. A mediocre story like Vereen's "Brag Dog," for example, appears in Berman, Caras, and Goodman.

10. The Negative Side of Our Friendship with Dogs

1. Sometimes the dog's unconcern with spiritual matters is really pointed. In Veronese's *Presentation of the Cuccina Family to the Virgin* (1570–72), the family papillon resolutely turns its back on the reverential group of adults worshiping the enthroned Virgin and Child. In the center foreground of Titian's *Adoration of the Magi* (Madrid version, 1559), a tiny white dog cocks his leg against the main post supporting the shed that shelters the Holy Family.

2. Keith Thomas, 38; "Against Quarrelling and Fighting" (1720), in *The Oxford Book of Eighteenth-Century Verse*, ed. David Nichol Smith (Oxford: Clarendon Press, 1926), 56.

3. *King Lear*, II.2.80, III.7.92–93, IV.6.160; *Julius Caesar*, III.1.40; *Antony and Cleopatra*, IV.10.33–36.

Surprisingly, in view of Shakespeare's lack of warm feeling for dogs and the callousness of his time, he did go out of his way to condemn experimentation on animals. The wicked queen in *Cymbeline* acquires poisons whose effects she will try on cats and dogs, and she is advised against such experiments on the grounds that they will harden her heart (I.5). Samuel Johnson, who did care for animals, emphasized the moral of this passage in his edition of Shakespeare.

4. "Bibbles," in Hawtree, 630–34.

5. "The Dog (As Seen by the Cat)," in Burtis, 15; "Earning a Collie Degree," in Winocur, 11. Even though Barry constantly makes fun of his two dogs, his columns reveal his genuine fondness for them.

6. Necker, 149, 151–52, 156–57.

7. Jean-Pierre Claris de Florian, "The Dog and the Cat," *Fables de Florian* (Paris: Briand, 1816), 41–42; Necker, 144, 147–48.

8. Necker, 293 (*Theory of the Leisure Class*, 1899).

9. H. P. Lovecraft, "Something About Cats" (1926), *Something About Cats and Other Pieces* (Sauk City, Wis.: Arkham House, 1949), 4.

10. William Plomer, *The Case Is Altered* (London: Hogarth Press, 1946), 101–102, 245, 337.

11. Ambrose Bierce, *The Devil's Dictionary* (1906), *Collected Writings* (New York: Citadel Press, 1946), 74; Parry, 24.

    Bierce's contrasting definition of cat—"A soft, indestructible automaton provided by nature to be kicked when things go wrong in the domestic circle" (47)—differs strikingly from the usual view, which has the cat privileged at the expense of the more deserving dog.

12. O. Henry, *Collected Stories* (New York: Gramercy Books, 1986), 439–40. The misogyny here is perhaps more genuine than the cynophobia. Although his story "Memoirs of a Yellow Dog" presents a similar picture, with a woman doting on her dog and forcing her henpecked husband to walk him, the canine protagonist is sympathetically presented and therefore despises the woman and allies himself with the man.

13. Raymond Hull, *Man's Best Fiend* (New York: Hippocrene Books, 1972), 14, 23–29, 159. The last section recalls Jonathan Swift's "Modest Proposal," but there is no evidence, as there is in Swift's essay, that it is meant to be ironic.

14. Ash, 1:113–16.

15. Théophile Gautier, *My Private Menagerie, The Complete Works*, trans. F. C. DeSumichrast (London: Postlethwaite, Taylor and Knowles, 1909), 10:319; Blaine, 124–26.

16. Walpole, 35: 306; Letter 119 of Goldsmith's *Citizen of the World*, in Hawtree, 125–27.

17. Taplin, *Sportsman's Cabinet*, 2:304.

18. Fortunately, George Angell, founder of the ASPCA, appeared and awed them into abandoning the idea (Caras, *Celebration*, 219–21).

19. Iris Nowell, *The Dog Crisis* (New York: St. Martin's Press, 1978), 146, 191–93, 201.

20. *Washington Post*, February 26, 2001, A1, 4 (pit bulls); January 29, 2002, A2, February 20, 2002, A3, June 18, 2002, A3 (Presa Canario); December 24, 2002, B2, December 27, 2002, B2 (dachshund).

    It is important to point out, however, that a dog that bites someone is not necessarily vicious. Bites from normal family dogs usually result from ill-judged human behavior, such as making advances to a dog that is giving plain signals of fear or aggression. Dogs cannot be expected to behave like humans or to recognize that a provocation is unintentional.

21. In Britain in 1989, a few serious rottweiler attacks prompted politicians to demand a blanket ban on rottweilers. This excitement died down, but two years later, two savage, apparently unprovoked, attacks on people by pit bull terriers provoked the Dangerous Dog Act of 1991, which banned the breeding, sale, or exchange of all pit bull terriers and required owners to destroy or neuter them and to keep them leashed and muzzled in public, even if they had never shown signs of aggressiveness.

11. Dogs as Equals

1. Spencer, 149.
2. Serpell, *Domestic Dog*, 2.

    Dave Barry often writes affectionately about his hopelessly imperfect dogs, who are as fallible as their "master." They "have been trained to respond immediately to my voice. For example, when we're outside, all I have to do is issue the following standard dog command: 'Here, Earnest! Here, Zippy! C'mon! Here! I said come *here*! You dogs *come here right now! Are you dogs listening to me?* Hey!!!' And instantly both dogs, in unison, like a precision drill team, will continue trotting in random directions, sniffing the ground" (Winocur, 89). Earnest was probably the model for the large mongrel Roger, one of the numerous stupid male characters in Barry's novel *Big Trouble.*

3. *Irish Memories,* in Menzies, 167; Woolf's essay on Shag (1904) in Hawtree, 548–49.
4. "Memories," in Bud Johns, ed., *Old Dogs Remembered* (New York: Carroll and Graf, 1993), 52, 54.
5. Woodhouse in *Treasury of Dogs,* 43; Singer in Peter Singer, ed., *In Defense of Animals* (New York: Basil Blackwell, 1985), 1, 4, 6, 9.
6. Winocur, 28; Lorenz, 52.
7. Joseph Duemer and Jim Simmerman, eds., *Dog Music: Poetry About Dogs* (New York: St. Martin's Press, 1996), 172.
8. Cohen and Taylor, ix, 8, 70, 100, 110.
9. J. R. Ackerley, *My Dog Tulip* (New York: Fleet Publishing Co., 1965), 39, 48, 95, 119–20, 124–25; *My Father and Myself*, in Garber, 132. William Plomer, creator of the antidog Miss Haymer, told a mutual friend that " 'that bloody dog' had taken possession of Joe to such an extent that he and [E. M.] Forster were loath to visit the flat in Putney that Ackerley shared with his adored Queenie." See Paul Bailey, *A Dog's Life* (London: Hamish Hamilton, 2003).

    In *The Dogs Who Came to Stay* (1995), George Pitcher described a relationship much like Ackerley's with Queenie. Pitcher, too, had been a cold intellectual and was freed to express affection by a stray bitch he took in. So tender were his feelings for her that he was glad when his partner kept her from helping him when he was being beaten up by thugs; she might have got hurt.

10. Letters to David Garnett, November 25, December 1944, in Spencer, 168–70. Happily, when White fictionalized Brownie as the cook's dog, Captain, in *Mistress Masham's Repose,* he was able to portray her complacent, dog-centered benevolence with comic detachment.

11. Elizabeth Marshall Thomas, *The Social Lives of Dogs: The Grace of Canine Company* (New York: Simon & Schuster, 2000), 46, 87, 94–95.

   Compare Ackerley's self-abasement when he once failed to understand Tulip's indications that she wanted to go out: "How wonderful to have had an animal come to one to communicate," and "How wretched to have failed!" to understand her. "Oh yes, I could throw my arms about her as I did, fondle and praise her in my efforts to reassure her that it was all my fault and she was the cleverest person in the world. But . . . I had failed to take her meaning, and nothing I could ever do could put that right" (54).

   In keeping with her general sentimentality, Thomas is convinced that humans and dogs communicate by extrasensory perception.

   In some writers, vague modern-age spirituality joins with sentimental imaginings about canine virtue to produce a mystical overestimation of doggy intuition and power to elevate humanity. Brad Steiger writes in *Man and Dog* (New York: Donald J. Fine, 1995): "In my forty years of research into the paranormal, the metaphysical, and the unknown, I have even collected numerous accounts of instances in which it appears that angelic beings, higher intelligences, have been able temporarily to enter dogs and to accomplish miracles through their physical vehicles." In one case, a grieving family looking at a snapshot taken after their dog's death saw his image sitting beneath "the caretaking hands of an angel or guide" and thereby "knew that on a higher plane of existence he was healthy and happy— and waiting for them to join him." It was typical of their considerate dog to let them know (5, 150–51).

   Rupert Sheldrake's *Dogs That Know When Their Owners Are Coming Home and Other Unexplained Powers of Animals* (New York: Crown, 1999) is based on his faith that all animals, including at least unsophisticated humans, have extrasensory powers. His "most convincing" evidence is the alleged capacity for dogs to know when their owners are coming home, in the absence of any external clues. He also reports that, when a woman was leaving her house in the morning, her normally quiet dog jumped up on her, pushed her, leaned against the door—did everything he could to stop her. She ignored his warnings and, sure enough, was soon badly injured in a traffic accident. In the hospital, she felt his anguish and sent him a mental message of reassurance, on which, according to her husband, the agitated dog calmed right down (262–63).

12. Jeffrey Moussaieff Masson, *Dogs Never Lie About Love: Reflections on the Emotional World of Dogs* (New York: Crown, 1997), 124–25.

13. Susan Conant, *Black Ribbon: A Dog Lover's Mystery* (New York: Bantam, 1995), 228.

14. In *Two for the Lions* (1998), Davis introduces the wonderful dog act performed before Vespasian and described by Plutarch, in which a dog pretends to be poisoned.

   The murder motive in Robert Barnard's *Fête Fatale* (New York: Dell, 1985) is a woman's need to keep her dog with her in spite of British quarantine law, and her crime is extenuated because "She murdered for love" (181). Since the narrator is the local veterinarian's wife, the book is filled with reports on all the neighborhood dogs.

15. Susan Conant, *Bloodlines* (New York: Doubleday, 1992), 207–208.

16. Michael Bond, *Monsieur Pamplemousse Aloft* (New York: Fawcett, 1989), 2–3.

17. Johns, 48.

18. John Steinbeck, *Travels with Charley in Search of America* (New York: Viking Press, 1962), 31–32.

19. Stephen Budiansky, *The Truth About Dogs: An Inquiry into the Ancestry, Social Conventions, Mental Habits and Moral Fiber of Canis familiaris* (New York: Viking, 2000), 1, 78.

20. Carl Hiaasen, *Sick Puppy* (New York: Knopf, 1999), 190.

21. Essay of 1952, in Maloney and Suarès, 58.

22. A. R. Gurney, *Sylvia* (New York: Dramatists Play Service, 1996), 8, 27, 35, 37, 42.

23. Peter Mayle, *A Dog's Life* (New York: Knopf, 1995), 86, 88–89, 168–69.

24. Michael Z. Lewin, *Rover's Tales: A Canine Crusader and His Travels in the Dog World* (New York: St. Martin's Press, 1998), 29, 76, 158–59.

Two other works that illuminate canine and human nature by giving dogs a voice are C. G. Learoyd's "Descent to the Beasts" and Olaf Stapledon's *Sirius: A Fantasy of Love and Discord.* In Learoyd's story, a dog-loving journalist who wondered whether the sentimental dog stories he read "ever remotely approximated the truth" went out with his fox terrier, Jorrocks, to listen in on canine conversations. When Jorrocks lingered to sniff at a wall and the journalist tried to hustle him along, the dog protested: "Well, that's pretty cool from a newspaper man! You like to know what's going on, don't you? So do I. And what do I find here? Bingo was here last, probably took his bloke to the post last thing. Before him was old Max and that sap Sandy. And before him that well-behaved young lady Dorothea the Dachshund. Her message is not quite complete—she was probably as usual on a string. And before her—oh, it's myself. And if you weren't in such a blasted hurry I could tell you what they'd all been eating" (Aymar, 283–86).

Stapledon's *Sirius* is a somber story about an outsized German shepherd mix scientifically endowed with a human-quality brain. He is raised with the scientist's daughter and they form a close bond, but their relationship cannot last in human society, and ultimately Sirius is shot for killing a man who pursued him. Sirius's canine characteristics are well worked out—he was capable of unambivalent love and so sensitive to tones of voice that he "could distinguish unerringly between spontaneous praise and mere kindly encouragement"; yet he was constantly frustrated by the lack of hands and precise near vision (*Odd John & Sirius: Two Science Fiction Novels by Olaf Stapledon* [New York: Dover, 1972], 186). But Stapledon was more interested in philosophical issues than in what a dog might actually experience in Sirius's situation.

25. Rudyard Kipling, "Thy Servant a Dog" (1930), *Collected Dog Stories* (Garden City, N.Y.: Doubleday, 1935), 167, 183–84.

26. Virginia Woolf, *Flush: A Biography* (New York: Harcourt Brace Jovanovich, 1983), 30–31, 60. Woolf started the book as a parody of the biographies by her friend Lytton Strachey, but she came to be genuinely engaged by the Browning dog.

27. King did sporadically associate Cujo with a serial killer policeman and an undefined monster at the back of the boy's closet, but I believe the story is effective on a realistic level and is actually weakened by these attempts to make Cujo more horrible.

12. Myth and Reality

1. The others were kept primarily for hunting or farming. In addition to the owned dogs, there are an estimated ten million strays (petfoodinstitute.org; Phillips, 23).

2. Peter Carlson, "Chow Hounds," *Washington Post*, September 3, 1999, C1, 5.

3. Sherri S. Tepper, *The Companions* (New York: HarperCollins, 2003), 24–25. This very recent novel breaks with the traditional presentation of dogs in science fiction—that is, as loyal servants of man, despite radical changes in circumstances.

4. Jon Katz, *The New Work of Dogs: Tending to Life, Love, and Family* (New York: Villard, 2003), 23. Despite the soundness of his general thesis, Katz's account suffers from unawareness of history. There are many examples of intense bonding between humans and dogs in the nineteenth century, such as Elizabeth Barrett and Flush; and there were undoubtedly cases in earlier times, although it was not yet customary to write about them in detail. Similarly, there must have been many people who had to do without emotional support from humans even in the closer knit societies of the past.

5. "The Idolatrous Dog," in Ollie Depew, ed., *Here Are Dogs: A Collection of Essays* (New York: Century Co., 1931), 252–54.

6. "The Better I Like Dogs," in Berman, 115–16; Ben Hur Lampman, in Brown, *All Dogs*, 493.

7. Poem of 1921, in Stephens, 100.

8. *Table-Talk,* in Hawtree, 603–604, Emmanuel Dieudonné, Comte de las Cases, *Memoirs of the Life, Exile, and Conversations of the Emperor Napoleon* (New York: W. J. Widdleton, 1879), 1:248.

9. Olaf Stapledon, *Odd John & Sirius: Two Science Fiction Novels by Olaf Stapledon* (New York: Dover, 1972), 202.

10. Patrick, 26.

11. Johns, 39.

12. "Dog's Death," in Duemer.

13. Johns, 31–32.

14. Robert Westall, *The Kingdom by the Sea* (New York: Farrar, Straus, Giroux, 1990), 38.

Bibliography

Ackerley, J. R. *My Dog Tulip* (1956). New York: Fleet Publishing Co., 1965.

Adams, Richard. *The Plague Dogs.* New York: Knopf, 1978.

Addison, Joseph, and Richard Steele. *The Spectator.* London: J. M. Dent, 1945. 4 vols.

Aelianus, Claudius. *On the Characteristics of Animals* (third century CE). Trans. A. F. Scholfield. Cambridge: Harvard University Press, 1958. 3 vols.

Aesop. *The Fables of Aesop.* Told anew by Joseph Jacobs. New York: Macmillan, 1964.

Alcott, Louisa May. *Under the Lilacs* (1877). Boston: Little, Brown, 1928.

American Humane Association. *Advocate* 17:1 (1999), 8–9, 23.

American Kennel Club. *Complete Dog Book*, 19th ed. New York: Howell Book House, 1997.

Ancient Laws and Institutes of Wales; Comprising Laws Supposed to Be Enacted by Howel the Good, Modified by Subsequent Regulations Under the Native Princes prior to the Conquest by Edward I. Printed by command of his late majesty King William IV under the direction of the Commissioners of the Public Records, 1841.

Aristotle. *Aristotle's History of Animals* (fourth century BCE). Trans. Richard Cresswell. London: George Bell, 1891.

Ash, Edward Cecil. *Dogs: Their History and Development.* New York: Benjamin Blom, 1972. 2 vols.

Ashley, Maurice. *Rupert of the Rhine.* London: Hart Davis, MacGibbon, 1976.

Austen, Jane. *Mansfield Park* (1814). New York: New American Library, 1964.

―――. *Sense and Sensibility* (1811). New York: New American Library, 1961.

Aymar, Brandt, and Edward Sagarin, eds. *The Personality of the Dog.* New York: Crown Publishers, 1964.

Babrius and Phaedrus. Trans. Ben Edwin Perry. Cambridge: Harvard University Press, 1965.

Baer, Nancy, and Steve Duno. *Choosing a Dog: Your Guide to Picking the Perfect Breed.* New York: Berkley Books, 1995.

Bailey, Paul. *A Dog's Life.* London: Hamish Hamilton, 2003.

Baker, Steve. *Picturing the Beast: Animals, Identity and Representation.* Manchester: Manchester University Press, 1993.

Ballantyne, Robert Michael. *The Dog Crusoe* (1861). London: J. M. Dent, 1966.

Barnard, Robert. *Fête Fatale.* New York: Dell, 1985.

Barry, Dave. *Big Trouble.* Thorndike, Maine: G. K. Hall, 2000.

Bass, Rick. *Colter: The True Story of the Best Dog I Ever Had.* Boston: Houghton Mifflin, 2000.

Beck, Alan, and Aaron Katcher. *Between Pets and People: The Importance of Animal Companionship.* New York: Putnam, 1983.

Beerbohm, Max. *Zuleika Dobson: or an Oxford Love Story* (1911). New York: Dodd, Mead, 1946.

Beilby, Ralph. *A General History of Quadrupeds.* Illus. Thomas Bewick. Newcastle upon Tyne: T. Bewick and S. Hodgson, 1790.

Bell, Thomas. *A History of British Quaduupeds.* London: John Van Voorst, 1837.

Bentham, Jeremy. *The Principles of Morals and Legislation* (1780). Buffalo: Prometheus Books, 1988.

(Berger, John). *King: A Street Story.* New York: Pantheon, 1999.

Berman, Harold, ed. *The Pocket Book of Dog Stories.* New York: Pocket Books, 1942.

Berners, Juliana. *The Book of St. Albans.* Reprint of 1496 edition. New York, 1966.

Best in Show. Film of 2000.

Bible, The. King James version.

Bicknell, Ethel E, ed. *Praise of the Dog: An Anthology.* London: Grant Richards, 1902.

Bierce, Ambrose. *Collected Writings.* New York: Citadel Press, 1946.

Blaine, Delabere. *Canine Pathology, or a Full Description of the Diseases of Dogs.* London: T. Boosey, 1817.

Bloch, Marguerite, ed. *Favorite Dog Stories.* Cleveland: World Publishing Co., 1950.

Blount, Margaret. *Animal Land: The Creatures of Children's Fiction.* New York: William Morrow, 1975.

Bond, Michael. *Monsieur Pamplemousse Aloft.* New York: Fawcett, 1989.

Bond, Simon. *Odd Dogs: 101 Scenes of Canine Life.* New York: Harper & Row, 1989.

Boswell, James. *Boswell on the Grand Tour, Germany and Switzerland, 1764.* New York: McGraw-Hill, 1953.

Bradford, Arthur. *Dogwalker.* New York: Knopf, 2001.

Briggs, Katharine. *An Encyclopedia of Fairies.* New York: Pantheon Books, 1976.

Brontë, Anne. *Agnes Grey* (1847). Oxford: Oxford University Press, 1988.

Brontë, Charlotte. *Jane Eyre* (1847). New York: W. W. Norton, 1971.

———. *Shirley* (1849). London: Penguin Books, 1974.

———. *Villette* (1853). New York: Harper & Row, 1972.

————. *The Letters of Charlotte Brontë*. Ed. Margaret Smith. Oxford: Clarendon, 1995, 2000, 2 vols.

Brontë, Emily. *Wuthering Heights* (1847). New York: New American Library, 1959.

Broughton, Rhoda. *Belinda: A Novel*. New York: D. Appleton, 1884. Reprinted by Scholarly Press, 1970.

————. *Mrs. Bligh: A Novel*. New York: D. Appleton, 1892.

————. *Red as a Rose Is She*. New York: D. Appleton, 1870.

————. *A Waif's Progress*. London: Macmillan, 1905.

Brown, Beth, ed. *All Dogs Go to Heaven*. New York: Grosset and Dunlap, 1961.

————. *The Wonderful World of Dogs*. New York: Harper & Brothers, 1961.

Browning, Elizabeth. *The Complete Poetical Works*. Boston: Houghton Mifflin, 1900.

Bryant, Traphes, and Frances Spatz Leighton. *Dog Days at the White House: The Outrageous Memoirs of the Presidential Kennel-Keeper*. New York: Macmillan, 1975.

Budiansky, Stephen. *The Covenant of the Wild: Why Animals Chose Domestication*. New York: Morrow, 1992.

————. *The Truth About Dogs: An Inquiry into the Ancestry, Social Conventions, Mental Habits, and Moral Fiber of Canis familiaris*. New York: Viking, 2000.

Bueler, Lois E. *Wild Dogs of the World*. New York: Stein & Day, 1973.

Buffon, Georges-Louis Leclerc de. *Histoire Naturelle, Generale et Particulière* (1749–67). Paris: F. Dufart, 1799. Vol. 23.

Burke, Edmund. *A Philosophical Enquiry into the Origin of Our Ideas of the Sublime and Beautiful* (1757). London: George Bell, 1889.

Burnford, Sheila. *The Incredible Journey*. Boston: Little, Brown, 1960.

Burtis, Edwin S., ed. *All the Best Dog Poems: An Anthology of Poetry About Dogs*. New York: Thomas Y. Crowell, 1946.

Bush, Barbara. *C. Fred's Story*. Garden City, N.Y.: Doubleday, 1984.

————. *Millie's Book, as Dictated to Barbara Bush*. New York: William Morrow, 1990.

Caius, Johannes. *Of Englishe Dogges, the Diversities, the Names, the Natures, and the Properties*. Trans. Abraham Fleming (1576). Amsterdam: Theatrum Orbis Terrarum, 1969.

Caras, Roger. *A Celebration of Dogs*. New York: Times Books, 1982.

————. *A Dog Is Listening: The Way Some of Our Closest Friends View Us*. New York: Summit Books, 1992.

————. *Going for the Blue: Inside the World of Show Dogs and Dog Shows*. New York: Warner Books, 2001.

————, ed. *Roger Caras' Treasury of Great Dog Stories*. New York: E. P. Dutton, 1987.

Carlson, Peter. "Chow Hounds: Not-So-Finicky Canines Put Gourmet Treats to the Taste Test." *Washington Post*, September 3, 1999, C1, 5.

Carr, Samuel, ed. *The Poetry of Dogs*. London: Batsford, 1975.

Carroll, William Meredith. *Animal Conventions in English Renaissance Non-Religious Prose*. New York: Bookman Associates, 1954.

Cases, Emmanuel Dieudonné, Comte de las. *Memoirs of the Life, Exile, and Conversations of the Emperor Napoleon.* Newark: W. J. Widdleton, 1879. 4 vols.

Cavanah, Frances, and Ruth Cromer Weir, eds. *A Treasury of Dog Stories.* Chicago: Rand McNally, 1947.

Chaucer, Geoffrey. *The Canterbury Tales.* Trans. Neville Coghill. Harmondsworth, Middlesex: Penguin Books, 1951.

Clark, Kenneth. *Animals and Men: Their Relationship as Reflected in Western Art from Prehistory to the Present Day.* New York: William Morrow, 1977.

Clarke, Timothy, ed. *The Dog Lover's Reader.* New York: Hart Publishing Co., 1974.

Clutton-Brock, Juliet. *Dog: Eyewitness Books.* New York: Knopf, 1991.

———. *Domesticated Animals from Early Times.* Austin: University of Texas, 1983.

Cohen, Barbara, and Louise Taylor. *Dogs and Their Women.* Boston: Little, Brown, 1989.

Cole, William, ed. *Good Dog Poems.* New York: Scribner, 1981.

———. *Man's Funniest Friend: The Dog in Stories, Reminiscences, Poems and Cartoons.* Cleveland: World Publishing Co., 1967.

Colette. *Creatures Great and Small.* Trans. Enid McLeod. New York: Farrar, Straus & Giroux, 1951.

Collins, Emanuel. "The Fatal Dream: or, The Unhappy Favourite. An Elegy" (1762), in *The New Oxford Book of Eighteenth-Century Verse.* Ed. Roger Lonsdale. Oxford: Oxford University Press, 1984.

Collins, Wilkie. *Heart and Science: A Story of the Present Time* (1883). Peterborough, Ontario, Canada: Broadview Press, 1996.

Columbia University College of Physicians and Surgeons Complete Home Medical Guide. Ed. Donald F. Tapley et al. 3rd rev. ed. New York: Crown, 1995.

Columella, Lucius Junius Moderatus. *On Agriculture* (first century CE). Trans. E. S. Forster and Edward H. Heffner. Cambridge: Harvard University Press, 1954. 3 vols.

Conant, Susan. *Animal Appetite.* New York: Bantam Books, 1997.

———. *Black Ribbon: A Dog Lover's Mystery.* New York: Bantam Books, 1995.

———. *Bloodlines.* New York: Doubleday, 1992.

Cooper, Page, ed. *Famous Dog Stories.* Garden City, N.Y.: Doubleday, 1948.

Coppinger, Raymond P., and Lorna Coppinger. *Dogs: A Startling New Understanding of Canine Origin, Behavior and Evolution.* New York: Scribner, 2001.

———. "Dogs in Sheep's Clothing Guard Flocks." *Smithsonian* 13:1 (April 1982), 64–73.

Coppinger, Raymond, and Mark Feinstein. "'Hark! Hark! The Dogs Do Bark . . .' and Bark and Bark and Bark." *Smithsonian* 21 (January 1991), 119–29.

Coren, Stanley. *How to Speak Dog: Mastering the Art of Dog-Human Communication.* New York: Simon & Schuster, 2001.

———. *The Intelligence of Dogs: A Guide to the Thoughts, Emotions, and Inner Lives of Our Canine Companions.* New York: Bantam Books, 1995.

———. *The Pawprints of History: Dogs and the Course of Human Events.* New York: Free Press, 2002.

Coventry, Francis. *The History of Pompey the Little: or, The Life and Adventures of a Lap-Dog* (1751). London: Oxford University Press, 1974.

Cowper, William. *Poems.* London: J. M. Dent, 1931.

———. *The Selected Letters.* Ed. Mark Van Doren. New York: Farrar, Straus and Young, 1951.

Cox, Nicholas. *The Gentleman's Recreation* (1677). Yorkshire: E. P. Publishing, 1973.

Crockford, Susan Janet, ed. *Dogs Through Time: An Archaeological Perspective.* Proceedings of the First ICAZ Symposium on the History of the Domestic Dog. Eighth Congress of the International Council for Archaeozoology. August 23–29, 1998. Oxford: Archaeopress, 2000.

Crusie, Jennifer. *Crazy for You.* New York: St. Martin's Press, 1999.

"Cynics," *Concise Routledge Encyclopedia of Philosophy.* London: Routledge, 2000, 186.

"Cynics," *Encyclopaedia of Religion and Ethics.* Ed. James Hastings. Edinburgh: T. and T. Clark, 1911. 4:378–83.

Dante Alighieri. *The Inferno.* Trans. John Ciardi. New York: New American Library, 1954.

D'Arblay, Frances Burney. *Cecilia, or the Memoirs of an Heiress* (1782). Oxford: Oxford University Press, 1988.

———. *The Journals and Letters of Fanny Burney (Mme. d'Arblay).* Oxford: Clarendon, 1982. Vol. 10.

———. *The Wanderer or, Female Difficulties* (1814). London: Pandora, 1988.

Darwin, Charles. *The Descent of Man, and Selection in Relation to Sex.* New York: Appleton, 1871. 2 vols.

———. *The Expression of the Emotions in Man and Animals* (1872). New York: New York University Press, 1989.

Davies, Nina M. *Ancient Egyptian Paintings, Selected, Copied, and Described.* Chicago: University of Chicago Press, 1936. 3 vols.

Davis, Lindsey. *Two for the Lions.* New York: Warner Books, 1998.

Defoe, Daniel. *The Life and Adventures of Robinson Crusoe.* Baltimore: Penguin Books, 1965.

Depew, Ollie, ed. *Here Are Dogs: A Collection of Essays.* New York: Century Co., 1931.

DeQuoy, Alfred W. *The Irish Wolfhound in Irish Literature and Law.* Alfred W. DeQuoy, 1971.

Derr, Mark. *Dog's Best Friend: Annals of the Dog-Human Relationship.* New York: Henry Holt, 1997.

Desberg, Peter. *No Good Dogs: Surefire Dog-Training Techniques.* Illus. Betsy Rodden. New York: Simon & Schuster, 1982.

Descartes, René. *Oeuvres de Descartes.* Ed. Charles Adam and Paul Tannery. Paris, 1899.

Dickens, Charles. *Barnaby Rudge: A Tale of the Riots of '80* (1841). New York: Heritage Press, 1941.

———. *Bleak House* (1852–53). New York: W. W. Norton, 1977.

———. *The Personal History of David Copperfield* (1849–50). Baltimore: Penguin Books, 1966.

———. *Dealings with the Firm of Dombey and Son, Wholesale, Retail, and for Exportation* (1848). London: Oxford University Press, 1953.

———. *Hard Times* (1854). New York: W. W. Norton, 1966.

————. *The Old Curiosity Shop* (1840–41). London: Oxford University Press, 1957.

————. *Oliver Twist* (1837–38). In *The Works of Charles Dickens.* Boston: Jefferson Press, 1908.

Downey, Fairfax Davies, ed. *Great Dog Stories of All Time.* Garden City, N.Y.: Doubleday, 1962.

Doyle, Conan. *The Annotated Sherlock Holmes.* New York: Clarkson N. Potter. Vol. 2.

Duemer, Joseph, and Jim Simmerman, eds. *Dog Music: Poetry About Dogs.* New York: St. Martin's Press, 1996.

Edward, Second Duke of York. *The Master of Game* (1406–13). Ed. William A. and F. Baillie-Grohman. With foreword by Theodore Roosevelt. London: Ballantyne, Hanson, 1904.

Edwards, Sydenham Teak. *Cynographia Britannica* (1801). Leeds: Peregrine Books, 1992.

Eliot, George. *Adam Bede* (1859). New York: Washington Square Press, 1956.

————. *Middlemarch* (1871–72). New York: W. W. Norton, 1977.

————. *The Mill on the Floss* (1860). New York: New American Library, 1965.

Evans, Pauline Rush, ed. *Best Book of Dog Stories.* Garden City, N.Y.: Doubleday, 1964.

Evelyn, John. *The Diary of John Evelyn.* Oxford: Clarendon, 1955.

Faulkner, William. "The Bear" (1942), in *Bear, Man, and God: Seven Approaches to William Faulkner's "The Bear."* Ed. Francis Lee Utley, Lyn Z. Bloom, and Arthur F. Kinney. New York: Random House, 1964.

Fielding, Henry. *Joseph Andrews* (1742). Boston: Houghton Mifflin, 1961.

Flanagan, Mary. "Beyond Barking," in *The Blue Woman and Other Stories.* New York: W. W. Norton, 1994.

Florian, Jean-Pierre Claris de. *Fables de Florian.* Paris: Briand, 1816.

Fogle, Bruce. *The New Encyclopedia of the Dog.* London: Dorling Kindersley, 2000.

————, ed. *Interrelations Between People and Pets.* Springfield, Ill.: Charles C Thomas, 1981.

Forster, John. *The Life of Charles Dickens.* London: J. M. Dent, 1927.

Fox, Michael W. *Canine Behavior: A History of Domestication, Behavioral Development and Adult Behavior Patterns.* Springfield, Ill.: Charles C Thomas, 1965.

————. *The Dog: Its Domestication and Behavior.* New York: Garland, 1978.

Fox-Davies, A. C. *A Complete Guide to Heraldry.* Rev. J. P. Brooke-Little. London: Nelson, 1969.

Garber, Marjorie. *Dog Love.* New York: Simon & Schuster, 1997.

Gaskell, Elizabeth. *The Life of Charlotte Brontë* (1857). London: Oxford University Press, 1951.

Gaston de Foix (Gaston Phoebus). *Le Livre de la Chasse.* Manuscrit français 616. Trans. Robert and André Bossuat. Graz: Akademische Druck u. Verlagsanstalt, 1976.

Gautier, Théophile. *My Private Menagerie*, in *The Complete Works.* Trans. and ed. F. C. DeSumichrast. London: Postlethwaite, Taylor and Knowles, 1909. Vol. 10.

Gay, John. *Poetry and Prose.* Oxford: Clarendon, 1974. Vol. 2.

Gerhardt, Pamela. "Heal, Doggie, Heal." *Washington Post Health,* July 25, 2000, 10–15.

Gerhart, Ann. "Wagging the Dog." *Washington Post,* February 13, 2002, C1, 3.

Godden, Rumer. *The Butterfly Lions: The Story of the Pekingese in History, Legend, and Art.* New York: Viking Press, 1977.

Goldsmith, Oliver. *A History of the Earth and Animated Nature* (1774). Edinburgh: A. Fullarton, 1879. Vol. 1.

Goodman, Jack, ed. *The Fireside Book of Dog Stories.* New York: Simon & Schuster, 1943.

Gray, Charles Wright, ed. *"Dawgs!" An Anthology of Stories About Them.* Garden City, N.Y: Sun Dial Press, 1937.

———. *Real Dogs: An Anthology.* Garden City, N.Y.: Garden City Publishing Co., 1926.

Great Dog Stories. New York: Ballantine Books, 1955.

Greene, Graham. *The Human Factor.* New York: Simon & Schuster, 1978.

Griffith, Beatrice Fox. *Historic Dogs: An Outline in Pictures of the Story of the Dog.* Haverford, Pa.: Clinton L. Mellor, 1953.

Gross, Sam, ed. *Dogs, Dogs, Dogs: A Collection of Great Dog Cartoons.* New York: Harper & Row, 1985.

Guisewite, Cathy. *Cathy* cartoons, *Washington Post,* August 12, September 8, 2000; March 5, March 16, 2001; February 8, 2002.

Gurney, A. R. *Sylvia.* New York: Dramatists Play Service, 1996.

Haddon, Celia. *Faithful to the End: An Illustrated Anthology About Dogs and Their Owners.* New York: St. Martin's Press, 1991.

Hamerton, Philip G. *Chapters on Animals.* Boston: Roberts Brothers, 1882.

Hammett, Dashiell. *The Thin Man.* New York: Vintage Books, 1989.

Hardy, Thomas. "Ah, Are You Digging on My Grave?" in Louis Untermeyer, ed. *Modern British Poetry.* New York: Harcourt, Brace, 1942.

———. *Far from the Madding Crowd* (1874). New York: Rinehart, 1959.

Hare, Brian, et al. "The Domestication of Social Cognition in Dogs." *Science* 298 (November 22, 2002): 1634–36.

Harper, Wilhelmina, ed. *Dog Show: A Selection of Favorite Dog Stories.* Boston: Houghton Mifflin, 1950.

Hastings, Hester. *Man and Beast in French Thought of the 18th Century.* Baltimore: Johns Hopkins, 1936.

Hawtree, Christopher, ed. *The Literary Companion to Dogs: From Homer to Hockney.* London: Sinclair-Stevenson, 1993.

Hearne, Vicki. *Adam's Task: Calling Animals by Name.* New York: Knopf, 1986.

Henry, O. *Collected Stories.* New York: Gramercy Books, 1986.

Herbert, Henry. *Frank Forester's Field Sports of the United States, and the British Provinces of North America.* New York: W. A. Townsend, 1858. 2 vols.

Herodotus. *The Histories* (fifth century BCE). Trans. Robin Waterfield. Oxford: Oxford University Press, 1998.

Hiaasen, Carl. *Sick Puppy.* New York: Knopf, 1999.

Hogg, James. *The Shepherd's Calendar.* Edinburgh: University Press, 1995.

Homer. *The Iliad* (c. eighth century BCE). Trans. Richmond Lattimore. Chicago: University of Chicago Press, 1951.

———. *The Odyssey* (c. eighth century BCE). Trans. F. V. Rieu. Baltimore: Penguin Books, 1946.

Hubbard, Clifford. *A Kennel of Dogs.* London: Elek, 1977.

———. *Working Dogs of the World.* London: Sidgwick and Jackson, 1947.

Hull, Denison Bingham. *Hounds and Hunting in Ancient Greece.* Chicago: University of Chicago Press, 1964.

Hull, Raymond. *Man's Best Fiend.* New York: Hippocrene Books, 1972.

International Encyclopedia of Dogs, The. Ed. Stanley Dangerfield and Elsworth Howell. New York: McGraw-Hill, 1971.

"It's a Dog's Life," *The Economist,* December 21, 2002, 61–63.

Jerome, Jerome K. *3 Men in a Boat (To Say Nothing of the Dog).* Gloucester: Alan Sutton, 1982.

Jesse, George R. *Researches into the History of the British Dog, from Ancient Laws, Charters and Historical Records.* London: Robert Hardwicke, 1866. 2 vols.

Johns, Bud, ed. *Old Dogs Remembered.* New York: Carroll and Graf, 1993.

Johnson, Edgar. *Sir Walter Scott: The Great Unknown.* New York: Macmillan, 1970. 2 vols.

Johnson, Samuel. *Dictionary of the English Language.* Hildesheim: George Olms, 1968.

———. *Selected Writings.* Ed. Katharine Rogers. New York: New American Library, 1981.

Jones, Arthur Frederick, and John Rendel, eds. *The Treasury of Dogs.* New York: Golden Press, 1964.

Katcher, Aaron H., and Alan M. Beck, eds. *New Perspectives on Our Lives with Companion Animals.* Philadelphia: University of Pennsylvania Press, 1983.

Katz, Jon. *The New Work of Dogs: Tending to Life, Love, and Family.* New York: Villard, 2003.

Kendall, Edward Augustus. *Keeper's Travels in Search of His Master* (1798). Boston: Lilly, Wait, 1833.

King, Stephen. *Cujo.* New York: Viking Press, 1981.

Kipling, Rudyard. "The Cat That Walked by Himself," in *Just So Stories.* New York: Books of Wonder, 1996.

———. *Collected Dog Stories.* Garden City, N.Y.: Doubleday, 1935.

Kismaric, Carole, and Martin Heiferman. *Growing Up with Dick and Jane: Learning and Living the American Dream.* San Francisco: Collins Publishers, 1996.

Kjelgaard, Jim. *Big Red.* New York: Holiday House, 1945.

———, ed. *Hound Dogs and Others: A Collection of Stories by Members of Western Writers of America.* New York: Dodd, Mead, 1958.

Knapp, Caroline. *Pack of Two: The Intricate Bond Between People and Dogs.* New York: Dial, 1998.

Knight, Eric. *Lassie Come-Home* (1940). Thorndike, Maine: G.K. Hall, 1996.

Krutch, Joseph Wood, ed. *The World of Animals: A Treasury of Love, Legend and Literature by Great Writers and Naturalists from the Fifth Century B.C. to the Present.* New York: Simon & Schuster, 1961.

Lang, Andrew, ed. *The Blue Fairy Book.* New York: Viking Press, 1975.

Lansbury, Coral. *The Old Brown Dog: Women, Workers, and Vivisection in Edwardian England.* Madison: University of Wisconsin Press, 1985.

Leach, Maria. *God Had a Dog: Folklore of the Dog.* New Brunswick, N.J.: Rutgers University Press, 1961.

Lee, Rawdon B. *A History and Description of the Modern Dogs of Great Britain and Ireland.* London: Horace Cox, 1906. 2 vols.

Lee, Richard B., and Irven DeVore, eds. *Man the Hunter.* Chicago: Aldine, 1968.

Lemish, Michael G. *War Dogs: Canines in Combat.* Washington, D.C.: Brassey's, 1996.

Lewin, Michael Z. *Rover's Tales: A Canine Crusader and His Travels in the Dog World.* New York: St. Martin's Press, 1998.

Lewis, C. S. *The Last Battle.* New York: Macmillan, 1956.

Lindsay, Joyce, and Maurice Lindsay, eds. *The Scottish Dog.* Aberdeen, Scot.: Aberdeen University Press, 1989.

Linnaeus (Carl von Linné). *A General System of Nature.* Trans. William Turton. Swansea: Voss and Morris, 1800. Vol. 1.

London, Jack. *Novels and Stories.* Library of America. New York: Viking, 1982.

Lorenz, Konrad. *Man Meets Dog.* Trans. Marjorie Kerr Wilson. Baltimore: Penguin Books, 1964.

Lovecraft, H. P. *Something About Cats and Other Pieces.* Collected A. Derleth. Sauk City, Wis.: Arkham House, 1949.

Lucretius. *On the Nature of the Universe* (first century BCE). Trans. Ronald Latham. Baltimore: Penguin Books, 1951.

Lurie, Alison. *Foreign Affairs.* New York: Avon Books, 1990.

Lytton, Judith. *Toy Dogs and Their Ancestors.* London: Duckworth, 1911.

McCaig, Donald. *Nop's Trials.* New York: Crown, 1984.

Macdonald, George. *The Princess and Curdie* (1883). New York: Macmillan, 1954.

MacDonogh, Katharine. *Reigning Cats and Dogs.* New York: St. Martin's Press, 1999.

McKie, Roy. *The Dog: A Cartoon Inquiry Concerning Man's Relationship to His Best Friend.* New York: Simon & Schuster, 1954.

McLoughlin, John C. *The Canine Clan: A New Look at Man's Best Friend.* New York: Viking, 1983.

Maloney, William E., and Jean-Claude Suarès. *The Literary Dog.* New York: Push Pin Press, 1978.

Manning, Roger B. *Hunters and Poachers: A Social and Cultural History of Unlawful Hunting in England, 1485–1640.* Oxford: Clarendon, 1993.

Man's Best Friend: The National Geographic Book of Dogs. Rev. ed. Washington, D.C.: National Geographical Society, 1974.

Manson, Cynthia, ed. *Canine Crimes II.* New York: Berkley, 1997.

Marks, Jeffrey, ed. *Canine Crimes.* New York: Ballantine Books, 1998.

Martialis, Marcus Valerius. *Epigrams* (first century CE). Trans. D. R. Shackleton Bailey. Cambridge: Harvard University Press, 1993. Vol. 1.

Mason, Ian L., ed. *Evolution of Domesticated Animals.* London: Longman, 1984.

Masson, Jeffrey Moussaieff. *Dogs Never Lie About Love: Reflections on the Emotional World of Dogs.* New York: Crown, 1997.

Maxwell, William. *So Long, See You Tomorrow.* New York: Knopf, 1980.

Mayle, Peter. *A Dog's Life.* Illus. Edward Koren. New York: Knopf, 1995.

Meadows, Robin. "Scat-Sniffing Dogs." *Zoogoer*, September/October 2002, 22–27.

Meddaugh, Susan. *Martha and Skits.* Boston: Houghton Mifflin, 2000.

Menzies, Lucy, ed. *The First Friend: An Anthology of the Friendship of Man and Dog, Compiled from the Literature of All Ages 1400 B.C.–1921 A.D.* London: George Allen and Unwin, 1922.

Mercatante, Anthony S. *Who's Who in Egyptian Mythology.* New York: Clarkson N. Potter, 1978.

Messent, Peter. *Understanding Your Dog.* New York: Stein & Day, 1979.

Milton, John. *Complete Poetry and Selected Prose.* Glasgow: Nonesuch Press, 1948.

Montaigne, Michel de. "Of Crueltie," "An Apologie of Raymond Sebond," in *Essays* (1580). Trans. John Florio. London: J. M. Dent, 1910. Vol. 2.

Montgomery, John. *Royal Dogs: The Pets of the British Sovereigns from Victoria to Elizabeth II.* London: Max Parrish, 1962.

Morris, Desmond. *The Animal Contract: An Impassioned and Rational Guide to Sharing the Planet and Saving Our Common World.* New York: Warner Books, 1990.

Morris, Willie. *My Dog Skip.* New York: Random House, 1995.

Mowat, Farley. *The Dog Who Wouldn't Be.* Boston: Little, Brown, 1957.

Munsche, P. B. *Gentlemen and Poachers: The English Game Laws 1671–1831.* Cambridge: Cambridge University Press, 1981.

Necker, Claire. *Cats and Dogs.* New York: A. S. Barnes, 1969.

New York Times, The. April 10, 1998, A17.

New Yorker Book of Dog Cartoons, The. New York: Knopf, 1995.

Nowell, Iris. *The Dog Crisis.* New York: St. Martin's Press, 1978.

Olsen, Stanley J. *Origins of the Domestic Dog: The Fossil Record.* Tucson: University of Arizona Press, 1985.

O'Mara, Lesley, ed. *Best Dog Stories.* New York: Wings Books, 1990.

O'Neill, Eugene. "The Last Will and Testament of Silverdene Emblem O'Neill." In *The Unknown O'Neill.* Ed. Travis Bogard. New Haven: Yale University Press, 1988.

Orwell, George. *Animal Farm.* New York: New American Library, 1946.

Ouida (Louise de la Ramee). *A Dog of Flanders* (1872), in *English Stories.* Ed. Edward Everett Hale. Freeport, N.Y.: Books for Libraries, 1969.

Ovid. *Metamorphoses* (2–8 CE). Trans. Rolfe Humphries. Bloomington: Indiana University Press, 1968.

Owst, G. R. *Literature and Pulpit in Medieval England: A Neglected Chapter in the History of English Letters and of the English People.* Oxford: Basil Blackwell, 1966.

Papashvily, Helen, and George Papashvily. *Dogs and People.* Philadelphia: J.B. Lippincott, 1954.

Parker, Eric, ed. *Best of Dogs: Stories of Many Famous Friends.* London: Hutchinson, 1949.

Parry, Michel, ed. *The Hounds of Hell: Weird Tales About Dogs.* London: Victor Gollancz, 1974.

Patrick, Ted. *The Thinking Dog's Man.* New York: Random House, 1964.

Pepys, Samuel. *The Diary of Samuel Pepys.* Berkeley: University of California Press, 1970–   .

Phillips, Angus. "Wolf to Woof: The Evolution of Dogs." *National Geographic*, January 2002, 2–31.

Pitcher, George. *The Dogs Who Came to Stay*. New York: Dutton, 1995.

Plato, *The Republic* (fourth century BCE). Trans. Francis MacDonald Cornford. London: Oxford University Press, 1945.

Pliny the Elder (C. Plinius Secundus). *Natural History* (first century CE). Trans. H. Rackham. Cambridge: Harvard University Press, 1947. 10 vols.

Plomer, William. *The Case Is Altered*. London: Hogarth Press, 1946.

Plutarch, *Moralia* (first–second century CE). Trans. Harold Cherniss and William C. Helmbold. Cambridge: Harvard University Press, 1957. 15 vols.

Podberscek, Anthony L., Elizabeth S. Paul, and James A. Serpell, eds. *Companion Animals and Us: Exploring the Relationships Between People and Pets*. Cambridge: Cambridge University Press, 2000.

Pope, Alexander. *Collected Poems*. London: J. M. Dent and Sons, 1983.

Power, Eileen. *Medieval People*. London: Methuen, 1963.

Putney, William. *Always Faithful: A Memoir of the Marine Dogs of World War II*. New York: Free Press, 2001.

Radford, E., and M. A Radford. *Encyclopedia of Superstitions*. Ed. and rev. Christina Hole. Chester Springs, Pa.: Dufour Editions, 1969.

Reed, Christopher. "Best Friend Bests Chimp." *Harvard Magazine*, April 2003.

Regan, Tom, and Peter Singer, eds. *Animal Rights and Human Obligations*. Englewood Cliffs, N.J.: Prentice-Hall, 1976.

Rhodes, Dan. *Timoleon Vieta Come Home: A Sentimental Journey*. Edinburgh: Canongate, 2003.

Richardson, Elizabeth, ed. *Poets' Dogs*. New York: G. P. Putnam's, 1895.

Richardson, H. D. *Dogs: Their Origin and Varieties*. New York: Orange Judd, 1874.

Rine, Josephine Z. *The World of Dogs*. Garden City, N.Y.: Doubleday, 1965.

Ritvo, Harriet. *The Animal Estate: The English and Other Creatures in the Victorian Age*. Cambridge: Harvard University Press, 1987.

Rosen, Michael J., ed. *The Company of Dogs*. New York: Doubleday, 1990.

Rosenblum, Robert. *The Dog in Art: From Rococo to Post-Modernism*. New York: Harry N. Abrams, 1988.

Rosenfield, Leonora Cohen. *From Beast-Machine to Man-Machine: Animal Soul in French Letters from Descartes to La Mettrie*. New York: Oxford University Press, 1941.

Rousselet-Blanc, Pierre, ed. *Larousse du Chien*. Paris: Librairie Larousse, 1974.

Rowan, Andrew N., ed. *Animals and People Sharing the World*. Hanover: University Press of New England, 1988.

Rowan, Roy, and Brooke Janis. *First Dogs: American Presidents and Their Best Friends*. Chapel Hill, N.C.: Algonquin Books, 1997.

Rubin, James H. *Impressionist Cats and Dogs: Pets in the Painting of Modern Life*. New Haven: Yale University Press, 2003.

Sanders, Clinton R. *Understanding Dogs: Living and Working with Canine Companions,* Philadelphia: Temple University Press, 1999.

Saunders, (Margaret) Marshall. *Beautiful Joe* (1893). In Blanche Cirker, ed. *Five Great Dog Novels.* New York: Dover, 1961.

Savolainen, Peter, et al. "Genetic Evidence for an East Asian Origin of Domestic Dogs." *Science* 298 (November 22, 2002):1610–13.

Schinto, Jeanne, ed. *The Literary Dog: Great Contemporary Dog Stories.* New York: Atlantic Monthly Press, 1990.

Scholtmeijer, Marian. *Animal Victims in Modern Fiction: From Sanctity to Sacrifice.* Toronto: University of Toronto Press, 1993.

Schwartz, Marion. *A History of Dogs in the Early Americas.* New Haven: Yale University Press, 1997.

Scott, John Paul. "Evolution and Domestication of the Dog." In Theodosius Dobzhansky et al., eds. *Evolutionary Biology* 2:243–75. New York: Appleton-Century-Crofts, 1968.

Scott, John Paul, and John L. Fuller. *Genetics and the Social Behavior of the Dog.* Chicago: University of Chicago Press, 1965.

Scott, Walter. *Guy Mannering: or The Astrologer* (1815). London: Adam and Charles Black, 1897.

———. *Ivanhoe* (1819). New York: Dodd, Mead, 1941.

———. *The Talisman* (1825). New York: Dodd, Mead, 1943.

———. *Woodstock, or The Cavalier: A Tale of the Year 1651* (1826). Edinburgh: Adam and Charles Black, 1871.

Secord, William. *A Breed Apart: The Art Collection of the American Kennel Club and the American Kennel Club Museum of the Dog.* Woodbridge, Suffolk: Antique Collectors Club, 2001.

———. *Dog Painting 1840–1940: A Social History of the Dog in Art.* Woodbridge, Suffolk: Antique Collectors Club, 1992.

Serpell, James, ed. *The Domestic Dog: Its Evolution, Behaviour, and Interactions with People.* Cambridge: Cambridge University Press, 1995.

———. *In the Company of Animals: A Study of Human-Animal Relationships.* Oxford: Basil Blackwell, 1986.

Shakespeare, William. *The Comedies.* London: Oxford University Press, 1911.

———. *The Histories and Poems.* London: Oxford University Press, 1912.

———. *The Tragedies.* London: Oxford University Press, 1912.

Shaler, Nathaniel Southgate. *Domesticated Animals: Their Relation to Man and to His Advancement in Civilization.* New York: Charles Scribner's, 1895.

Shaw, Vero. *The Classic Encyclopedia of the Dog.* New York: Bonanza Books, 1984.

Sheldrake, Rupert. *Dogs That Know When Their Owners Are Coming Home, and Other Unexplained Powers of Animals.* New York: Crown, 1999.

Singer, Peter. *Animal Liberation: A New Ethic for Our Treatment of Animals.* New York: Avon Books, 1975.

———, ed. *In Defense of Animals.* New York: Basil Blackwell, 1985.

Sit! The Dog Portraits of Thierry Poncelet. Text Bruce McCall. New York: Workman, 1993.

Smith, Dodie. *The One Hundred and One Dalmatians* (1956). New York: Penguin Puffin, 1989.

Smith, Wayne. *Thor.* New York: St. Martin's, 1992.

Smollett, Tobias. *The Expedition of Humphry Clinker* (1771). London: Oxford University Press, 1925.

Somervile, William. *The Chace* (1735). Garden City, N.Y.: Doubleday, Doran, 1929.

Spencer, Benjamin T., ed. *Memorable Dogs: An Anthology.* New York: Harper and Row, 1985.

Stables, Gordon. *Our Friend the Dog.* 5th ed. London: Dean and Son, 1990.

Stapledon, Olaf. *Sirius: A Fantasy of Love and Discord* (1944), in *Odd John & Sirius: Two Science Fiction Novels by Olaf Stapledon.* New York: Dover, 1972.

Steadman, Ralph. *No Good Dogs.* New York: Perigee Books, 1970.

Steiger, Brad. *Man and Dog.* New York: Donald J. Fine, 1995.

Steinbeck, John. *Travels with Charley in Search of America.* New York: Viking Press, 1962.

Steinhart, Peter. *In the Company of Wolves.* New York: Knopf, 1995.

Stephanitz, Max von. *The German Shepherd Dog in Word and Picture.* American ed., revised by J. Schwabacker. Jena, Germany: Anton Kampfe, 1923.

Stephens, John Richards, ed., *The Dog Lovers' Literary Companion.* Rocklin, Calif.: Prima Publishing, 1992.

Stern, Jane, and Michael Stern. *Dog Eat Dog: A Very Human Book about Dogs and Dog Shows.* New York: Scribner, 1997.

Stoker, Bram. *Dracula* (1897), in *Frankenstein, Dracula, Dr. Jekyll and Mr. Hyde.* New York: Penguin, 1978.

Stowe, Harriet Beecher. *Uncle Tom's Cabin or Life among the Lowly* (1852). New York: Penguin Books, 1981.

Strachey, John St. Loe, ed. *Dog Stories from the "Spectator": Being Anecdotes of the Intelligence, Reasoning Power, Affection and Sympathy of Dogs, Selected from the Correspondence Columns of "The Spectator."* 2nd ed. London: T. Fisher Unwin, 1896.

Strutt, Joseph. *The Sports and Pastimes of the People of England.* New ed. by J. Charles Cox. New York: Augustus M. Kelley, 1970.

Taber, Gladys. *Long Tails and Short.* Philadelphia: Macrae Smith, 1938.

———. *When Dogs Meet People.* Philadelphia: Macrae Smith, 1952.

Taplin, William. *The Sportsman's Cabinet, or a Correct Delineation of the Canine Race.* Illus. J. Reinagle. London, 1803. 2 vols.

———. *The Sporting Dictionary, and Rural Repository.* London: Vernor and Hood et al., 1803. 2 vols.

Tarkington, Booth. *Penrod.* New York: Grosset & Dunlap, 1914.

Taylor, George B. *Man's Friend, the Dog.* New York: Frederick A. Stokes, 1891.

Taylor, Joseph. *The General Character of the Dog: Illustrated by a Variety of Original and Interesting Anecdotes of That Beautiful and Useful Animal.* Philadelphia: Benjamin Johnson, 1807.

Tepper, Sheri S. *The Companions.* New York: HarperCollins, 2003.

Terhune, Albert Payson. *Lad, a Dog* (1919). New York: Puffin, 1987.

Thomas, Elizabeth Marshall. *The Hidden Life of Dogs.* Boston: Houghton Mifflin, 1993.

———. *The Social Lives of Dogs: The Grace of Canine Company.* New York: Simon & Schuster, 2000.

Thomas, Keith. *Man and the Natural World: A History of the Modern Sensibility.* New York: Pantheon, 1983.

Thomas Aquinas. *The Summa Theologica* (1265–74). Trans. Lawrence Shapcote. Chicago: Encyclopaedia Britannica, 1990.

Thomson, Keith Stewart. "The Fall and Rise of the English Bulldog." *American Scientist* 84 (May–June 1996), 220–23.

Thurber, James. *Thurber's Dogs: A Collection of the Master's Dogs, Written and Drawn, Real and Imaginary, Living and Long Ago.* New York: Simon & Schuster, 1955.

Thurston, Mary Elizabeth. *The Lost History of the Canine Race: Our 15,000-Year Love Affair with Dogs.* Kansas City: Andrews and McMeel, 1996.

Tinniswood, Adrian. *His Invention So Fertile: A Life of Sir Christopher Wren.* Oxford: Oxford University Press, 2001.

Tobit, The Book of. In *The Apocrypha, An American Translation.* Trans. Edgar J. Goodspeed. Chicago: University of Chicago Press, 1938.

Tongue, Ruth L. *Forgotten Folk-tales of the English Counties.* London: Routledge & Kegan Paul, 1970.

Top Dogs, including Mel Ellis, *Run, Rainey, Run,* and Dion Henderson, *Algonquin.* Madison, Wis.: Northwood, 1985.

Toynbee, Jocelyn M. C. *Animals in Roman Life and Art.* Ithaca: Cornell University Press, 1973.

Trapman, Arthur H. *Man's Best Friend: The Story of the Dog.* New York: Macmillan, 1928.

Travers, P. L. *Mary Poppins.* New York: Harcourt, Brace & World, 1934.

Treasury of Dogs, The. London: Octopus Books, 1972.

Trimmer, Sarah Kirby. *Fabulous Histories, Designed for the Instruction of Children, Respecting Their Treatment of Animals.* London: T. Longman and G. G. J. and J. Robinson, 1793.

Trut, Lyudmila. N. "Early Canid Domestication: The Farm-Fox Experiment." *American Scientist* 87 (March–April 1999), 160–69.

Tucker, Michael. *The Eyes That Lead: The Story of Guide Dogs for the Blind.* London: Robert Hale, 1984.

Uglow, Jenny. *Hogarth: A Life and a World.* New York: Farrar, Straus & Giroux, 1997.

Varro, Marcus Terentius. *Varro on Farming* (first century BCE). Trans. Lloyd Storr-Best. London: G. Bell, 1912.

Veblen, Thorstein. *The Theory of the Leisure Class: An Economic Study of Institutions* (1899). New York: New American Library, 1953.

Vesey-Fitzgerald, Brian, ed. *The Book of the Dog.* London: Nicholson & Watson, 1948.

———. *The Domestic Dog: An Introduction to Its History.* London: Routledge and Kegan Paul, 1957.

Vines, G. "Wolves in Dogs' Clothing." *New Scientist* 91: 1270 (September 10, 1981), 648–52.

Virgil (Publius Virgilius Maro). *The Aeneid* (first century BCE). Trans. W. F. Jackson Knight. Baltimore: Penguin, 1956.

Voltaire. "Bêtes: Animals," *Philosophical Dictionary.* Trans. Theodore Besterman. New York: Penguin Books, 1971.

Walpole, Horace. *Correspondence.* New Haven: Yale University Press, 1937–74. 48 vols.

Walsh, John Henry ("Stonehenge"). *The Dogs of the British Islands.* London: Horace Cox, 1872.

Washington Post, The. February 26, 2001, A1, 4; January 29, 2002, A2; February 20, 2002, A3; June 18, 2002, A3; December 24, 2002, B2; December 27, 2002, B2; November 19, 2004, A15.

Watkins, Dwight Everett, and Charles H. Raymond, eds. *Best Dog Stories.* Chicago: Rand McNally, 1925.

Watson, Bruce. "The Dogs of War," *Smithsonian* (December 2000), 100–11.

Watts, Isaac. "Against Quarrelling and Fighting," in *The Oxford Book of Eighteenth-Century Verse.* Ed. David Nichol Smith. Oxford: Clarendon, 1926.

Webb, Stephen H. *On God and Dogs: A Christian Theology of Compassion for Animals.* New York: Oxford University Press, 1998.

Westall, Robert. *The Kingdom by the Sea.* New York: Farrar, Straus & Giroux, 1990.

White, T. H. *Mistress Masham's Repose.* New York: Capricorn, 1960.

Wilcox, Bonnie, and Chris Walkowicz. *Atlas of Dog Breeds of the World.* 4th ed. Neptune City, N.J.: T. F. H. Publications, 1993.

Winokur, Jon, ed. *Mondo Canine.* New York: Dutton, 1991.

Wollstonecraft, Mary. *A Vindication of the Rights of Woman.* New York: W. W. Norton, 1988.

Woolf, Virginia. *Flush: A Biography* (1933). New York: Harcourt Brace Jovanovich, 1983.

Wright, Patrick. *Walkies.* New York: St. Martin's Press, 1982.

Wyett, Jodi L. "The Lap of Luxury: Lapdogs, Literature, and Social Meaning in the 'Long' Eighteenth Century." *Lit* 10:4 (2000), 275–301.

Xenophon. *Cynegetica,* in *Scripta Minora.* Trans. E. C. Marchant. Cambridge: Harvard University Press, 1925.

Youatt, William. *The Dog.* London: Longman et al., 1852.

Zeuner, F. E. *A History of Domesticated Animals.* New York: Harper & Row, 1963.

Zistel, Era. *Golden Book of Dog Stories.* Chicago: Ziff-Davis, 1947.

Zweifel, Karyn Kay. *Dog-gone Ghost Stories.* Birmingham, Ala.: Crane Hill Publishers, 1996.

Credits for the Photographs

The author gratefully acknowledges the following sources for the material reprinted in the photo section.

Photo numbers:

1, 2 Copyright the Trustees of the British Museum

3, 12 National Gallery of London

4 Scuola Dalmata dei Santi Giorgio e Trifone, Venezia

5 Galleria Sabauda, Torino

6, 21 Musée du Louvre, Paris

7, 8, 17 Kunsthistorisches Museum, Wien

9 The Metropolitan Museum of Art, New York. Catharine Lorillard Wolfe Collection, Wolfe Fund, 1907 (07.122)

10 Museo del Prado, Madrid

11 The Metropolitan Museum of Art, New York. The Jules Bache Collection, 1949 (49.7.49)

13 Staatliche Museen, Kassel

14 The Metropolitan Museum of Art, New York. Marquand Collection, Gift of Henry G. Marquand, 1889 (89.15.16)

15, 24 Tate Gallery, London

16 The Royal Collection, Her Majesty Queen Elizabeth II, Windsor

18 National Gallery of Art, Washington, D.C.

19 Musée Malraux, Le Havre

20 Philadelphia Museum of Art. Gift of John G. Johnson for the W.P. Wilstach Collection, 1900

22 Photograph © Museum of Fine Arts, Boston

23 Copyright IRPA-KIK, Brussels. KBC Bank, the Rockox House, Antwerp

25 © Nicolas Mathéus. Musée de la Chasse et de la Nature, Paris

26 National Gallery of Scotland, Edinburgh

27 Victoria and Albert Picture Library, London

28 Copyright © 2000 by Susan Meddaugh. Reprinted by permission of Houghton Mifflin Co., New York

29 Museum of Modern Art, New York. Copyright Estate of Rufino Tamayo

30 The Samuel Courtauld Trust, Courtauld Institute of Art Gallery, London

Index